Seventh
Edition

MANAGING POLICE ORGANIZATIONS

Paul M. Whisenand, Ph.D.

PEARSON

Prentice
Hall

Upper Saddle River, New Jersey
Columbus, Ohio

Library of Congress Cataloging-in-Publication Data

Whisenand, Paul M.
   Managing police organizations / Paul M. Whisenand. —7th ed.
      p. cm.
   Includes bibliographical references and index.
   ISBN-13: 978-0-13-159086-1
   ISBN-10:   0-13-159086-3
  1. Police administration. 2.   Police administration—United States.   I. Title.
   HV7935.W43 2009
   363.2068—dc22   2007028801

Vice President and Executive Publisher: Vernon Anthony
Senior Acquisitions Editor: Tim Peyton
Editorial Assistant: Alicia Kelly
Project Manager: Jessica Sykes
Production Coordinaton: TexTech
Design Coordinator: Diane Y. Ernsberger
Cover Designer: Ali Mohrman
Senior Operations Specialist: Pat Tonneman
Director of Marketing: David Gesell
Marketing Manager: Adam Kloza
Marketing Coordinator: Alicia Dysert

This book was set in 10/12 Sabon-Roman by TexTech. It was printed and bound by Courier/Westford.
The cover was printed by Phoenix.

Pearson Education Ltd.   Pearson Education Australia Pty. Limited
Pearson Education Singapore Pte. Ltd.   Pearson Education North Asia Ltd
Pearson Education Canada, Ltd.   Pearson Educación de Mexico, S.A. de C.V.
Pearson Education—Japan   Pearson Education Malaysia Pte. Ltd.

                                              10 9 8 7 6 5 4
                                        ISBN-13: 978-0-13-159086-1
                                        ISBN-10:   0-13-159086-3

TO MY WIFE, MARILYN, FOR HER LOVE AND TO MY FRIEND, FRED FERGUSON, FOR HIS INTEGRITY AND SUPPORT

Fred and I first met at the University of Southern California in January 1968. We were participating in a graduation ceremony. He was being awarded a bachelor's degree, and I received a Ph.D.—both in public administration. Fred was at that time the chief of police in Covina, CA, while I was an assistant professor, California State University, Long Beach. No more about me; this is about my long-term, prized friend, and co-author. Here's why.

As I write this tribute to a man of honorable character, inspiring leadership, extraordinary imagination, and splendid wit, he's alive but unable to cerebrate. Fred is ill with Alzheimer's. This horrible disease took several years to erase his mental faculties, but it finally prevailed. It did not conquer his spirit or love for others. You can clearly sense both when you're visiting him. He continues to be surrounded by the love of his family and friends.

Fred started his police career in 1950 in Lynwood, CA. In 1957 he moved to Downey as a police sergeant. His first job as a chief was in Covina in 1962. In Covina he always experimented with exciting and at times controversial programs. He even earned the label "maverick," which is today referred to as a "change agent." He earned his master's degree, and in 1973 we co-authored our first edition of this book. Of all the chapters he wrote, he liked (and to this day I consider it a centerpiece) "Politics." Yes, with 36 (24 as a police chief) years in police work, Fred saw, wrestled with, lost a couple of battles, but typically won in tough times.

In 1971 Fred was selected as chief in Riverside, CA. He held that job for five years. His final chief's position was in Salinas, CA, 1976–1986. Along his career path Fred mentored hundreds of officers. He actively served in numerous service clubs and befriended many people. Most of all he is a great dad to Perry and Sunny, and is Marilou's husband and best friend for 61+ years.

Fred is of the traditional generation, serving in the USN during WWII. Everything that we, and now I, write about in this book, he believed in and lived it. Fred was a leader by anyone's definition. No one ever questioned his integrity. All of us who know him are aware that if you ask him a question, you'll get the truth (even if it hurts a bit). By now, I assume, you realize how much I admire and love my buddy Fred. He was and is still a blessing to his family, others, and me.

CONTENTS

PREFACE

I'm blessed with managing and training in a state-certified (POST) police management course for newly promoted lieutenants—nine courses per year, each containing 22 participants, equals approximately 200 managers. They represent city, county, and state agencies—large, medium, and small. They bring to the classroom ideas, inspiration, vision, and teamwork. *They* are the reason this book has entered its 7th edition. After meeting and listening to them for 40 of the 104 hours that comprise each class, writing this book is a snap.

I've changed the book a lot, adding two new chapters that start ("Decisions") and end it ("Performance"). Also, the chapters have been segmented into leadership, management, and results. Here's the logic—leadership depends on *values* and *ethics* that can be communicated as a *vision* along with the power and energy necessary to fulfill it. Now management includes controlling your *time* and *problem employees*, coping with *politics* and *unions* while keeping your eye on securing adequate *budget* dollars. Why the leading; why the managing? The answer: to get the *results* your community expects in an *organized* way and then being able to prove your *performance*.

It is the first chapter that links and pervades all of the other 14. Clearly, all of the thoughts and acts involved in leading, managing, and measuring police work depend on *decisions*—rational ones, efficient ones, honest ones, and emotional ones. You'll learn that police leaders and managers have loads of choices. Those that are character driven are the *right* ones.

On the last day of each police management course, I depart fully convinced that no matter what society throws at these men and women they'll handle it. They're intellectually smart, emotionally stable, technically competent, and most importantly—trustworthy. As I write, I'm probably including you in this assessment. When you finish this book, you'll know if I did or not.

This is not the product of one author. It was a team effort. Key members of the team are Pat David, my buddy and computer genius; new guy Tim Peyton, the Prentice Hall coach and motivator; the outside insightful and helpful manuscript critics: Alex Del Carmen, University of Texas—Arlington, Arlington, TX; Steve Egger, University of Houston—Clearlake, Houston, TX; William Fraher, John Jay College of Criminal Justice, New York, NY; David Kotajarvi, Lakeshore Technical College, Cleveland, WI; Mark Marsouais, Northern Kentucky University, Highland Heights, KY; Rosie O'Shea, my pal who stood by me faithfully; and several police leaders/managers whom I admire and who hammered on my work very hard. Simply and sincerely—thank you.

Paul M. Whisenand, Ph.D.
San Clemente, CA

*Whatever you can do or dream you can do, begin it. Boldness
has genius, power, and magic in it.*
— *Goethe*

Register today at www.prenhall.com
to access instructor resources digitally.

To access supplementary materials online, instructors need to request an instructor access code. Go to **www.prenhall.com**, click the **Instructor Resource Center** link, and then click **Register Today** for an instructor access code. Within 48 hours after registering you will receive a confirming e-mail including an instructor access code. Once you have received your code, go to the site and log on for full instructions on downloading the materials you wish to use.

ABOUT THE AUTHOR

Paul Whisenand is the president of PMW Associates, a law enforcement and training firm located in San Clemente, California. He is a professor emeritus of criminal justice, California State University, Long Beach. Paul served as a police officer, City of Los Angeles, and reserve deputy sheriff, County of Los Angeles Sheriff's Department. He has authored 14 books on police work. Further, he has trained and lectured to hundreds of police agencies across this nation and abroad on the subjects of leadership, team building, strategic planning, and empowerment. Paul is a University of Southern California "Trojan" holding his Ph.D. in public administration. You can learn more about him and his firm by consulting: www.pmwassociates.com.

1 | DECISIONS

The most important responsibility for any police leader and manager is that of making decisions.

Our decisions serve as a transparent window that reveals the very substance of our character and competency.

Always remember that your own resolution to succeed is more important than anything else.
—*Abraham Lincoln*

CHAPTER OUTLINE

1. Choices
2. Space
3. Character and Competency
    a. Trust
    b. Character
    c. Competence
4. Management and Leadership
    a. Manager or Leader?
    b. Police Leadership
    c. Police Management
    d. An Ideal Choice
5. Character-Driven Decisions: Seven Reasons for Making Them
    a. Trust Revisited
    b. Courage
    c. Purpose
    d. Metrics
    e. Focus
    f. Motivation
    g. Rewarding
6. Four Intelligences

E ven if you decide not to make a decision—that is still a decision. Police managers are paid to make them. I'm convinced that more than ever, *decision making* is the foundation and essential characteristic of leadership. Unfortunately, there are some of us who postpone strategic decisions for quick fixes that allow us the comfort of lingering in long-term denial.

Please reread Lincoln's opening maxim. When doing so, substitute the word *decision* for *resolution*. What meaning does this quote now hold for you? What is your decision about your success as a manager and leader? *You have a choice; choose well.*

One of the biggest complaints among rank-and-file police personnel is about their bosses who, for some reason, decide *not* to decide. This is referred to as procrastination and indecisiveness. Indecisive police managers typically offer such lame excuses as "not enough time"; "it's not my decision to make"; "gee, I don't see any need for a decision." The reasons for such irresponsible thinking include laziness, cowardice, ignorance, and/or apathy. Whatever the reason, such thinking on the part of a police manager is intolerable. As a manager, the most critical part of your job, first and foremost, is to *make decisions*. As a manager, you've been selected and are being paid to make decisions—often tough ones. Major Richard "Dick" Winters (Band of Brothers—the leader of Easy Company, "Band of Brothers," 101st Airborne, World War II) puts it this way . . .

> **You get it done by making a decision quick, getting to it, and getting the thing done. Don't sit back and let the other guy make a decision that will put you on the defensive. Make up your mind quickly and get it done, right or wrong.**

If you have not already discovered, you will, that the truly tough, risky, and confusing calls are not about policies, budget, or technological issues (the "what"); they are about people (the "who"). In selecting, motivating, and directing the "who," you will not experience clear-cut, easy answers. On the contrary, you will be seeing more than one right and more than one wrong choice. The fully rational decision you seek will be bounded by uncertainties, emotions, and a host of other intervening influences. When it comes to making your best choice, choose well; your success depends on it.

The key to managing your future is having the right people working with and for you. Your job carries with it the opportunity and the responsibility to understand and make decisions about the people you lead and the community you serve.

Good management and good leadership require good decisions and good choices. Your success as a manager and a leader will be measured by your timely and accurate choices.

The usefulness of all the following chapters of this book will depend on what *you* decide to do about the contents of this chapter. Critical choices await you.

CHOICES

> *The history of free man is never written by chance,*
> *but by choice—their choice.*
> —*Dwight D. Eisenhower*

We were all given magnificent "birth gifts" such as talents, capacities, privileges, intelligence, and opportunities that would remain largely unopened but for our own decisions and efforts. However, next to life itself, the greatest gift of all is that we are free to choose.

Certainly our genes, our culture, and our socialization influence our choices, but they do not determine them. The essence of *being human* is being able to make choices about *our own lives*. The essence of being a manager and leader is being able to influence the choices of others.

Making choices about our own lives is awesome enough, but being able to influence the choices of scores of others is truly incredible. Making choices is the leader in action. The power of choice means that we are *not* merely a product of our genetic heredity or social acculturation. We are not an outcome of how others have treated or defined us. While our past, our genes, and our experiences all influence our choices, they do *not* determine them.

Through our choices we exercise self-determination. We are a product of our decisions, not our conditions.

As a police manager, the freedom and power to choose is affirming because it excites a sense of potential and achievement. It can also make a leader anxious due to a sudden heightened awareness of responsibility. We become accountable. Perhaps, in the past, we have been sheltered by the impression that our managerial problems are due to past or present circumstances beyond our control. Suddenly we have no excuses. Leaders know that they have both the freedom and responsibility to make choices. This freedom and responsibility produce a *stimulus* and a need for a *response*—a decision.

SPACE

- Watch your thoughts; they lead to attitudes.
- Watch your attitudes; they lead to words.
- Watch your words; they lead to actions.
- Watch your actions; they lead to habits.
- Watch your habits; they form your character.
- Watch your character; it determines your destiny.

Between stimulus and response is a space. Within that space is the freedom to stop for a moment. In it resides the power to choose our response. If even a fraction of a second exists between stimulus and response, that space provides us with the opportunity to reflect and then choose the best response to any situation. In essence, functioning within this "space" are your decisions about your character.

Between a stimulus (a personnel problem, for example) and your decision as a leader is the space within which you must make a choice. That choice is driven by your character. How a police manager uses his or her character within that space to evaluate the problem and make a decision determines the quality of the decision. Marginal managers see their "space for choice" as limited. Superior managers see their "space for choice" as flexible, expandable, and morally driven. This capacity is one of the qualities that separate the weak and unethical decision makers from the strong and moral ones.

Think long and hard about the gift of choice—reflect on what kind of character you have developed and nurtured as a police leader. Is it small and rigid? Or is it large and expandable? The manner in which you use your space to drive your choice will determine the quantity and quality of your managerial decisions. Each good decision, therefore, should start with a stop—a forced space for reflection to let us clarify our goals, evaluate the completeness and credibility of our information, and devise alternative strategies to achieve the best possible result. This stop can also allow us to muster our moral willpower to overcome temptations and emotions that can lead to rash, foolish, or ill-considered decisions.

A lot of scientific evidence can be found that discounts the notion of character in the use of free will. We are told that how well we decide and act is highly susceptible to outside influences. It is reported that our unconscious mind can override our conscious decision making with snap judgments. While I appreciate that there is empirical data to this effect and agree with it to some extent, I believe that we are given the freedom within our "space for choice," however brief, to exercise our character in our power to decide. Your use of character within your space for choice can be perfected and enlarged until the very nature of your responses will begin to shape the stimulus—literally creating the type of world in which you wish to live and work.

CHARACTER AND COMPETENCY

*To lead in the 21st century . . . you will be required to
have both character and competence.*
—H. Norman Schwarzkopf

Decisions about your character as well as your competency should be given prime time within your space for choice. Depending on your choices about these two facets of your life, you'll either build or destroy your trustworthiness as a manager, which enables me to trust you and you to trust me. Before a closer look at how character and competency fit into our discussion of managerial decision making, we'll explore trust in more detail.

Trust

Every police manager I work with talks freely and frequently about the importance of trust as an operational asset. No one seems to doubt how important trust is to professional or personal relationships, and everyone seems equally aware of the tremendous costs of distrust. Yet, despite enlightened rhetoric about trust, some police managers regularly engage in conduct that undermines trust and damages credibility, demonstrating a lack of character and/or competence as a leader.

Trust is the key to all human relationships. If there is a lack of trust between a manager and his or her staff, the working relationship will be doomed. Trust is the glue that holds relationships together. Likewise, it is a binding agent for police organizations. Without it, they fail to meet their mission and fulfill their potential. Specifically, character and competency are the primal pillars of police leadership and management. The deeper, the larger, the stronger these twin pillars are, the greater the leader and the better the manager.

Lack of trust guarantees disaster for a police organization. Some believe that the only things needed for success are talent, skills, energy, and personality. This is wrong thinking. Experience has repeatedly shown us and continues to teach us that who we *are* is more important than who we *appear* to be.

The Industrial Age (1830–1947) provided an operational path of personality, technology, situational ethics, and an emphasis on the "bottom line." The slogan of the age was "What's in it for me?" I sense a new path emerging as police leaders experience the miserable fruits of a personality ethic and a valueless organizational culture. More and more departments are recognizing the urgency of building trustworthiness through a demonstration of both character and competency. Forging a work environment that manifests trust is a matter of personal relationships. *Can I trust you? Can you trust me?* Second, it is a matter of organizational systems and procedures. *Do we trust our department? Does our department trust us?* Third, it is a matter of human communications. *Am I being heard? Am I hearing you?*

We've learned how important foundational trust is to the daily operations of a police agency. We've also learned that it comes from employees being trustworthy. Now, how do we best measure the trustworthiness of others? The answer is—by observing both their character and their competency.

Character

Five birds are sitting on a telephone wire. Two of them decide to fly south. How many are left? Three, you say? No, it's five. You see, deciding to fly south is not the same as doing it. If a bird really wants to go somewhere, it's got to point itself in the right direction, jump off the wire, and flap its wings. Good intentions are not enough. Our character is defined and our lives are determined not by what we want, say, or think, but by what we do.

Though character surely shapes one's destiny, character itself is not predestined; it's not inborn. It is developed. Character is the product of habits we form and choices we make about values, attitudes, and conduct. While not identical, conduct and character are closely related. In fact, what we say and do, especially as police leaders, generally reveals and often reinforces our character. So we expect kind managers to act kindly and honest managers to tell the truth and keep their promises.

The three components of a trustworthy character are: (1) integrity; (2) maturity; and (3) "win-win" behavior.

Integrity: Integrity means behaving in a manner that is grounded in sound principles, ethics, and honesty. Honesty is the characteristic of being truthful. Integrity is acting on the commitments made to yourself and others. Note: The word *integrity* won the award for the word most often searched for in the Merriam-Webster online dictionary in 2006. This subject permeates Chapter 3, "Ethics."

Maturity: In this case, we are referring to *emotional maturity* as distinguished from chronological maturity. A manager's character depends in large part on understanding self and others. He relates to co-workers with conviction and compassion. He is seen as self-disciplined.

Win-Win: Thinking win-win (we both win) is a mind-set and so is thinking win-lose (I win, you lose). Regrettably, the majority of us tend to think win-lose. Fortunately, there is a proven method for reaching agreements that are win-win. It actually works!

Win-win is a belief in the "Third Alternative." The Third Alternative means that the solution isn't your way or my way; it's a *better* way, a higher way. (If a Third Alternative can't be reached, there is "No Deal" (which means if you and I can't find a solution that would benefit us both, we agree to disagree agreeably—No Deal!).

Win-win is never a victory over other people. It is a decision that brings mutually beneficial results to everyone involved.

STRUCTURED EXERCISE 1-1

The use of the Third Alternative requires three commitments. As you review them, rate yourself on a scale of 1 to 7, 7 being high:

- *Integrity:* Integrity is the value I place on myself and others _____.
- *Emotional Maturity:* This commitment requires that I express my feelings with conviction and courage balanced with consideration for the feelings and convictions of others _____.
- *Abundance Mentality:* This is the belief that there is enough for everyone. The opposite is the mentality of scarcity—the belief that the more I get, the less you have, or the happier I am, the unhappier you are. My abundance mentality is _____.

STRUCTURED EXERCISE 1-2

Let us see how you rate your competence. Based on your current job, how do you see yourself in terms of (1–7, 7 is high):

- *Technical:* My technical skills and abilities are _____.

- *Knowledge:* My conceptual and applied knowledge base is _____.

- *Teamwork:* My ability to either lead or perform as a member of a team is _____.

Competence

Competency is both what we perform and how well we perform it. There are three parts of the competence side of trustworthiness: (1) technical; (2) knowledge; and (3) teamwork.

Technical: Technical competence is the skill and ability to accomplish managerial tasks (e.g., Chapter 12, "Budget"). It also means deploying your birth-given talents to solve problems. It is an excellent opportunity for a manager to showcase what she expects from her staff in the way of a work product—a police service. Displaying technical competence is one critical step a manager must take to elevate trustworthiness.

Knowledge: There is your innate conceptual knowledge that enables you to envision a goal, think about it strategically, and apply your imagination to its attainment (e.g., Chapter 4, "Vision"). You also have self-acquired knowledge that stems from job-related experiences, in-service training, and formal education. Again, a strong knowledge base used with wisdom is a trust builder.

Teamwork: Teamwork is building complementary teams in a police agency. It is the installation of a work ethic that flourishes on a covenant to pull together and share in the rewards of a job well done (e.g., Chapter 6, "Empowerment"). Building a team definitely isn't easy. It is complex and at times frustrating, and always challenging, always changing. Teamwork and empowerment are interrelated. You have to have both in order to get one.

MANAGEMENT AND LEADERSHIP

> *Nothing is more difficult and therefore more*
> *precious than to be able to decide.*
> —*Napoleon Bonaparte*

A police manager and a police leader can be the same individual. Or one can be a police manager and not a leader, or a police leader but not a manager. One responsibility that they share is the need to *make decisions*. Two others are modeling *values* and *ethics*.

These three responsibilities are foundational. They pertain to both management and leadership. Remember . . .

Police managers and police leaders are expected to make decisions, and these include the critical ones of modeling values and ethics.

Manager or Leader?

Both management and leadership are needed in a police agency. Unfortunately, many of us have succumbed to an overemphasis on leadership and a neglect of the importance of management. The cliché of the day is, "We're overmanaged and underled." I disagree. I believe too many of our police organizations are poorly managed and misled. Here's why. Managing pertains to *things* such as money, costs, time organization, physical resources, and statistics. Leading is about *people*—their vision, empowerment, teamwork, communication, vitality, and service. The former is mundane and routine while the latter is exciting and challenging. Many police personnel decide that they want to lead but skip the "ho-hum" stuff of managing things. In other words, "I've decided to do the necessary 25 push-ups required to be a police leader, but I want to skip the 25 push-ups required to be a manager." In the vast majority of cases, this is a bad decision. Things and people are interrelated. To do a good job with one requires the ability to do a good job with the other. When you pick up one end of a barbell, you must pick up the other as well. Being an effective boss requires competence in both areas—things and people.

When we start leading things and managing people, police organizations suffer.

Earlier, I mentioned that the truly hard decisions a manager makes involve "who" as distinguished from "what." Since leadership emphasizes people, Part One will center on decisions about the human element—human resources. Part Two deals more with decisions on the "what" or physical resources. Combined they will give you the full 50 push-ups needed to be a good police manager and leader.

Police Leadership

Leadership is the capacity to command.

There are two choices when considering leadership: Do you want to lead, and do you want to lead effectively?

Here is the trickology of leading others—you don't have to be a police manager to be a police leader. While managing is positional, leading is personal. While managing depends on authority, leading requires power. While managing focuses on a thing, leading concentrates on people. It is capacity!

In a police organization anyone can exert leadership—anyone. It all depends on the capacity to model values and ethics and reflect a motivating vision. The leader builds teams, empowers others, emphasizes purposes, and listens. If the leader is performing all of these functions and is a police manager, you are witnessing a manager/leader, which is as good as it's going to get! Concisely, a leader commands based on an individually developed capacity to use power, not the power of the police agency but his or her own.

Police Management

Management is the right to command.

There are two choices when it comes to being a police manager. First, do you want to be one, and second, do you want to be a good one?

When your police department awards you a bar or a star, it simultaneously grants you the right to command things and people. The agency acknowledges that you have the delegated authority and shared responsibility for controlling structure, expenses, methods, and people's behavior. Your authority is based on your position and rank. It is your right!

If you exercise your right with fairness, wisdom, and care, you will be respected and followed. If you execute this right with coercion, fear, and callousness, you will be feared and avoided. Briefly, a manager commands based on an agency-granted right to a person in a particular management position holding a certain rank to dispense authority—not his or hers but that of the agency.

An Ideal Choice

In a perfect world, the police officer who decides to be a manager also chooses to be a leader. This requires a blending of the position with the person—authority and power. It is possible to be both a good manager and a good leader. Right now, you can set about acquiring the competency necessary to be a winning police manager. Likewise, you can choose to develop the character required to be a great police leader. It's a choice you can make—the ideal choice.

Having explored choices, character, competency, management, and leadership, we are now positioned to probe further into the adhesive that binds and drives them—decision making.

CHARACTER-DRIVEN DECISIONS: SEVEN REASONS FOR MAKING THEM

Character is much easier kept than recovered.
—*Linda Goldzimer*

We begin this section with Structured Exercise 1-3. *Do not skip it!* You'll find out why in a few minutes. (Incidentally, this exercise works well in a group setting. Independently complete the exercise and then reach group consensus on the rank ordering of the characteristics.)

Steven Covey (*The 8th Habit*) had nearly 15,000 people complete the questionnaire in Structured Exercise 1-3. They represented a highly diverse cross section of American workers. The vast majority had "integrity" as their first choice. A distant second, third, and fourth were: communicator, people focused, and visionary. Initially, I resolutely concurred. I have changed my mind, deciding that "decision maker" was number one, and here is why.

In choosing integrity, or any other characteristic, *you* made a *decision*. Which comes first—your integrity or your decision to have it as a leader? I believe that *your*

STRUCTURED EXERCISE 1-3

Carefully study the following list of *essential qualities of a leader*. You are welcome to add one of your own. Next, rank order them ("1" is high, "2" second highest, etc.).

_____ Caring

_____ Dedicated

_____ Integrity

_____ People focused

_____ Communicator

_____ Decision maker

_____ Model

_____ Visionary

_____ Motivator

_____ Courageous

_____ Expert

_____ Other (Your turn)

decision to be (or not to be) a character-driven leader is paramount. In other words, your choices shape, drive, and reveal your character. Obviously this is a circular and reinforcing process—moral decisions lead to an honest leader, which leads to moral decisions. But it has to start somewhere. For me, its genesis occurs when we opt to think and act with integrity. Long ago, Samuel Johnson wrote, "Integrity without knowledge is weak and useless, but knowledge without integrity is dangerous and dreadful." Warren Buffett updated this proposition when he said, "In looking for people to hire, look for three qualities: integrity, intelligence, and energy. But if they don't have the first, the other two will kill you."

There are seven solid reasons for making character-driven decisions:

- Trust
- Courage
- Purpose
- Metrics
- Focus
- Motivation
- Rewarding

Trust Revisited

Trust was covered a few pages ago, but merits another look. Briefly, when those who work for you consistently see a clear-cut example of trustworthiness, they are apt to trust you. With their trust you'll gain their followership. Yes, as the ethicist Michael Josephson constantly reminds us—character counts. For a police leader and manager, generating trust by manifesting a good character counts big time.

Courage

Managing and leading others frequently is an act of courage. As a manager, you're deciding about such things as budget expenditures, deployment of personnel, disciplinary problems, promotions, and the like. There is some risk involved. Usually there isn't any manual, authority person, or proven standard to judge by. When leading, it is even more risky—even fearful. In this case you are confronted with decisions about ethical dilemmas, clarity of vision, empowerment, team building, and more. Here the benchmarks and guidelines are either vague or nonexistent.

Without fear there would not be any courage. The police manager who exclaims, "I'm not afraid of anything" is either a liar, stupid, or clinically stoned. A character-based decision does not remove the risk or fear, but it does help you to overcome it. Overcoming fear and adversity not only builds character . . . it reveals it.

Purpose

Without purpose, leadership lacks meaning. Purpose is as essential as air and water. Hope comes from having a purpose, and we need hope to cope. When leadership shows purpose, everyone can bear tremendous burdens to achieve it. Without purpose these burdens can seem unbearable. To be effective, it must be transparent, and it must be demonstrated by the example you set.

Metrics

Your character as a police manager defines what you will and will not do. It sets the metric you use to evaluate those tasks that are essential and those that are not. Without clear metrics, there are no benchmarks by which you can make decisions, allocate your time, and commit your resources. Leaders who do not know their metrics take on unnecessary projects that cause stress, fatigue, and hostility. Proven leadership wisdom is, "What gets measured gets done."

Focus

For your leadership to have impact, you must focus it. With your purposes firmly in mind, you are able to concentrate your decisions and your energy on what is vital. Without a laser beam on your purposes, you tend to procrastinate and become easily distracted by minor issues, spinning at a frenetic pace but going nowhere. Good intentions that are unfocused rarely become a reality.

Motivation

Character-based decisions frequently generate enthusiasm. Nothing promotes inspiration more than doing the right thing for the right reasons. Meaningless work typically wears us down faster than hard work. The majority of police employees are ready to commit themselves—but only when they know why. As a police leader, if you project a vivid picture of the rightness of your efforts, those you lead are likely to follow. Without an expressed reason for your decision, the most you can expect is blind obedience with a ho-hum attitude. Explain the reason for your decision, and motivation is apt to occur.

Rewarding

In the long run, character-driven decisions are rewarding. Everyone can win—the staff, the department, the community, and the police manager. However, at times the job of leader and manager can be lonely or frustrating, fatiguing, or all three in a toxic mix. If you know that you made the best decision for the greatest good, what more reward is needed? Others may not know about it or even damn your decision. But you have the sense of fulfillment and self-efficacy that your integrity prevailed and drove the decision. That is character at its best.

FOUR INTELLIGENCES

> *Minds are like parachutes—they only function when open.*
> —*Lord Thomas Dewar*

When we encounter a situation that commands we make a decision, we will deploy one or more of our four intelligences:

- Intellectual (e.g., "$7 \times 7 = 49$"; "H_2O = Water")
- Physical (e.g., "Ouch! That hurts"; "The volume is too loud.")
- Spiritual (e.g., "What would God, or Allah, or Buddha tell me to do?")
- Emotional (e.g., "Be happy, don't worry;" "I'm proud of you!")

Most times we endeavor to apply our intellect or IQ. Managers want to be seen as linear, objective, logical, and rational, when, in fact, their decisions are a mixture of zigzagging, subjectivity, psychology, and emotions.

The seminal thinker and researcher Daniel Goleman asserts that decisions by managers and leaders are mainly shaped and driven by our emotional intelligence (EI). And when our four intelligences collide over a choice, our EI usually prevails over the other three. Daniel Goleman researched (*Emotional Intelligence*) how much IQ accounts for career success. What do you think he discovered? Grab a pen and take a guess. IQ accounts for what portion of career success?

   a. 50%–60%
   b. 35%–45%
   c. 23%–29%
   d. 15%–20%

The answer: between 4% and 10%. Surprise! He found IQ can influence the profession you enter (e.g., astrophysics), but within a profession, mastery of a high IQ matters relatively little. More important to professional growth within a profession are integrity, imagination, social dexterity, vision, active listening, sense of humor, optimism, enthusiasm, and really caring about the welfare of others.

FIVE RULES FOR MAKING A DECISION

> *A leader must be part of the team and yet be able to step back and see clearly. Enough distance is required to make the tough calls.*
> —*Carly Fiorina*

There are five general rules for a police manager to consider when making a decision.

Rule 1. Never Make a Decision That Should Be Delegated

When presented with the need for a decision, you should first ask yourself, "Is this decision mine to make, or should one of my staff make it?"

Unfortunately, some police managers believe that since they have the authority to decide a certain issue and the responsibility for the decision, they must personally make the decision.

Some managers fear that a subordinate may make a bad decision; therefore, they make a decision themselves that would be better left to others. They feel that because they are better trained, more experienced, more expert, and ultimately accountable, they must make all the decisions. This kind of thinking is the downfall of a police manager. This type of thinking is that of an individual who is not ready to manage or lead.

Why delegate? There are three compelling reasons to delegate decision making:

1. *Empowerment.* When you empower others to do their job, you actually expand your own power base. Also, the decisions made by those you have empowered are apt to be more accurate and timely because the personnel closest to the problem or situation are engaged in making the choices. Through empowerment, you build a more coherent and stronger work team. In addition, you are building trust, morale, and expertise among your team. (More on this subject in Chapter 6.)
2. *Time.* Making good decisions is difficult and time consuming. No leader can make all of them. The sheer weight and number of decisions confronting a police manager force delegation. The manager who will not delegate is destined to "crash and burn." Nondelegation is a setup for failure. You must carefully reserve for yourself only those decisions that clearly need your attention, and cheerfully delegate the rest. In this manner, everyone benefits—the department, the management team, and the police officers. (More on this subject in Chapter 8.)
3. *Mentoring.* When you delegate, you cause others to mature professionally, and you enrich their job satisfaction. A leader can't expect his staff to grow in expertise and judgment unless he gives them the opportunity to make real decisions that have real consequences for the department. Being second-guessed and micromanaged by a police manager is demeaning and demoralizing to an employee. It will produce turned-off and tuned-out employees who do not feel respected. True delegation—really letting go—is an inspiring, appreciated, and empowering experience for all involved. (More on this subject in Chapter 6.)

Delegation and leadership are interoperable.

Rule 2. Never Make a Decision Today That Can Be Reasonably Delayed

The operative word in this rule is "reasonably." To the average police employee, this rule probably appears ridiculous, even dangerous. It doesn't mean that you ignore critical incidents that demand an immediate decision. Nor does it mean you suspend thinking about them. However, most managerial decisions (personnel issues, as an example) do not require speeding to judgment. President Harry Truman was constantly pressured for snap decisions. The first thing he would ask his staff was, "How much time do I have?"

In other words, is it essential that the decision be made now, in an hour, a day, next week? Truman recognized that all decisions are not equal in priority and that the timing of a decision is as important as the decision itself.

The timing of a leader's decision is as important as the decision itself.

This decision rule is not "artful procrastination"; rather, it is "strategic timing," which avoids the risk of rushing into a fast (and wrong) fix. The advantage of Rule 2 is that it usually opens up many more choices for the leader. The downside to Rule 2 is that by waiting too long, options may be foreclosed. Timing a decision is an art, not a science. Decisive timing is an act of courage because it involves risk taking. Surrendering a decision to fate or to others amounts to cowardly procrastination.

Rule 3. Decide If the Decision Is Yours to Make

When required to make a decision immediately, ask yourself, "Do I have the authority and/or the responsibility to make this decision?" Perhaps the decision is beyond your purview. Some police managers get into trouble for overstepping the bounds of their authority—they make brilliant decisions with respect to issues that lie outside their jurisdiction and then they are embarrassed and reproached. The message in this example is clear—or should be.

If it is your decision to make, make it or delegate the making of it. If not, express an opinion, if invited to do so, but beyond that—butt out!

Rule 4. Take Extra Care with "Big Ticket" Decisions

Certain decisions are considered "big ticket" items. These decisions involve the likelihood of extreme consequences to the decision maker as well as all other stakeholders in the matter. In these cases, the leader must slow down, focus, and take extra care to think long term.

A decision merits this special time and attention if the answer to any of the following questions is yes.

- **Could the decision cause serious financial, physical, or emotional damage?**
- **Could the decision jeopardize important relationships?**
- **Could the decision undermine or trash reputations or credibility?**
- **Could the values, integrity, and vision of the department be adversely affected by the decision?**

Rule 5. Enforce the Rules

Leadership in any environment, from parenting to leading a group of police officers, requires that the leader lay down the rules and evenhandedly enforce them. While it may seem counter to our current warm and fuzzy, feel-good culture, fair but strong discipline administered by a leader with the proper respect for justice will give rise to a stronger sense of security and teamwork among the staff.

I am *not* recommending that you punish all rule violators. Neither am I suggesting that you suspend compassion and forgiveness. I am simply pointing out that the failure of a leader to enforce the rules due to a desire to remain popular or to avoid negative emotions can bring that leader to ruin in a hurry. Remember . . .

What you do not enforce you encourage!

THE DECISION-MAKING PROCESS: SIX STEPS

We are a product of our decisions, not our conditions.
—*Steve Covey*

With the above five rules serving as a decision-making framework, you are now prepared to take the requisite six concurrent steps for actually deciding. Although covered in sequential order, the steps are an integrated process and are taken simultaneously. The steps are:

- Participation
- Chance
- Intuition
- Future
- Satisfying
- Conscience

Step 1. Participation

Carefully considering the values, needs, and desires of those likely to be affected by the decision is vital. Even more critical is that all those who will be affected by the decision participate in some way in the decision-making process. This does *not* mean that others make your decision. That remains your responsibility. However, allowing others to participate in the process assures them an opportunity to voice their ideas, concerns, opinions, and hopes. In this manner they feel more a part of the process. Ultimately, even though others may not like the decision you make, they are more apt to understand it and be supportive of it if they have been a part of the process.

> **Abraham Lincoln once took a vote among his cabinet on an issue that he favored. When he had counted the votes, Lincoln announced, "One aye and seven nays—the ayes have it!"**

Although Lincoln disagreed with his staff, he made certain that they participated in the process. At least they were asked for their opinions and ideas. Obviously it was Abe's decision to make. You may be thinking, "Hey, he asked for their input, and he ignored it! He should have decided in favor of their option." Nonsense. It was their responsibility to candidly express recommendations. It was his responsibility to involve them in helping him make decisions that affect the nation, but it remained Lincoln's responsibility to actually decide on which route to take.

Have you ever been offended, put down, or angered by a boss or peer who did not ask your counsel when making a decision about your work or your expertise? It happens all too often. When it occurs, the decision-making process is damaged and needs repair. Although it may happen to you, do not victimize others with the same insensitive behavior. If you do, your effectiveness as a police leader will take a dive.

Step 2. Chance

Every decision includes some element of risk or chance. Decision making is a game of chance in which the leader is betting on success versus failure. Some police managers become anxious about the sheer speculation inherent in a decision. All of us prefer to make a safe, 100% guaranteed accurate decision. Only naïve people would delude themselves by thinking that their decision can be measured and calculated to ensure this level of certainty.

> **Niccolo Machiavelli wrote that slightly more than half the outcome of any bold undertaking is due to luck.**

This step can be referred to as the "slippery rock" step. You can significantly reduce your chance of slipping by strong analysis, concentrated focus, and most of all by allowing others to participate in the process.

Step 3. Intuition

An important tool used in making a decision (taking a risk) is that of personal judgment—*intuition*. Police managers must select choices that are sometimes based as much on intuition (gut feelings) as on precise analysis and objective logic. In most decision-making situations, facts are incomplete and frequently inaccurate. You must rely instead on your own good sense and instinctive feelings.

In his much celebrated book *Blink,* Malcolm Gladwell argues that snap decisions (rapid cognition) are frequently as good—even better—than decisions made after lengthy deliberation. Deliberate decisions are useful in certain situations, but we actually use intuitive decisions more often.

> **Truly successful decision making relies on a balance between deliberate and intuitive thinking.**

Snap decisions are made when our brain reaches a conclusion before it informs our consciousness. The part of our brain that jumps to judgment is the "adaptive unconsciousness," and the study of this kind of decision making is an important new field of psychology. The term *adaptive unconsciousness* does not refer to the unconscious described by Freud as a dark, murky place full of disturbing desires, fantasies, and memories, but rather a kind of giant computer that rapidly and quietly processes a lot of data that we need to function as human beings. It "thin slices" our experiences, searching for what is meaningful and discarding superfluous information that would impair our ability to solve problems or know our own mind. At times too much information can result in bad or poorly timed decisions.

Rapid cognition has incredible power for good as well as bad. Snap judgments are generated by our experiences and our environment. If we rely only on experiences that are negative, we will intuit wrong, stupid, or unethical decisions about events and people.

Good news! We can alter the way we thin slice—by substituting new, positive experiences for old, negative information. This requires that we take active steps to manage and control what resides in our adaptive unconsciousness.

We need both analytical and intuitive decision making. Where we err is in using one or the other in inappropriate circumstances. For example, suppose you are in a situation involving a barricaded suspect with a hostage. Do you consult a strategic plan or the police chief for assistance in making your decision? Of course not! You experience rapid cognition; you thin slice your past experiences and information and quickly make a snap, and hopefully correct, decision.

> **If you get caught up in the production of information in order to make a decision, you risk drowning in the data.**

Deliberate thinking is a wonderful tool when we have the luxury of time, a computer, the Internet, and a clearly defined task. The results of that type of deliberative analysis can set the stage for *accurate,* rapid cognition and *correct* first impressions.

Our snap decisions come out of a locked room, and we cannot look inside that room. But with experience—in this case supervisory experience—we become expert at using our behaviors and our training to interpret, and we decode what lies behind our snap judgments and first impressions.

Whenever we have something that we are good at—something we care about—that experience and passion fundamentally changes the nature of our thin slicing. With self-discipline, experience, and care, we can be assured of making successful snap decisions as police supervisors.

Step 4. Future

This step requires looking ahead—foresight. Decisions by a police leader can only influence the future, not the past! What's done cannot be undone, and a leader must steel herself to that fact and look forward. Even though there may be huge emotional or political pressures urging the boss to justify past decisions and commitments, she must have the courage to take a fresh look and disregard past mistakes. Bad past decisions must not be allowed to define your future decisions or limit the future choices that you possess.

> **The wrong decisions of the past, even those that involve reputation, time, and money, must be acknowledged as wrong in order not to repeat them and thus to free yourself to succeed in the future.**

Step 5. Satisfying

This step asks the question, "How much is enough?" For example, if you were responsible for overseeing the design of a new police facility, how many police facilities, design architects, and construction firms would you consult and consider? Or, if you were deciding on new computer monitors, how much time would you commit? The time, energy, and concentration on a decision should vary in direct relationship to the significance of the decision. Again, "How much time is enough?" It is the efficient manager and wise leader who knows the answer to this question.

Step 6. Conscience

As mentioned earlier, when making tough decisions, a leader will carefully listen to those who will be affected. When making the *really* tough, gut-wrenching, and soul-searching decisions, he will also carefully listen to his heart. The operative word here is *listen.*

The hardest thing to do and the right thing to do are often the same thing!

Unfortunately, when most of us consult our inner voice, we do all the talking. That's because some of us are afraid of what we might hear. However, if we are quiet and patient, and carefully listen to our conscience, our "inner voice" can be a strong ally in making good decisions in difficult times.

The final forming of a person's character lies in their own hands.
—*Anne Frank*

CENTERPIECE

Decision making is the centerpiece of police leadership and management. It serves as a start and end point. It is the driving force of self-efficacy and organizational results. It is the life blood of all ideas, practices, and challenges that follow. Our ability to choose—to make decisions—is to be forever prized and always appreciated.

The decisions you'll be making about running a police department can be roughly segmented into three parts, as you'll soon experience.

Part One—Leadership (Chapters 2–7)
Part Two—Management (Chapters 8–12)
Part Three—Results (Chapters 13–15)

The great things a man does appear to be great only after they are done.
When they're at hand, they are normal decisions and are done without
knowledge of their greatness.
—*General George S. Patton*

Competency Checkpoints

- The key characteristic of a police leader/manager is making decisions.
- The freedom of choice is one of our richest birth gifts.
- Between a demand for a decision and our response to it there is a "space" that guarantees us our freedom of choice.
- Our character and competency determines our trustworthiness.
- Trust is the linchpin for all human relationships.

- Our character is a unique and fluid blend of our: (1) integrity; (2) maturity; and (3) win-win behavior.
- Our competency is a mix of our: (1) technical skills; (2) knowledge; and (3) teamwork.
- Our character is shaped to the degree that we evidence, or not, the above six factors.
- Both police management and police leadership are needed for a police department to be successful.
- Leadership is the capacity to command; management is the right to do so.
- Character-driven decisions at once inculcate: (1) trust; (2) courage; (3) purpose; (4) metrics; (5) focus; (6) motivation; and (7) a rewarding feeling.
- We have four intelligences: (1) intellectual; (2) physical; (3) spiritual; and (4) emotional. The latter typically supersedes the other three.
- There are five rules for making decisions:
  Never make a decision that should be delegated.
  Never make a decision today that can be reasonably delayed.
  Decide if the decision is yours to make.
  Take extra care with "big ticket" decisions.
  Enforce the rules.
- There are six decision-making steps: (1) participation; (2) chance; (3) intuition; (4) future; (5) satisfying; and (6) conscience.

Flexing the Message

1. Do you agree with the notion of "freedom of choice," or are we in reality constrained by our circumstances?
2. What do you do to protect your needed "space" to make accurate decisions?
3. Explain how trust or being trustworthy binds one's character together with one's competency.
4. Have you ever experienced making a decision that yielded a win-win result?
5. Explain the differences between leading and managing. Is one more important to policing than the other? Why?
6. When the vast majority of managers select "integrity" as their number one quality of a leader (see Structured Exercise 1-3), how can I argue that "decision making" ought to be first? Whom do you agree with?
7. List five people you know who have a high EI. Now list five with a low EI. Which attributes do you find in common among the first five as compared to the second five? How do you rate yourself on EI?
8. Among the "Five Rules for Making a Decision," which one is the most important to obey? Why?
9. How often do you think you rely on "intuition" or snap decisions as compared to analytical, thoughtful ones? Are you comfortable with rapid cognition?
10. What was not covered in this chapter that should have been included? Write down your thoughts and discuss them with a colleague.

PART

I

LEADERSHIP

CHAPTER

2 ‖ VALUES

Becoming a leader requires that you first understand your own values. Second, it requires that you understand the values of others.

Times change, but values endure.

What lies behind us and what lies before us are tiny matters compared to what lies within us.
—Oliver Wendell Holmes

CHAPTER OUTLINE

1. Walk the Talk
2. Values: What They Are, Where They Come From, and How We Can Change Them
   a. Values Defined
   b. The Birthplace of Our Values
   c. Changing Our Values
3. Identifying Our Values
4. We Are What We Value and . . .
5. Values: What They Provide for Us
   a. Values Act as Filters
   b. Values Create Generation Gaps
   c. Values Produce Our Individual Differences
   d. Values Serve as a Map and Compass
   e. Values Cause or Resolve Conflict
   f. Values Trigger Our Emotional Intelligence
   g. Values Are Thought-Provokers
   h. Values Motivate Us
6. Values-Led Police Work
   a. Which Values Lead?
   b. Being Open
   c. Being Accountable
   d. Understanding and Respect

The most important decision that you and I must make is—what are my values? Our beliefs, attitudes, destiny, and *character* depend on the decisions we make about our values. We are what we value, and we manage/lead ourselves and others according to our value system. You and I have an important responsibility at work—and chances are it's not listed on any of our job descriptions—sharing the responsibility for making human values a part of our work life.

Values trigger our thinking and drive our behavior. Some of them are ethical in nature (e.g., integrity), which is the focus of Chapter 3. The police leader is *the* person most accountable for providing an example of correct police work values. In a valuational sense, the leader is challenged to day by day, hour by hour, "walk the talk."

WALK THE TALK

> *As I grow older, I pay less attention to what people say. I just watch what they do.*
> —Andrew Carnegie

All of us have values and a sense of what is right or wrong. Values make us different from other living things on our planet . . . they are what make us human. But while having values (several values equals a value system) is natural, practicing them isn't. Behaving in line with our values—"walking the talk"—is one of the biggest challenges each of us faces 24/7. It's true for every aspect of our lives. It's especially true in police work. And, even more significant, true for police leaders, who are expected to set the example.

Look and listen around your police agency. What's hanging on the walls, posted on bulletin boards, and published in manuals and handbooks? Do you see or hear words like *quality, service, teamwork,* and *commitment*? Many police employees do. Those are really *good* words. They're *right* words. They are excellent reminders of what police departments stand for. But we've learned that the real worth of values—the real value of values—can only be realized by practicing what we say and write.

Stating our values is easy. Behaving those values is the tough reality. It is the core and challenge of police leadership, and it must be met head on.

Here are seven points worth remembering:

1. *Everyone.* The responsibility for walking the talk doesn't rest just with police leaders. We're all responsible for bringing human values to life. (This involves empowerment, which is covered later.)
2. *Practice.* Regardless of who created the workplace values, if they're good and right, we need to *support* them.
3. *Everything.* No matter what our job is in a police department, values have everything to do with it.
4. *Accidents.* With a few exceptions, workers do *not* intentionally violate established values.
5. *Demanding.* Walking the talk is just as tough for others as it is for *you*.
6. *Perfection.* No one walks the talk all the time. There's always room for improvement.
7. *One.* Although you're only one person, you can make a difference right *now* by setting the example for others.

Leaders convey their values to their staff by everything they say and then do. Unfortunately, sometimes they are unaware of what values they are actually imparting to others. The real issue is not whether police leaders should communicate values. They can't avoid it! Policing is laden with value messages that influence the character of police employees. The issue is whether the leaders are willing to intentionally provide examples of the *correct* values.

STRUCTURED EXERCISE 2-1

Find a peaceful spot to read and carefully think about the next few paragraphs. Make a concentrated effort to project yourself into the following situation.

Visualize yourself driving to a dinner for a co-worker who is also a close friend. He has recently been selected to be the police chief in a neighboring community. You park your car and walk into the restaurant. You locate the assigned banquet room and enter. As you walk in, you see the banners and flags. You spot the smiling faces of your co-workers and their spouses. You sense a lot of happiness in the room.

As you approach your colleagues, you notice the head table and see your name card on it. You also see the name cards of your spouse and three children.

Overhead, a banner displays in large letters your name and "Congratulations for 20 Years of Service." Below that banner is another that reads "A Happy New Career to You." This celebration is in your honor! And all of these people have come on your behalf to express feelings of appreciation for your work.

You're directed to the head table, where your spouse and children join you. You're handed a program. There are five speakers. The first is your spouse. The second is one of your children. The third speaker is your closest friend. The fourth speaker is an employee who is currently working for you. The final speaker is your boss. All of these people know you very well, but in different ways.

(Continued)

STRUCTURED EXERCISE 2-1   (*Cont.*)

Now, think carefully. What would you expect each of these speakers to say about you and your life? What kind of spouse, father, and friend would you like their words to reflect? What kind of police manager? What kind of subordinate?

What values would you like them to have seen in you? What contributions, what achievements would you want them to remember? Look carefully at the people who have gathered to wish you well. What difference would you like to have made in their lives?

Five people spoke on your behalf. What values did each of them express about you? Think carefully and then list the values you believe they would have proffered.

Spouse	Child	Friend	Co-Worker	Boss
1.	1.	1.	1.	1.
2.	2.	2.	2.	2.
3.	3.	3.	3.	3.
4.	4.	4.	4.	4.
5.	5.	5.	5.	5.

What did you learn about yourself from this exercise? Take a few moments and write down your observations and feelings.

_____
_____
_____
_____
_____
_____

We live within the confines of our values, which are expressed by our words, seen in our deeds, and secluded in our thoughts.

VALUES: WHAT THEY ARE, WHERE THEY COME FROM, AND HOW WE CAN CHANGE THEM

Knowledge is of no value unless you put it into practice.
—*Heber J. Grant*

The term *value* has a variety of meanings. For example, we may value our family, value our leisure time, value our reputation, value our position as a police manager, and value jogging. Each of these five values is different in several ways. One is a goal-oriented value: our reputation. Another value, jogging, is a means to another desired state: our physical and mental health. Yet another value, our position as a police leader, is temporary; that is, it is an impermanent position. We tend to forget that what some of us may value highly, others may not. (For example, you may place a high value on the promise of a promotion, while someone else, satisfied with his or her present job, may not.) In fact, people are alike or different according to the similarities or differences among their professional, personal, and societal values.

Values Defined

A value is an enduring belief that we have in a goal and the action we must take to attain it.

The key words in the above definition are *enduring belief, goal,* and *action.* For a value to be in fact a value, all four words (or similar concepts) must prevail. Having a goal/target alone is not a value; taking action/means alone is not a value. Possessing an enduring belief/faith alone won't cut it. For example, if you very much want (enduring belief) to be promoted (goal), and you are studying very hard to get promoted (action), then "getting promoted" is one of your values. It's not your only value, but it's one of them.

Since each of us possesses more than a single value, it is essential that we think in terms of a *value system,* which is an enduring organization of beliefs concerning preferable modes of conduct or end states of existence in a hierarchical ranking of relative importance. There is not always a one-to-one connection between a means and a goal. We can have up to 20 end-state values (goals) and 60 to 70 modes of action values (means).

The Birthplace of Our Values

The process of value creation may actually begin before birth. (Many experts suggest that some behavior patterns in our ancestors might have been encoded in the DNA that now guides some of our present behavior.) Our main concern here is with behavior patterns that are learned from the moment of birth forward.

Our value learning, or *programming,* occurs in three ways: (1) imprinting, (2) modeling, and (3) socialization.

Imprinting/Parents (Birth to Age 6 or 7)

In addition to physical behavior development, a tremendous amount of mental development takes place during the imprinting period. The early years of our childhood may be compared to the foundation and frame of a building. The foundation determines the quality and strength of the structure that goes on top. The completed structure depends on its base, even if additions are built. The key figures here are Mom and Dad and a few others. Even though formal learning does not start in the preschool period, there are many important stages that determine how, how much, how well, and what we will learn as we develop. The question that we must answer and comprehend is: *Who* imprinted us, and *how,* in our formative years?

Modeling/Heroes (Age 7 or 8 to 13 or 14)

The process of identification—initially with the mother, then the father and important others around the child—expands. We shift into intense *modeling:* relating to family, friends, and external "heroes" in the world around us. We observe people we would "like to be like" carefully. As a result, our initial close models give way to more expanded contacts. Soon, group membership begins to exert its influence. We identify not only with play groups or gangs as a whole but also with certain important individuals within them. New values and behavior patterns are blended with the ones we garnered from our family. Once in school, the process of identifying expands to the heroes of history and fictional stories. Further, our increasing involvement with various media during this period will bring in characters from movies and television as additional heroes. We use these models to construct our internal ego ideal, the person we would like to become. The programming accelerates.

The hero models in our lives are very critical people. They are the people that we want to be like when we become adults. The modeling period is a critical period during which we absorb values from a diverse selection of models. Do you remember your own modeling activities? When you were 10 years old, whom did you want to grow up to be like? Further, what about your co-workers? Who were their potential role models at age 10 or 11?

Socialization/Peers (Age 13 or 14 to About Age 20)

In our early teens, our social life becomes concerned primarily with our friends. This intense *socialization* with our peers produces people with common interests (values) who group together for reinforcement. During this period of adolescence, we define and integrate the values, beliefs, and standards of our particular culture into our own personalities. At this time we achieve full physical maturity and a dominant value system. This system serves as our basic personality. During this period of socialization, we engage in experimentation, verification, and validation of our basic life plan. From about age 20 on, our value system programmed during childhood and adolescence is locked in, and we then repeatedly "test" it against the reality of the world.

People of like interests, behavior, and developing value systems associate intensely with one another and reinforce each other in their development. Who were your friends? What was your "best friend" like? What did you talk about? Did your friends have a nickname for you? What did you do together? How long have your friendships lasted? *Address the same questions in regard to your co-workers.*

Changing Our Values

Our values, while enduring, can be changed. This transition can occur in one of two ways. The first is a traumatic episode or significant emotional event (SEE). The second revolves around major and persistent dissatisfaction. Let's look at each condition more closely.

Significant Emotional Events

The common denominator of SEEs is a challenge and a disruption of our present behavior patterns and beliefs. In job situations and family relationships, such challenges might be created artificially (e.g., being fired or promoted), but SEEs are more likely to occur in an unplanned or undirected manner (e.g., being seriously injured or winning an athletic contest).

We must be careful to distinguish between SEEs, which actually change our gut-level value system, and external events, which simply modify our behavior. For example, a departmental order imposed on us may demand that we pay more attention to the needs of employees. Our behavior may change accordingly, but our values remain the same. The closer such events occur to our early programming periods, the more likely it is that significant change will occur. The less dramatic the event, the longer we hold our programmed values, and any change in values will occur more slowly, if at all. *SEEs are neither good nor bad.* Their frequency and type, and how we cope with them, determine if they are positive or negative for us.

Profound Dissatisfaction

Success in this most difficult of transitions—psychological growth—requires a special combination of inner and, to a degree, outer circumstances. In order to make significant psychological changes, we must first be profoundly dissatisfied with the status quo, energetic enough to work on changing old habits, and insightful about redirecting our dissatisfaction.

- We must be *deeply dissatisfied.* Otherwise, why change?
- We must possess a lot of psychological and physical *energy.* Few things are harder to break than old bonds, old views, old prejudices, old convictions, old habits.
- We must acquire an *insight* for redirecting the driving dissatisfaction. Without this, the effort to change will be random and pointless.

Only when all three of these factors are present simultaneously will we have the motivation to change, the drive to act on the motivation, and the foresight to know where to go and when we have arrived. See Figure 2-1 for a graphic summary of this section.

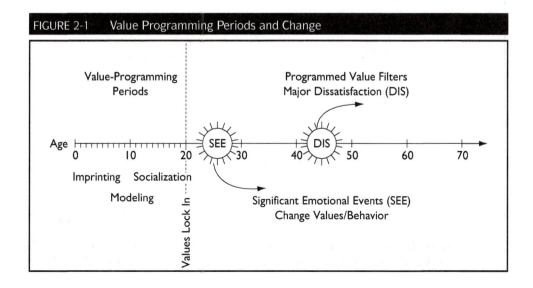

FIGURE 2-1   Value Programming Periods and Change

IDENTIFYING OUR VALUES

The only real difference between they and we is me.
—*Steve Ventura*

Take any one of your values (e.g., your job), and if you can answer each one of the following questions with a "yes," you have confirmed that it is indeed one of your values. (See Figure 2-2.) In terms of a particular value, are you

1. Choosing it *freely*?
2. Choosing it from *options*?
3. Choosing it after *thoughtful consideration* of the consequences of each option?
4. *Prizing* it (being happy with the choice)?
5. Willing to make a *public affirmation* of the choice?
6. Doing something with it: *performance*?
7. Using it in a *pattern of life*?

STRUCTURED EXERCISE 2-2

TEN OF OUR VALUES

Take the next few minutes to explore some of your individual values. The following two exercises can be accomplished either alone or in a group setting.

To begin, complete the value indicator list by quickly writing down the ten things that you enjoy (value) doing most in your professional, social, and personal life. In other words, of all the things you do in your life, list the ten that you enjoy the most.

Rank		Value	Symbol
_____	1.	_____	____
_____	2.	_____	____
_____	3.	_____	____
_____	4.	_____	____
_____	5.	_____	____
_____	6.	_____	____
_____	7.	_____	____
_____	8.	_____	____
_____	9.	_____	____
_____	10.	_____	____

Now study your list and rank your values on the left side of the list in order of priority: "1" indicates the most valued, "2" the next most valued, and so on.

Next, where they apply, place the following symbols on the right side of the list:

1. Put a "$" by any item that costs $50 or more each time you perform it. (Be certain to look for hidden costs.)
2. Put a "10" by any item that you would not have done ten years ago.
3. Put an "X" by any item that you would like to let others know you do.
4. Put a "T" by any item that you spend at least four hours a week doing.
5. Put an "M" by any item that you have actually done in the last month.
6. Put an "E" by any item that you spend time reading about, thinking about, worrying about, or planning for.
7. Put a "C" by any item that you consciously choose over other possible activities.
8. Put a "G" by any item that you think helps you to grow as a police manager.
9. Put an "R" by any item that involves some risk. (The risk may be physical, intellectual, or emotional.)

The more markings you have put next to an item, the more likely it is that the activity is one you value highly. This list is not necessarily a compilation of your values; rather, it may be an indication of where your values lie. Count the number of marks next to each item—the activity with the most marks being first, and so on. Now compare your first ranking (left side) with your second ranking (right side) and consider the following questions:

1. Do your rankings match?
2. Is your highest value in the first ranking the one that has the most marks next to it?
3. Can you see any patterns in your list?
4. Have you discovered anything new about yourself as a result of this activity?
5. Is there anything you would like to change about your preferences as a result of this exercise?

If you are studying as a group, you may want to divide into subgroups of four or five members each and share what you have learned about your values.

FIGURE 2-2   How Our Values Affect Our Attitudes and Behavior

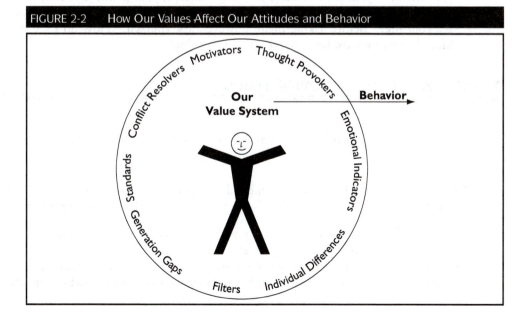

WE ARE WHAT WE VALUE AND . . .

> *It's great to be great, but it's greater to be human.*
> —Will Rogers

We are what we value, and we lead ourselves, and we lead others according to our value system.

The statement above is the center point of this discussion on values. In other words, our own unique value system determines how we lead ourselves. This same value system likewise dictates how we lead others.

Some people value work as a means of survival or attaining wealth. Their work is simply a means to an end. Others consider their work an intrinsic part of their lives. They value their jobs and the way they work as an expression of their personhood. The most fortunate of all are those who find value in their labor. These people value their jobs as careers.

Police leaders value their job as a leader, and they value those whom they lead. They comprehend that their values provide both a compass and a map for influencing the work, self-worth, and happiness of others. They strive to make police work more meaningful, thereby making our lives more meaningful.

The leadership values that result in excellence when acted on are not new. They've been with us for centuries to a greater or lesser degree. A "newness" occurs, however, when the police leader makes a *commitment* to apply them in nurturing a culture and in thinking strategically for the sheer joy of pursuing *excellence*.

The way you value your life shapes your life. Your values in life determine your destiny—your expectations, your relationships, your goals, your purposes. One of the best ways to understand other people is to ask them, "How do you see your life?" Before asking them, however, ask yourself, "How do I see my life?" In other words, honestly, what do you value?

VALUES: WHAT THEY PROVIDE FOR US

> *To know what is right and not do it is the worst cowardice.*
> —Confucius

Values tell us about who we are—as individuals, as citizens, as consumers, as a nation, and as police leaders. As you explore further, keep in mind the following points:

- The total number of values that we possess is relatively small (60 to 90).
- Values are organized into value systems.
- The origin of human values can be traced to our formative years, culture, institutions, society, and—to some limited extent—our unique genetic makeup.

- The consequences of our values will be manifested in virtually all that we feel, think, and do.
- A large part of a police manager's effectiveness, or lack of it, depends on his or her value system.
- *Enhanced or continued leadership is linked directly to our awareness of our values and the values of our co-workers.*

Values Act as Filters

Our values cause subjective reactions to the world around us. While some items are purely functional and can be viewed rationally and objectively (chalkboards, light bulbs, rulers, and so on), most items involve a valuational judgment reaction, especially when our feelings come into play. Gut-level value systems automatically *filter* the way we view reality. When values act as filters, they operate in degrees and shades of good/bad, right/wrong, normal/not normal, or acceptance/rejection.

Values Create Generation Gaps

In recent decades, the acceleration in the rate of change of technology, legal dimensions, social behavior, education, and economic systems has created vastly diverse programming experiences between generations. The differences in these experiences have created a spectrum of widely varying value systems within our society. In volumes of material, people have attempted to reconcile differences between generations that, in reality, are irreconcilable—perhaps *understandable,* but virtually *nonnegotiable.* Police organizations can reflect as many as four or five generations (major differences in value systems) within their employees. Obviously, this can, and usually does, present a problem for police management.

Values Produce Our Individual Differences

Value programming is not simply a process of indoctrination. (Nor is the behavior of people the result of processes that overlay a particular culture on a biological core.) Rather, society shapes our inherited temperament, but it does not transform us into the complete opposite of our own basic nature. We each emerge with somewhat distinctive ways of behaving, despite the influences of our generational programming. Our basic physical and mental abilities are influenced by a wide range of inputs. In broad categories, the major sources of programming experiences for all of us are (1) family, (2) formal education, (3) religious inputs, (4) the media, (5) our friends, (6) where we grew up geographically, and (7) socioeconomic conditions that provided a base for these other factors.

Values Serve as a Map and Compass

A value system serves as a moral map and compass and thus guides our conduct. It causes us to take a position or to abandon one, predisposes us to accept or reject certain ideas or activities, and gives us a sense of being right or wrong. Value systems help us make comparisons, act as a basis from which we attempt to influence others, and afford us an opportunity to justify our actions. A value system is our code of conduct. It gives us a true north. It points out the right path as compared to the wrong ones.

Values Cause or Resolve Conflict

We frequently find ourselves in conflict with another person because of differences in our individual value systems. In a personal way, however, value systems more often than not help us make choices. "I prefer blue over brown," for example, or "I choose to allocate my police personnel in a crime-prevention program over a crime-specific program." Briefly, our value system assists us in making decisions. However, when two or more of us possess different values, we are apt to conflict with one another.

Values Trigger Our Emotional Intelligence

The vast majority of us give the value of "fairness" a high rank. As a consequence, when seeing or experiencing wrongful personnel practices, our emotional intelligence threshold is normally breached and we feel angry, depressed, threatened, or a combination of all three. If we have acted unjustly, the emotion of guilt is probably triggered within us. The police manager who disciplines an errant employee with reasonable cause may feel some sadness for the employee's family; the manager may feel that the employee deserved being disciplined but feel sorry for the employee's spouse and children.

Values Are Thought-Provokers

If we value being peak-performing police leaders, shouldn't this value provoke us into thinking about what approach (enhancing job knowledge, for example) would best achieve the desired outcome (success)? Fortunately, there are techniques for recording and exploring our thoughts in a meaningful way so that we can put these thoughts to use. We will show you some of these techniques later; in the meantime, remember that values generate thoughts as well as guide them.

Values Motivate Us

The terms *motivation* and *motive* denote desired or actual movement toward an identified end. Our value system motivates us to choose one path (means) over others. Thus we can see our motivations by inspecting our behavior. Naturally, we can do this by carefully observing others. As a result, if we value management, it is reasonable for us to be motivated to become police managers. This sense of being motivated further serves as a motivation for acquiring the skills, knowledge, and abilities necessary for managing a group of police officers (Figure 2-2).

VALUES-LED POLICE WORK

> *Leadership is about empathy. It is about having the ability to relate and to connect with people for the purpose of inspiring and improving their lives.*
> —*Oprah Winfrey*

Values-led police work is based on the premise that the police leader has a fundamental responsibility to the staff and to the community to ensure that such work is necessary and appreciated. Values-led leadership seeks to maximize its efforts by integrating prized values into as many of its day-to-day activities as possible. In order to do that, values must lead and be seen in a department's (1) mission statement, (2) strategy, (3) operating plan, and, most importantly, (4) services.

By incorporating an agency's responsibility to the community into its strategic and operating plans, the values-led police leaders are able to make everyday decisions more reliably and decisively. Instead of choosing an activity based solely on the short term, the values-led police manager recognizes that by addressing community problems along with efficiency concerns, a police department can earn a respected place in the community and a special place with individual citizens.

Which Values Lead?

The values we're referring to are progressive community values. We see values-led police work, in general, as promoting individual safety for the common good; advocating for the many people in our society whose human rights are jeopardized; protecting people who are vulnerable; and helping to address the root causes of crime. Most citizens would prefer to be policed by a department that shares these values.

Being Open

Values-led police agencies must be open about—better still, must *broadcast*—their mission and goals. How can people support an agency if it is secretive about its programs and activities? When departments act covertly, the community is locked out of the process. Community members are deprived of the opportunity to use their power to support the police programs they endorsed. The degree to which a police agency can be values-led depends on how completely the police employees and community have embraced and bought into the department's mission.

Being Accountable

It is not enough to rely on leadership to enforce moral and legal behavior. The truly core values have to be instilled in a police employee and the department. Often we hear the contrary: A police department should be an efficiency instrument, a bureaucratic machine that totally maximizes its output within rules totally set by the community. This argument holds: Departments that get distracted from this goal by community responsibilities end up ineffective. Our own belief is that just the opposite is true.

> **No community can control a police institution as well as the institution itself, and if a department places outcomes above core values, then that organization is vulnerable to violating community standards, no matter how stringently laws and codes are written.**

Those violations will produce demoralization of the workforce, ill will in the community, and perhaps lawsuits that will have a long-term negative impact on results. On the other hand, the police agency that orients itself toward serving its community will reap long-term rewards in the form of loyal customers and positive community relations. Police leaders must never lose sight of the purpose of the job, and they must not compromise their values for the sake of expediency. If they do, both a police agency and its leaders are in danger of losing their direction, given the continually changing landscape they must negotiate.

The concept of community-oriented policing (COP) is well over 30 years old. Many police agencies have described their delivery systems (methods of providing service) as being "community oriented." When questioned about COP, most chiefs and sheriffs respond that it is a philosophy more than a set of prescribed practices or operations. Frequently the words *partnership, teamwork, vision, mission,* and *quality services* are used.

Many of us struggle to define COP. The definition eludes us when it shouldn't, because the answer has been in front of us all the time. All we have to do is clarify our values. What does the agency—*your* agency—really stand for? What are the values of your community? Are they congruent or different? Does your community know your values, and vice versa?

Then what is, or should be, community-oriented policing? By casting aside verbal fluff and operational window dressing, we are finally able to expose COP for what it truly is—*values-oriented policing*. Once you know your values, those of your staff, and those of your community, you know what COP ought to look like in action.

Understanding and Respect

As an evolving police leader, your ability to perform your job successfully is linked directly to your understanding and respect for your values and attitudes and those of your assigned personnel. With this understanding and respect, you are fortified to influence and lead others in the accomplishment of their assigned duties. The focus must be twofold, however. You must first comprehend your own values and attitudes. Once you have done that, you are in a better position to understand clearly those held by other employees.

Why is the emphasis on mutual understanding? The first step, the very first step, in becoming a leader is to know—know very well—the people you are leading. And the very best way to develop this "knowing" is to know a person's values.

Agreement

Let's pause here for a reality check. First, I as a leader understand what I stand for (values). Second, I should understand what you stand for. Hopefully, we concur; hence our values are similar. However, the opposite may occur. I understand your values (and vice versa), but we differ, even conflict, over them. In summary, we understand each other's values, but we don't agree on them.

Values-led policing is not necessarily agreement. But if we clearly understand our differences, we've achieved a platform from which we may get agreement. (If we don't, at least we know why we are arguing.)

Optimism

I have never met a leader who was pessimistic. Doomsayers are a turn-off. "If the boss doesn't have hope in our mission, how can I?" Here's a cold fact: Naturally occurring optimism is rare among people. Yet values-led policing depends on a strong dosage of it because leaders most definitely affect the levels of optimism among their followers.

From the early Greek philosophers to Abraham Lincoln to today's leading researchers, we know that we choose our own emotions—one of which is optimism.

There are all kinds of benefits for those of us who accentuate the positive; for example, fewer major diseases, better chance of promotion, and better human relations. Research has repeatedly shown that leaders in the workplace are leaders at home first. So too, if you want to be optimistic as a police leader, you have to nurture it at home.

> **The key to increasing optimism as a police leader is recognizing the importance of what you feel about what you are exposed to. State of mind can regulate perception, not the other way around!**

Optimism is contagious. Seek out other leaders who exude it. The very nature of police work makes a positive mental attitude difficult but *not* impossible. Hence, opt for optimism; you'll benefit and so will those who want to follow your lead.

Empathy

Please reread the earlier quote by Oprah Winfrey. It's a strong assertion by a very bright person. Another reason to acknowledge its influence in leading others involves our *emotional intelligence (EI)*. Later we'll spend prime time on EI and how it matters as much (some would argue more) as our intelligence quotient (IQ).

Empathy is the ability to imagine oneself in someone else's position and actually feel what that person is feeling. It is the ability to stand for what that person believes in, to see with their eyes, and to feel with their hearts. It is more spontaneous than deliberate, more natural than rational.

> **Empathy is not sympathy. It's not "for" but "with."**

Sympathy is feeling bad for someone else. Empathy is feeling with someone else—good or bad—sensing what it would be like to be that person. It is a stunning emotional experience of sensing what it would be like to be that person at that moment. It is feeling the world as that person is feeling it.

Empathy moves a police leader to see the other side of an argument, comfort someone who is in distress, and either say nothing or say something at the right moment. It builds self-awareness, forges teamwork, and serves as a compass when faced with ethical decisions.

But empathy is often considered a soft-sided weakness in police work. Some believe that police leadership requires hardheaded detachment and none of that liberal touchy-feely stuff. All decisions must be emotion-free and based solely on cool reason. This approach may have worked in the twentieth century, but it is dysfunctional—that is, if you want to lead people as compared to managing them.

Empathy is an ethic for leading. It means understanding people. It makes a leader human and fosters happiness in the workplace. Empathy supplements objective knowledge and the use of technology and other mechanistic skills for making decisions. As values-led leadership takes hold, empathy is destined to emerge in the forefront of a whole new system of values-driven policing.

How can you tell if you're capable of empathizing? Easy. Are you concerned about your staff or only yourself? Do you make time to make a difference, to encourage others? Remember, leadership is an art, which means there is always ample space for inspiration and caring about others. When you ask someone, "How can I help?" then you are leading!

STRUCTURED EXERCISE 2-3

CASE STUDY: I DON'T KNOW WHERE YOU'RE COMING FROM

Tina Clark (age 30) was recently promoted to lieutenant and assigned to the early-morning patrol by the watch commander. She submitted a vacation request to Captain Bill Roe (age 52) for the Fourth of July weekend. It was denied, and she asked to see Captain Roe.

TINA: Bill, why the denial of my vacation request? For many reasons I find this decision totally inappropriate! I demand an explanation.

BILL: Whoa, Tina. . . .

TINA: Don't tell me "Whoa." You owe me an explanation.

BILL: Listen up, Tina, I don't owe you anything.

TINA: I work miserable hours. On the Fourth my family is assembling for a picnic and I must be there. Come on, Bill, you've got a family—have some compassion.

BILL: Stop interrupting me! Watch your demeanor. You're hereby ordered to work your assigned shift and you'd better not call in sick.

TINA: Are you threatening me?

BILL: (No answer)

TINA: You owe it to me, Bill.

BILL: What do I "owe" you? You've got a job, now do it or ask for a reduction in rank.

TINA: Are you telling me that my job comes before my family?

BILL: (No answer)

TINA: You just don't understand, do you? You have no clue! I guess older managers place their job first and family second.

BILL: I'll be with my family on the Fourth.

TINA: Yeah! And thanks to you, I won't.

BILL: Your work ethic is screwed up.

TINA: Maybe. But so is your family ethic. You owe me this one.

BILL: Enough said. Back to work, Tina.

Discussion

1. What values are expressed in this conversation? How and why do they conflict?

2. What might be done to collapse the gap between their polar positions?

3. Who's right? Who's wrong?

4. What do you feel intuitively about this case?

ATTITUDES

Words can never adequately convey the incredible impact of our attitude toward life. The longer I live the more convinced I become that life is 10 percent what happens to us and 90 percent how we respond to it.
—*Charles Swindoll*

Most research has been done on our attitudes rather than on our values. An attitude refers to several beliefs about an object or situation, while a value refers to a single belief of a very specific kind. A value transcends attitudes and serves to guide attitudes, judgments, and behavior. Hence

- A value is a single belief, whereas an attitude refers to several beliefs about a single object or situation.
- A value goes beyond objects and situations, whereas an attitude focuses on a specific object or situation.
- A value is a standard, whereas an attitude is not necessarily one.
- Values are few in number (and are enduring beliefs), whereas attitudes are many in number (and transiently involve various objects or situations).
- Values are more central to our personality and cognitive makeup than are attitudes.
- Values are more dynamic, whereas attitudes are more overtly linked to particular objects or situations.
- Values explicitly reflect adjustive, ego-defensive, and knowledge functions, whereas attitudes do so inferentially.

Attitudes About Your Job

Our personal values shape our work-related attitudes. We underscore the personal side because what we feel and think about our job are very much influenced by personal or private events—and vice versa. Even if we try to block this connection between one arena and the other, it happens. An understanding of job attitudes, attitude formation, and attitude change is important to police managers for three reasons:

- Attitudes can be found in every aspect of police work. We have job attitudes about most things that happen to us, as well as about most people we meet.
- Attitudes influence our job behavior. Much of how we behave at work is governed by how we feel about things. Therefore, an awareness of attitudes can help you understand human behavior at work.
- Bad attitudes on the job cause problems. Poor job attitudes can be reflected in subsequent poor performance, turnover, and absenteeism, all of which impede excellence in the police agency.

An *attitude* may be defined as a predisposition to respond in a favorable or unfavorable way to objects or persons in our environment. When we like or dislike something, we are, in effect, expressing our attitude toward the person or object. An attitude reflects our feelings toward other objects and people. Although we cannot see them, we can observe the results of an attitude: *behavior*.

Competency Checkpoints

- Our character depends on the decisions we make about our values.
- While the police leader is mainly accountable for setting an example—walking the talk—in reality we're all responsible for making values a reality in the workplace.
- A value is an enduring belief that we have in a goal and the action we must do to achieve it.

- We acquire our values from our parents, role models, and peers.
- While difficult to change, a significant emotional event and/or profound dissatisfaction can alter values.
- We are what we value, and we lead ourselves, and we lead others in accordance with our value system.
- Our values act as filters; create generations; produce individual differences; serve as a map and compass; create or resolve conflicts; activate our emotional intelligence; stimulate thinking; and motivate us.
- Values-led policing includes promoting our human rights; openness; accountability; understanding and respect; agreement; optimism; and empathy.
- Our values shape our job attitudes, and our attitudes produce our job behavior.

Flexing the Message

1. Many motion pictures contain powerful value statements. Some examples are *Gandhi, Remember the Titans, The Queen, Flag of Our Fathers, Apollo 13,* and *The Mutiny on the Bounty.* The films can be rented and shown in segments. At key points they can be stopped and viewers can discuss the values presented and how they relate to leadership. It is best to allow two hours of discussion for each film.
2. Many police agencies have their "vision," "mission," and "value" statements posted on their Web pages. Select five agencies and print out their statements. Examine them and highlight the cited values. Are any of the values also ethical standards? Which one of the five has the greatest appeal to you? Why?
3. Which two of your values have changed over the past few years? What caused them to change? Was it either an SEE or profound dissatisfaction that caused the change? How do you feel about the results?
4. Of the numerous values that comprise a police department's value system, which one is most important or fundamental? Why? What can be done to make this value more effective?
5. Return to Structured Exercise 2-1. Now, commit the necessary time to answer in writing each one of the questions that are posed. When finished, answer a final question—*What did you learn about yourself?*

The real meaning of our lives is likely to be defined by how we are remembered. So, if you want to know how to live (value) your life, just think about what you want people (family, friends, co-workers, and others) to say about you after you die, and then live backward.

CHAPTER 3

ETHICS

Police leaders must never compromise their ethics for the sake of expediency. Departmental integrity is forfeited when ethics are ignored.

No community can police a police department as well as the department itself. The compass of ethics is best located within the department and each employee.

I want to lead my life in such a way that if I sold my talking parrot to the town gossip, I wouldn't have to worry.
—*Will Rogers*

CHAPTER OUTLINE

1. Ethical Challenges
2. There Is No Such Thing as Police Ethics
   a. Setting the Standard
   b. Why Ethics?
   c. Ethics = Moral Duties
3. Courageous Choices
   a. Public Office
   b. Easier Said Than Done
   c. Easy Choices
4. Three Approaches
   a. Neglect
   b. Compliance-Based Programs
   c. Values-Oriented Programs
5. Ethical Dilemmas
   a. Competing Rights
   b. Coping with Competing Rights
6. Ethics Training
   a. Inspiration
   b. Collaboration
   c. Education

7. Don't Pee in the Pool
8. Competency Checkpoints
9. Flexing the Message

If your teammates were asked to choose five words to describe you, what words do you think they would choose?

1. _____
2. _____
3. _____
4. _____
5. _____

Circle the one that you're most proud of and put an "X" through the one that least pleases you. Look at your department's personnel today—its managers, supervisors and line officers, and civilian staff. List behaviors you'd like to see more of and less of.

Managers		Supervisors		Officers		Civilians	
+	−	+	−	+	−	+	−
1.	1	1	1	1	1	1	1
2.	2	2	2	2	2	2	2
3.	3	3	3	3	3	3	3

Write down the names of the three most ethical people you know.

1. _____
2. _____
3. _____

How many of the above people would include you on the list?

Okay. You've completed some individual foundational homework. Now it's time for class. Don't despair about being "should upon." I don't appreciate it either. We are, however, going to ponder, probe, and pursue what makes our character morally strong or flabby. In mentioning character . . .

Although character surely shapes one's destiny, character itself is *not* predestined; it's *not* inborn—it develops. Character is *not* hereditary; it's the product of habits we form and our ethical decisions and conduct. While not the same, conduct and character are closely related. In fact, our ethical conduct generally reveals and often reinforces our character. We expect leaders to make ethical decisions and thus serve as examples of integrity of character.

Character isn't a stable, easily identifiable set of closely related traits. It is more like a bundle of habits, values, and hopes loosely bound together and highly dependent on circumstances (what we're experiencing) and context (where we're experiencing it). In other words, our character is molded by very powerful internal and external forces.

ETHICAL CHALLENGES

I've always felt that a person's intelligence is directly reflected by the number of conflicting points of view he can entertain simultaneously on the same subject.
—*Abigail Adams*

Let's start by recognizing that ethical challenges come in two forms. Some are challenges of discernment, where it's difficult to determine what's right. Others are challenges of discipline, where it's clear what should be done but doing it is difficult.

Ethics are the guidelines or rules of conduct by which we aim to live. It is, of course, foolhardy to write about ethics at all because you open yourself to the charge of taking up a position of moral superiority, of failing to practice what you preach, or both. I am not in a position to preach, nor am I selling a specific code of conduct. I believe, however, that all of those who are responsible for police leadership acknowledge the part that ethics plays in those decisions and want to encourage discussion of how best to couple police work and ethical judgments. Leadership decisions involve some degree of ethical judgment; few can be taken solely on the basis of performance or "bottom-line" thinking.

What matters most is where we stand as individual leaders and how we behave when faced with ethical decisions. In approaching such decisions, I believe it is helpful to go through two steps. The first is to determine, as precisely as we can, what our personal rules of conduct are. This does not mean drawing up a list of virtuous notions. It does mean looking back at decisions we have made and working out from there what our rules actually are. The aim is to avoid confusing everyone by declaring one set of principles and acting on another. Our ethics are expressed in our actions, which is why they are usually clearer to others than to us.

Once we know where we stand personally, we can move on to the second step, which is to think through who else will be affected by the decision and how we should weigh their interest in it. Well-organized groups will represent some interests; others will have no one to state their case.

It is the police leader who must adroitly elicit the interests of all stockholders. It is the astute police leader who recognizes and accepts that there are rarely two sides in an ethical decision—there are usually several. And it is the successful police leader who can make a principled decision that encompasses all stakeholders.

THERE IS NO SUCH THING AS POLICE ETHICS

Never create by law what can be accomplished by morality.
—Charles-Louis de Secondat

Some people would argue that there is a distinction between ethics and a legal obligation. Further, they would allege that police ethics and business ethics are different. I believe that a legal obligation is an ethical one—not a simple business decision. A legal obligation is also an ethical duty—it's a part of being trustworthy, of having character. I also believe that there isn't any difference between police ethics and business ethics or any other type of ethics (medical, sports, spiritual, etc.). *Ethics is ethics!*

The idea of "police ethics" flourishes because some police employees compartmentalize their lives into personal and police domains, assuming each is governed by different standards of ethics. In police work, the argument goes, ethical principles such as trustworthiness, respect, responsibility, fairness, caring, and good citizenship are simply factors to be taken into account. As a result, fundamentally good people who would never lie, cheat, or break a promise in their personal lives could delude themselves into thinking that they can properly do so in police work. This rationale is fatally flawed.

Ethics is not concerned with descriptions of the way things are but *prescriptions for the way they ought to be.* Though we may face different sorts of ethical challenges at work, the standards do not change when we enter the workplace. There is no such thing as police ethics. There is only ethics.

What is most puzzling about most instances of police wrongdoing is that they clearly contradict both the values that are held by most of us as individuals and the collective standards that we have established for appropriate professional behavior.

Clearly, all of us feel strongly about ethics in the abstract. But at the same time, each of us is keenly aware of the struggle we face as ethical dilemmas arise. It is a common struggle between our own desire to be ethical and the competing pressures of police performance. Police leaders are challenged on how to nurture and maintain an organizational culture that promotes ethical behavior.

Setting the Standard

Instilling and maintaining an ethical standard in a police agency is a tough task for the best of leaders. It starts with attentiveness, but it's not just a matter of hanging posters or lists of virtues. It requires serious and sustained efforts to enhance the ethical consciousness, commitment, and competence of police personnel through pervasive, continual, and creative lessons and activities. It requires a clear vision of the desired outcomes in terms of explicitly identified ethical values and a coherent implementation strategy.

You can't force ethical conduct onto a police organization. Ethics are a function of the collective values of the employees. These values are cultivated and supported by a leaders:

- Commitment to *responsible* police conduct
- *Trust* in employees
- Mission/values statements that provide police workers with *clarity* about the organization's ethical expectations

- Open, honest, and timely *communications*
- A departmental culture that helps police employees resolve ethical problems
- Reward and recognition systems that *reinforce* the importance of ethics

Ultimately, high ethical standards can be maintained only if they are modeled by police leadership and woven into the fabric of the agency. Knowing this, the challenge is to cultivate the kind of work environment in which people automatically do the right thing. (See Figure 3-1.)

Ethics is about character and courage and how we meet the challenge when doing the right thing will cost more than we want to pay.

Why Ethics?

Why the concern for building a strategy to combat unlawful or unethical conduct? First, wrongful conduct reduces *public confidence* in the police and thus inhibits citizens from cooperating in crime prevention and control. Second, it enhances *criminal activity*. After all, if the police are corrupt, why not follow their example? Third, it destroys effective *police leadership*. Fourth, *departmental morale* goes down the drain. Finally, when police personnel do the right thing even when it is personally disadvantageous, they earn the priceless assets of trust, credibility, self-respect, and the esteem

---

FIGURE 3-1   Police Code of Conduct

LAW ENFORCEMENT CODE OF ETHICS

As a law enforcement officer, my fundamental duty is to serve the community; to safeguard lives and property; to protect the innocent against deception, the weak against oppression or intimidation and the peaceful against violence or disorder; and to respect the constitutional rights of all to liberty, equality and justice.

I will keep my private life unsullied as an example to all and will behave in a manner that does not bring discredit to me or to my agency. I will maintain courageous calm in the face of danger, scorn or ridicule; develop self-restraint; and be constantly mindful of the welfare of others. Honest in thought and deed both in my personal and official life, I will be exemplary in obeying the law and the regulations of my department. Whatever I see or hear of a confidential nature or that is confided to me in my official capacity will be kept ever secret unless revelation is necessary in the performance of my duty.

I will never act officiously or permit personal feelings, prejudices, political beliefs, aspirations, animosities or friendships to influence my decisions. With no compromise for crime and with relentless prosecution of criminals, I will enforce the law courteously and appropriately without fear or favor, malice or ill will, never employing unnecessary force or violence and never accepting gratuities.

I recognize the badge of my office as a symbol of public faith, and I accept it as a public trust to be held so long as I am true to the ethics of police service. I will never engage in acts of corruption or bribery, nor will I condone such acts by other police officers. I will cooperate with all legally authorized agencies and their representatives in the pursuit of justice.

I know that I alone am responsible for my own standard of professional performance and will take every reasonable opportunity to enhance and improve my level of knowledge and competence.

I will constantly strive to achieve these objectives and ideals, dedicating myself before God to my chosen profession . . . law enforcement.

Reprinted with permission of the International Association of Chiefs of Police.

STRUCTURED EXERCISE 3-1

Imagine that you are a police officer and you're at roll call training. Your newly assigned lieutenant starts the training by introducing himself and then adds, "If you have any doubts about how I want you to treat our citizens, treat them *exactly* the way I treat you!"

Now imagine that you're a chief of police and you've just introduced yourself

to your new staff. One officer raises her hand and asks, "How do you expect us to treat the citizens?" What is your reply? In the following space, write your answer to her question.

_____

_____

_____

_____

---

of their team members—the ideal foundation for lasting friendships and productive working relationships.

> Breaking the law and being unethical are not synonymous. If you break the law, it is also unethical on your part. However, a police employee can be dishonest, break commitments, and be unfair and unaccountable (e.g., abuse sick leave) without breaking the law. It is regrettable, but we expect too much from laws and demand too little from people.

Ethics = Moral Duties

Ethics is concerned with *moral duties* and how we *should* behave regarding both ends and means. Police work is an intrinsically practical service enterprise that judges its employees and actions only in terms of the effective use of power and the achievement of results.

Ethos is the distinguishing character, moral nature, or *guiding beliefs* of a person, group, or institution. What are your guiding beliefs, those of your work group, those of your department? Does the ethos (beliefs) support or conflict with the ethics (moral duties)?

Here are some useful definitions that will assist us as we progress with this responsibility:

- Ethics = Body of moral principles or values
- Moral = Right of conduct
- Honesty = Intending to act morally and thus subscribing to ethical principles
- Integrity = Behaving in a moral way and thus manifesting ethical principles

COURAGEOUS CHOICES

> *The leader's integrity is not idealistic. It rests on a pragmatic knowledge of how things work.*
> —*Tao Ti Ching* (500 B.C.)

Many of us espouse ethics about integrity, trust, loyalty, and the like, until challenged. Then, because of our particular circumstances, selfish needs, and uncomfortable feelings, ethics become negotiable. Clearly resisting the inner drive toward ethical compromising requires both a *moral code* that distinguishes good versus bad behavior along with *courage* to make the right choice.

Over the years we have all heard and read about officers, supervisors, and managers wrestling with some hard choices. There is a constant conflict between the practical realities of politics, personal ambition, and the democratic ideal of selfless public service. Ethics and the real world place very conflicting demands on us that are often tough to reconcile.

The problem in some police agencies is that stated ethical values are *neither consistently modeled nor enforced*. Despite a clear responsibility to uphold organizational standards, the culture of some departments reflects a don't-rock-the-boat, avoid-confrontation-at-any-cost philosophy that undermines institutional integrity. Thus, some police managers will find an endless array of excuses to look the other way. Police agencies need good managers—men and women of principle with the courage to do what is right in an honorable manner—even in the face of controversy and unpopularity.

> **Two basic rules of management are: (1) Whatever you allow you encourage, and (2) whatever employees will do for you, they will do to you. Remember, every time you let a bad police employee win, you weaken the resolve of dozens of dedicated staff members who need to know that playing by the rules is not just for suckers.**

Public Office

Public office is a public trust. This axiom, supported by the related idea that participatory democracy requires public confidence in the integrity of government, lays the very foundations for the ethical demands placed on police personnel and the laws establishing baseline standards of behavior. Laws and rules are especially useful when it comes to making choices on brutality, stealing, perjury, and bribe taking. Although the choice may not always be easy, it's *clear and straightforward*. Laws are needed to define *minimum* standards of conduct.

> **Referring to such laws and rules as "ethical laws" or "ethical standards" is misleading and actually counterproductive. It is misleading because the laws deal only with a narrow spectrum of ethical decisions facing police employees. It is counterproductive because it encourages us to accept only existing laws as ethics.**

Easier Said Than Done

One reason ethics is much easier said than done is that the legal kind of unethical behavior has become common, as we can see from these generic examples:

- Embellishing claims
- Scapegoating personal failures
- Shirking distasteful responsibilities
- Knowingly making unreasonable demands

- Stonewalling questions
- Acting insincerely
- Reneging on promises
- Covering up
- Making consequential decisions unilaterally
- Loafing and loitering

None of these behaviors is scandalous. But each, nonetheless, violates a sense of what is the morally correct behavior (e.g., the behaviors of personal responsibility, honesty, fairness, etc.), increases cynicism and distrust, undermines integrity, and can be a stepping-stone to wrongful behavior.

Although laws can secure compliance within limited margins, they are far too narrow or minimal to act as a substitute for ethics. To repeat, we expect too much from laws and demand too little from people!

Easy Choices

The easy choices typically involve clear-cut laws and rules. If you take a bribe, the choice may result in the obvious—you're fired and go to jail. The hard choices deal with moral issues and ethical considerations such as a discretion, a rule infraction (e.g., sleeping on duty), deception in police investigations, the use of deadly force, the use of physical force, off-duty behavior that may or may not be job related, and so on.

Ethical decisions—courageous choices—are much more difficult than we would like to think. It is not just a matter of character. Ethical decision making requires an alert and informed conscience. It requires the ability to resist self-deception and rationalization. It requires courage and persistence to risk the disapproval of others and the loss of power and prestige. Finally, it requires the capacity to evaluate incomplete or confusing facts and anticipate likely consequences under all kinds of pressure.

Some of us overestimate the costs of being ethical and underestimate the costs of compromise.

THREE APPROACHES

The unfortunate thing about this world is that the good habits are so much easier to give up than the bad ones.
—Somerset Maugham

When examining the ethics programs of police departments, it is useful to bear in mind the three very different approaches to dealing with ethical choices. These are

- Neglect, or the absence of any formal ethical programs
- Compliance-based programs
- Values-oriented programs

Neglect

It is hard to imagine that any police agency could deliberately ignore the importance of ethics or fail to develop management policies and programs, given the effect ethical breaches can have on performance, reputation, and community support.

The departments that ignore ethics view them either as fluff or as a costly and inconvenient luxury. They are wrong on both counts.

Compliance-Based Programs

Compliance-based programs are legal in context. They are based on rules and regulations with the goal of preventing, detecting, and punishing legal violations. The centerpiece of such programs is a comprehensive collection of regulations that spell out a universal code of police ethics. The code lays out rules for hiring practices, travel expenses, compliance with local laws, improper payments, gifts, and potential conflicts of interest. It is a long and weighty list of dos and don'ts for people to follow.

This approach doesn't work well. First, rules beget rules; regulations beget regulations. You become buried in paperwork, and any time you face a unique ethical issue, another rule or regulation is born. Second, a compliance-based program sends a disturbing message to the employees: "We don't respect your intelligence or trust you!"

One of the most compelling reasons for shedding this approach is that it doesn't keep police managers or employees from exercising poor judgment and making questionable decisions.

Values-Oriented Programs

The values-oriented approach relies on ethical principles. Each police agency is responsible for developing its own core ethical values. Like a lot of public agencies, I subscribe to the six advocated by the Josephson Institute, the Six Pillars of Character^{SM}. (See Figure 3-2.)

We can examine an ethical issue by first identifying which of the six ethical principles applies to a particular decision. Then we determine which internal and which external stakeholders' ethical concerns should influence the decision. This principle-based approach balances the ethical concerns of the community with the values of the police organization. Let's apply the Six Pillars to a hypothetical situation that involves you. Assume that you're a police chief/sheriff and you will soon select a new lieutenant from the promotional list. The "rule of three" allows you to promote anyone in the top three positions. How can the Six Pillars guide you in making the right decision?

When faced with a decision that involves ethics, ask the following questions of yourself or your work unit:

1. **Will the decision I make violate the rights or goodwill of others?**
2. **What is my personal motive and spirit behind my actions?**
3. **Will it add to or detract from my trustworthiness?**
4. **If I were asked to explain my decision in public, would I do so with pride or shame?**
5. **Even if what I do is not illegal, is it done at someone else's personal expense?**

FIGURE 3-2	Six Pillars of Character[SM]

TRUSTWORTHINESS

Ethical persons are worthy of trust. Trustworthiness is an especially important ethical value because it encompasses four separate ethical values: honesty, integrity, promise-keeping, and loyalty.

RESPECT

The ethical value of respect is fundamental. It imposes a moral duty to treat all persons with respect. This means we recognize and honor each person's rights to autonomy and self-determination, privacy, and dignity.

RESPONSIBILITY

Ethical persons are responsible, an ethical concept that embodies three separate values: accountability, self-restraint, and pursuit of excellence.

FAIRNESS

Another fundamental ethical value is fairness. The concept embodies the values of justice, equity, due process, openness, and consistency. Fairness is one of the most elusive ethical values since, in most cases, stakeholders with conflicting interests sharply disagree on what is fair.

CARING

At the core of many ethical values is concern for the interests of others. Persons who are totally self-centered tend to treat others simply as instruments of their own ends, and rarely do they feel an obligation to be honest, loyal, fair, or respectful.

CIVIC VIRTUE AND CITIZENSHIP

An ethical person acknowledges a civic duty that extends beyond his or her own self-interests, demonstrating social consciousness and recognizing his or her obligations to contribute to the overall public good. Responsible citizenship involves community service and doing one's share.

© 2007 Reprinted with permission of Josephson Institute. www.charactercounts.org.

STRUCTURED EXERCISE 3-2

TAKE THE ETHICAL CLIMATE SURVEY

Ethical decision making in government is essential to a community's health, vitality, and democracy. Ethical behavior and decisions maintain citizen trust and ensure effective and efficient use of resources. Yet an ethical environment does not happen overnight. Successful local government managers and leaders, as well as a policy that sets the pace for an ethical organization, also provide the necessary tools and establish the climate.

The first steps toward building and maintaining an ethical organization are to assess the current environment and identify any changes that are needed. How do you know where to start? What actions are most critical? Do employees think the local government is ethical?

Circle one number for each statement:

	Strongly Disagree	Disagree	Undecided	Agree	Strongly Agree
1. Ordinarily, we don't deviate from standard policies and procedures in my department.	1	2	3	4	5
2. My supervisor encourages employees to act in an ethical manner.	1	2	3	4	5
3. I do not have to ask my supervisor before I do almost anything.	1	2	3	4	5
4. Around here, there is encouragement to improve individual and group performance continually.	1	2	3	4	5
5. The employees in my department demonstrate high standards of personal integrity.	1	2	3	4	5
6. My department has a defined standard of integrity.	1	2	3	4	5
7. Individuals in my department accept responsibility for decisions they make.	1	2	3	4	5
8. It is wrong to accept gifts from persons who do business under my jurisdiction, even if those gifts do not influence how I do my job.	1	2	3	4	5
9. It is not usual for members of my department to accept small gifts for performing their duties.	1	2	3	4	5
10. Members of my department do not use their positions for private gain.	1	2	3	4	5
11. Members of my department have not used their positions to influence the hiring of their friends and relatives by the government.	1	2	3	4	5

(*Continued*)

STRUCTURED EXERCISE 3-2 *(Cont.)*

	Strongly Disagree	Disagree	Undecided	Agree	Strongly Agree
12. I would blow the whistle if someone in my department accepted a large gift ($50.00 or more in value; this amount varies by local government) from a person who does business with the government.	1	2	3	4	5
13. Promotions in my department are based on what you know or how you perform on the job rather than on whom you know.	1	2	3	4	5
14. I trust my supervisor.	1	2	3	4	5
15. The department has implemented a code of ethics.	1	2	3	4	5
16. There are no serious ethical problems in my department.	1	2	3	4	5
17. Co-workers in my department trust each other.	1	2	3	4	5
18. My superiors set a good example of ethical behavior.	1	2	3	4	5
19. I feel that I am a member of a well-functioning team.	1	2	3	4	5
20. All employees have equal opportunities for advancement.	1	2	3	4	5
21. Performance evaluations accurately reflect how employees have done their jobs.	1	2	3	4	5
22. Performance evaluations address ethical requirements as well as other measures.	1	2	3	4	5

23. Employees share negative information with supervisors without the worry of receiving a negative reaction from them.

    1   2   3   4   5

24. Supervisors are concerned with *how* employees achieve successful results rather than just with the results themselves.

    1   2   3   4   5

25. When there is a disagreement between employees and supervisors on how best to solve a problem, the employees' ideas are listened to and considered.

    1   2   3   4   5

26. When employees feel that they are being asked to do something that is ethically wrong, supervisors work with them on alternative ways to do the task.

    1   2   3   4   5

27. In this organization, it is much better to report a problem or error than it is to cover it up.

    1   2   3   4   5

28. When something goes wrong, the primary goal is to fix the problem and prevent it from happening again rather than to find someone to blame.

    1   2   3   4   5

29. The organization's decisions on how people are treated are clear and consistent.

    1   2   3   4   5

30. The organization's expectations concerning productivity, quality, and ethics are consistent.

    1   2   3   4   5

31. The same set of ethical standards is used in dealing with citizens, employees, and others.

    1   2   3   4   5

32. You can rely on the accuracy of the organization's information about what will or won't happen.

    1   2   3   4   5

(Continued)

STRUCTURED EXERCISE 3-2 (*Cont.*)

	Strongly Disagree	Disagree	Undecided	Agree	Strongly Agree
33. The organization publicly recognizes and rewards ethical behavior by employees when it occurs.	1	2	3	4	5
34. Doing what is right around here is more important than following the rules.	1	2	3	4	5
35. Ethical standards and practices are routinely discussed in employee meetings.	1	2	3	4	5
36. If there is suspicion that some employees may be violating ethical standards, the situation is dealt with openly and directly.	1	2	3	4	5
37. Employees are aware of where to obtain assistance when they need to resolve an ethical dilemma.	1	2	3	4	5
38. If one employee is doing something unethical, the other employees in the group will usually try to correct the situation before management gets involved.	1	2	3	4	5
39. Employees are encouraged to report their work results accurately even when the results are less than satisfactory.	1	2	3	4	5
40. Employees maintain the same ethical standards even when no one is observing their actions.	1	2	3	4	5

Use the scale below each statement to respond to the following items; circle the number that most closely represents your response. (1 is very low; 7 is very high.)

41. My ethical standards are

Very low   Very high

1	2	3	4	5	6	7

42. The ethical standards in my department are

Very low   Very high

1	2	3	4	5	6	7

Circle the answer that best represents your response to this statement:

43. My behavior as a public employee is regulated by state law.

Yes   No   Don't know

The first 40 questions of the ethical climate survey are organized in their relationship to seven important values that affect the nurturing and sustaining of an ethical work environment.

Values and Related Questions

Accountability	Responsiveness/Customer Service
1, 7, 12, 16, 22, 27, 38	4, 19, 28, 30, 34
Integrity/Honesty	Trust
5, 6, 8, 9, 10, 11, 40	3, 14, 17, 32
Fairness	Communication
13, 20, 21, 31	15, 29, 35, 36, 37
Leadership	
2, 18, 23, 24, 25, 26, 33, 39	

The questions are designed and evaluated based on an ideal and ethically healthy work environment, which would be reflected by "strongly agree" answers. Therefore, a strongly ethical work environment would be indicated by an average of the questions within each category with a result as close as possible to five. An average of all the category averages also can indicate an overall perception by employees of the total work environment, based on the factors listed.

Rating Values of Survey Responses
Responses to this survey indicate a local government's ethical strengths and weaknesses. For example, if you gave high responses to the questions under the fairness category, your organization probably treats its citizens and staff in a fair manner. If your scores for the communication category were relatively low, however, it might be in the best

(Continued)

STRUCTURED EXERCISE 3-2   (*Cont.*)

interest of your local government to write and implement a code of ethics or routinely discuss ethical issues during departmental meetings.

This survey is only the beginning. It might indicate that some work needs to be done, such as including ethics into the performance evaluation system. And by taking the survey and analyzing the scores annually, it also might help you maintain an organization that already has high ethical standards.

An ethical work environment is reflected in ethical decision making that results in important organizational values being addressed, such as productivity, responsiveness, accountability, and a sense of ownership in how the organization conducts its business. Ideally, the most effective organization has a high level of compatibility between the employees' ethical values and those of the organization. There also is a clear understanding of the manager's expectations of the organization and employee behavior and performance.

Reprinted with permission of the International City/County Management Association, Washington, D.C.

---

6. Does what I do violate another's honor?
7. If it were done to me, would I approve or would I take offense and react in pain?
8. What are the basic principles that govern my actions and decisions?
9. When I am in doubt, to whom can and will I go to check my decisions?
10. Will my decision give other people any reason to distrust me?
11. Will my decision build the credibility of my work or profession?

ETHICAL DILEMMAS

> *Remember that whenever you point your finger at someone else, three of your*
> *fingers are pointing back to you!*
> —*Louis Nizer*

Isn't it odd that most instances of police wrongdoing clearly contradict both the ethics that are held by most of us as individuals and the collective standards we have established for appropriate professional behavior?

Up to this point, we've examined information that summarizes and reinforces what each of us knows in our hearts: When choosing between right and wrong, you need to choose right. No degree in theology is required to get that one—it's clear-cut. And that's the way things are most of the time.

STRUCTURED EXERCISE 3-3

I'd like to conduct a brief quiz.

1. Do you consider yourself to be an ethical person?

   1 2 3 4 5 6 7 (7 = high)

2. Do you believe that it's important for police agencies to function in an ethical manner?

   1 2 3 4 5 6 7 (7 = high)

3. Do you believe that you know an ethical dilemma when you see it?

   1 2 3 4 5 6 7 (7 = high)

4. Do you feel there are clear answers to ethical problems?

   1 2 3 4 5 6 7 (7 = high)

5. Do you believe that you always know an ethical dilemma when it arises and always know how to resolve it?

   1 2 3 4 5 6 7 (7 = high)

6. Do you believe your above answers are really true?

   1 2 3 4 5 6 7 (7 = high)

But occasionally, there will be times when instead of having to choose between a right and a wrong, you find yourself torn between two apparent rights. It's where normal behavioral guidelines don't clearly or easily apply, where picking one of the rights means violating the other. There's the signpost up ahead—you're entering "the gray zone." And your moral compass appears uncertain because you're confronted with "competing rights."

Competing Rights

Issues involving competing rights are often referred to as "ethical dilemmas." Look up *dilemma* in the dictionary and you'll find definitions such as "a situation that requires one to choose between two equally balanced alternatives; a predicament that seemingly defies a satisfactory solution." In other words, there are no easy or obvious answers. The only rule of thumb here is: Don't look for any rules of thumb here!

Competing rights are issues that must be thought out, talked out, and worked out—using the resources available to you.

You know you have the potential for an ethical dilemma when you use the words "but it's also right to . . ." Here are some examples:

It's right to tell the truth

but it's also right to . . .

be kind and considerate of people's feelings and emotions.
It's right to apply rules and procedures equally, without favoritism,

but it's also right to . . .

give special consideration to hard-working, dependable, and productive employees.

It's right to spend additional time adding more quality to your work

but it's also right to . . .

meet deadlines and avoid "diminishing returns" on your efforts.
It's right to be concerned with short-term results

but it's also right to . . .

focus on long-term strategy.
It's right not to share information given to you in confidence

but it's also right to . . .

report violations of laws, rules, and ethical standards.

Coping with Competing Rights

When facing a situation involving competing rights, there are three basic tactics.

1. *Defuse the Conflict.* Imagine two senior sergeants conflicting over a prime assignment. They're butting heads and very angry due to their competitive instincts. Let's defuse the situation. First, you can flip a coin to see which one gets the nod. Second, you can select a third, nonengaged sergeant for the job. Third, you can eliminate the assignment. There are many additional steps available for you to be "right" when others see "right" as being a winner.

2. *Decide What's "More Right."* If the conflict between competing rights cannot be eliminated, it will be necessary to identify and choose that which seems the *more right* of the two. Here are some common criteria (questions to ask) when making that decision.

   Which of the competing rights . . .

   • Is most in line with laws, regulations, and corporate procedures?
   • Is most in sync with organizational values?
   • Provides the greatest benefit for the largest number of stakeholders?
   • Establishes the best precedent for guiding similar decisions in the future?

3. *Seek Advice.* These situations are, by their very nature, the most frustrating decisions you'll have to deal with. They can result in increased stress and lost sleep. So seek advice from whatever resources are available inside or outside your organization. An objective viewpoint can be invaluable in deciding what's right when there are no apparent wrongs.

The most challenging "right versus right" of all . . .
It's right to have solid relationships with your co-workers—to watch out for and help each other, to be friends, to be a team player

but it's also right to . . .

take a stand, refuse to "go along to get along" and be willing to take action when a police employee acts unethically or makes a mistake.

Accept the reality that on most significant issues or competing rights, intelligent people of character will disagree. While it's appropriate to advocate and defend one's "right" with passion, it's illogical and unethical to reflexively treat people who disagree with us as enemies or stupid or both. It's also a mistake to think that the *intensity* of our

---

STRUCTURED EXERCISE 3-4

You and your patrol car partner receive a Code-3 dispatch, "Officer down and needs help." You're driving and decide on a hairpin route, much shorter in time. It is a narrow, one-lane road with a rock wall on your right and a 100-yard sheer drop on the left side. At your best speed practical, you round a blind curve and see a little child playing in the road. There isn't time to brake! Your snap judgment options are to stay on the road and drive over the child, or veer left, lose your life, and kill your partner. The officer in distress may also die if you do not arrive soon. What is your decision? Let's change the situation to that of two young kids in the road. Now what is your decision? What are the competing rights in this scenario? If possible, discuss this exercise in a group setting.

---

convictions increases the likelihood that we're so right that we can seek to *destroy* the competing right of others.

ETHICS TRAINING

> We have a Bill of Rights. What we need is a Bill of Responsibilities.
> —*Bill Maher*

All of us have been trained to read, write, and calculate numbers. We've been trained to operate a personal computer, an iPod, a cell phone, and a CAD system. We've learned many, many more things. How many of us have taken a course on ethical conduct? Ethics training for police employees has been sparse, nonexistent, or superficial. This is changing. There is, fortunately, an accelerating trend toward ethics training.

It is possible for police agencies, by design, to create a positive ethical culture that nurtures and rewards moral behavior and discourages bad conduct. There are three ways to train ethics: (1) inspiration, (2) collaboration, and (3) education.

Inspiration

Inspiration is fostered in three ways:

1. *Leadership by Example. We preach a better sermon with our life than with our lips.* I've heard police managers comment with detectable frustration, "The officers don't pay attention to me." Nonsense. They do pay careful attention to managers. For most officers, leadership either occurs or not, based on their relationship to their manager.

   Remember, your staff does pay careful consideration to what you say and what you do!

2. *Value Orientation.* Make sure that everyone, especially newcomers, knows and understands the laws, rules, and values that should guide their heart

and behavior. This establishes a *culture of ethics*. If your agency has a mission statement, a code of ethics, or a set of goals, review it periodically with your staff. Reinforce it with your decisions—live it minute by minute.

With all cultures there are countercultures. Some of these may be good: for example, a group of officers who refuse to accept bribes even when others do so. Alternatively, we may see an agency striving very hard to provide high-quality services, while a counterculture of officers is advocating that the public (or most of it) is the enemy.

Culture building is not a one-shot endeavor. It takes time and a lot of reinforcement.

Police employees want to know the rules, the laws, the goals, and the values that guide and *measure* their work.

3. *Limitations of Laws and Rules.* Technical compliance with laws is necessary, but not always enough! Laws cannot replace the need for a sensitive conscience or free you of your moral duty to adhere to traditional *ethical principles*. To encourage good-faith acceptance of the moral obligation to abide by both the letter and spirit of the law, every opportunity must be used to (1) *clarify* the reasons for the rules and (2) *emphasize* the importance of the "appearance of wrongdoing" test.

Good ethics are expected and appreciated by leaders. The line personnel are no different—they expect and appreciate good ethics on the part of their bosses.

Those police leaders who use the legal "dos and don'ts," or who impose the "should and should not" of rules, are missing their main power source—ethical values.

Collaboration

Collaboration also can be achieved in three ways:

1. *Unifying the Group.* Unify individuals behind the traditional ethical values. One way is to appeal to the common interest that all personnel have in the ethical behavior of each person. The goal here is shared esteem for duty and honor with the hope that the group will not allow any member to place self-interest (e.g., taking extra rewards such as free meals) above the public trust.

I listened to a sheriff admonish his staff about not accepting gratuities. "Not one dime, not one cup of coffee," he asserted. Later, he signed a permit allowing one of his key campaign donors to carry a concealed weapon. Something doesn't jive here. A colleague of mine had the courage to tell a story on himself. He sermonized to a group of newly appointed sheriff's sergeants on the virtues of honesty. For 30 minutes he extolled morality. He then proceeded to play a pirated VCR tape. Naturally, the duplicated tape was politely called to his attention by members of the group. He was embarrassed, he blushed, he was speechless. He learned a lesson, however: If you're going to preach something, you'd darn well better be practicing it.

2. *Identifying Situations.* Identify situations in which values are likely to be tested. Typically, those in the best position to anticipate value challenges are leaders.

After all, they've recently experienced identical or similar hard choices. Any ethics program must be custom-built by and for a particular agency. What may be an ethics problem for one agency may not be for another.

Members of an agency should be surveyed to discover ethical problems and issues. Once the critical concerns have been spotted, training scenarios and simulations can be constructed.

Similar to a finely tuned and expertly trained athlete, all of us can be conditioned to make, when necessary, the right choices, which frequently are the hard choices.

3. *Specifying Guidelines.* Specify guidelines and approaches for deciding on hard choices. This task involves the development and pronouncement of minimum standards of behavior for various situations. It also involves guidelines for coping with totally unanticipated circumstances.

Hard choices require known guidelines.

Education

Educational programs should stress *issue spotting,* reasoning, and other decision-making skills. Here are seven steps to achieve this.

1. *No Sermonizing.* Moralizing about ethics is not very effective in sustaining or changing attitudes and behavior: No one likes to be "should upon"! Traditional lectures on ethics should be scrapped and replaced by group discussions. I'm confident that if police personnel had been asked, "Where might our major vulnerability for corruption be?" in the early 1980s, the answer would have been, in most cases, "drug money and drug use." The officers knew this, but, regrettably, few administrators asked them.

2. *Anticipate and Recognize Ethical Warning Signs.* All police employees should be educated in early detection of ethical issues. They should be sensitized to the eight conditions that tend to defeat ethical principles:

- Self-interest
- Self-protection
- Self-deception
- Self-righteousness
- Rationalization
- Groupthink
- Greed
- Envy

One or more of the above eight conditions are in such statements as:

"Everyone else does it."
"They'll never miss it."
"Nobody will care."
"The boss does it."
"No one will know."
"I don't have time to do it right."

"That's close enough."
"Some rules were meant to be broken."
"It's not *my* job."
"I'm usually honest."
"It's all relative."
"It's only a little white lie."

3. *Ethical Competence.* Seeing ethics is easier than doing ethics. The first involves *consciousness* and the second emphasizes *commitment.* We must learn how better to evaluate facts and make reasoned decisions on ethical conduct. Decisions that include deceit or coercion often cause secondary risks that are not seen or properly evaluated. If you wonder what I mean by this last statement, merely scan the front page, business, or sports section of a daily newspaper.

4. *Temptations.* Being ethical does not mean we're temptation-free. There are going to be exciting temptations toward which we will feel drawn. It is at that moment we have the opportunity to make a choice for time-honored rules of conduct. When tempted, think of Will Roger's words that opened this chapter.

5. *Motives* Assessing motives is usually pointless and often harmful. It is pointless because motives are almost impossible to determine. We often don't know our own motives, let alone those of others. It is harmful because we almost always exaggerate the purity of our own motives and label others' motives as evil.

The solution to this problem is: We should judge *actions*—our own and those of others—not motives. An ethics course should emphasize that it is what we *do*, not what we *intend*, that counts!

6. *Basically Good.* The belief that employees are inherently good is one of the most widely held beliefs in society. Yet it is both untrue and destructive. As far as the proposition about "inherently good," look around and you'll detect numerous infractions of rules and policies. The destructiveness occurs when people concentrate on the external forces (e.g., "It's my sergeant's fault") rather than our human will. Those who believe in innate human goodness view the battle for a better world as primarily a conflict between the individual and society. I'm convinced that especially in a free society, the battle is between the individual and his or her character. A police department can survive a serious crime condition but not its officers' lack of ethical conduct.

7. *Accountability.* Despite a code of ethics, ethics training programs, and all the rules and laws—police departments don't make decisions about ethics. Ethical choices are made by individuals.

Question: When it comes to ethics, which police activities, functions, decisions, and behaviors are truly important?
Answer: All of them!

Think about it. When is it okay to be unethical? The answer is *never!* What are the parts of our job—and our human interactions—to which fairness, honesty, respect, and "doing right" don't apply? *There are none!* Ethics is *not* a sometimes thing. It's an *all the time* thing—and it's reflected in everything we do. There are no time outs, no "too small to matter" issues, no "too busy to do it" excuses, and no "too low on the police hierarchy to make a difference" people. Everyone is responsible—*everything counts!*

We paint the self-portrait that we call character by our actions. We can choose to paint that portrait in the pale watercolors of unearned successes and short-lived pleasures or in the deep, rich oils of integrity, duty, and honor for our human character.

DON'T PEE IN THE POOL

Yes, in summary—don't pee in the pool. As a kid, remember the many "dos and don'ts" your parents imparted? For example, "Clean your plate because there are children starving in India." "Respect your elders!" and "Always wear clean underwear." In being told "Don't pee in the pool," your parents were conveying not one but two messages—the second being the more vital.

The first message was intended to keep you from polluting your environment for yourself and others as well. While important, these words also contained a broader and more fundamental meaning: Don't pollute (corrupt) your life or those of others by unethical choices and wrongful actions, even though you may not get caught. It is your choices and actions that count for or against your character, not whether or not you're detected. So, if you're set on becoming a leader, don't pee in the pool. Your parents told you so; I'm merely reminding you of their sage advice!

Competency Checkpoints

- Our character is not hereditary; it's the result of the habits we acquire.
- Ethical challenges come in two forms: one of determining what is right (consciousness), and the other doing what is right (discipline).
- There is no such thing as police ethics.
- Ethics is about character and courage.
- Ethics focuses on moral duties and how we should behave.
- Ethos constitutes the moral nature or guiding beliefs of a person or institution.
- The three approaches to handling ethical dilemmas are (1) neglect, (2) compliance-based programs, and (3) values-oriented programs.
- Laws present a minimum standard of conduct; ethical decisions require courage, character, and sound judgment.
- Ethical dilemmas occur when there are competing rights.
- Ethics training involves inspiration, collaboration, and education.
- When is it okay to be unethical? *Never!*

Flexing the Message

1. Review the section "There Is No Such Thing as Police Ethics." Do you agree or disagree with our proposition? If there is, in your opinion, a difference—how and why?
2. Complete and compare the results of Structured Exercise 3-2 (Take the Ethical Climate Survey) with your associates. Besides bottom-line results, what were the

extreme answers—"Strongly Disagree" and/or "Strongly Agree"? Can you discern any commonalities or patterns? What did you learn?

3. Review your answers to the five questions posed at the beginning of the "Ethical Dilemmas" section. Share your responses with other co-workers (students). Any surprises?

4. Create four "competing rights" scenarios and then debate what is the best decision.

5. Is lying ever justified? Think carefully. When might lying be appropriate, even helpful?

6. Police personnel are most frequently subjected to temptation when confronted by _____ (complete this sentence).

4 | VISION

Effective police leaders determine where they want to be tomorrow and continually focus on the results and performance that's needed to get there.

Police leadership does not begin with power but rather with a set of values that are cast into a department's mission. Together they create a compelling vision statement of intended excellence.

The insight to see new paths, the courage to try them, and judgment to measure results—these are the qualities of a leader.
—*Mary Parker Follett*

CHAPTER OUTLINE

Have you ever met a leader who did not have a vision? I haven't, and you won't either. A leader without a vision is no longer a leader. A vision without a leader is no longer a vision.

POLICE AGENCIES GET INTO TROUBLE

The future isn't what it used to be.
—*Yogi Berra*

We have arrived at a milestone where you and I are able to galvanize what we've learned about making decisions, acquiring values, and examining ethics into creating a vision, formatting a strategy, combating a resistant organizational culture, prospecting on how to pursue it, and prospecting the future. Sounds formidable? It is! But leaders do it all the time, only they're not just thinking about it; they're actually doing it.

There are five key reasons that police agencies (and all organizations, for that matter) get into trouble. First, they toss aside *foundational integrity* for the easy, fast, clever, and low-risk route to success. Second, there isn't any *shared vision* (note the word *shared*). Third, even if there is a shared vision, there isn't a *clear strategy* on how to achieve it. Fourth, the leader (change agent) ignores the existing, firmly entrenched culture ("the way we've always done things here"). Fifth and finally, they fail miserably and flunk *future testing*. We've already covered the first reason, and we are well positioned to explore the other four.

- Vision
- Strategy
- Culture
- Prospection

Change is frequent.

VISION

If you have built castles in the air, your work need not be lost; that is where they should be. Now put the foundations under them.
—*Henry David Thoreau*

Are you wondering why this chapter is entitled "Vision," yet it encompasses "Strategy" and "Prospection" as well? Here's the reason. Vision without a strategy is vapid. Strategy without a vision is rudderless. And without prospection, both can be knocked senseless.

With a shared vision a police agency achieves a desired balance and a continuity of purpose. If an organization frequently changes its vision, it would cause chaos for the participants. Some employees would be immobilized; others would be rushing around in circles. Vision, because it is values-centered, presents an enduring mission for a police department. It doesn't change easily or often, if at all. Shared vision lets everyone know (staff, elected officials, and most importantly the community) why and where the organization is headed. Without a shared vision a police agency is going to experience the harmful crosscurrents and headwinds of change.

There are four key considerations when it comes to building a shared vision: (1) What should it consist of? (2) What is the best approach? (3) Are there helpful examples? and (4) How do we actually make it work on a daily operational basis?

Recipe
A viable vision (as opposed to a vacuous one) contains at least the following ingredients.

Purpose/Mission
Whether you call it a mission or a purpose, a vision statement must clearly articulate the fundamental reason for the organization's existence. It explains exactly what the involved employees and volunteers are here to do together.

Future
A vision statement paints an inspiring future that is not out of sight but slightly out of reach. It is not an idle dream but rather a compelling picture of the way it ought to look.

Values
A vision statement is backed with values. It tells the reader precisely what the organization stands for and is prepared to be measured on.

Principled Decision Making
A shared vision should be judged on its ability to encourage principled decisions. Here's the question, "Does my vision statement help me to avoid the wrong decision while pointing to the right one?" When you study your shared vision, are you comfortable that it propels you toward the moral high ground?

Change Agent
A shared vision of a desirable future will automatically nudge the department for measurable progress. If a vision does not produce change, then it's not a vision.

Conflict Resolution
All police departments struggle over issues. It's natural the staff will differ on the best means to resolve a problem. When this occurs, cast your attention to the shared vision, allowing it to assist in problem resolution.

The Big Picture

A shared vision will keep the employees focused on what is really significant. It resists the inclination to emphasize day-to-day minutiae (tunnel vision).

Excellence

Finally, any shared vision should mandate a transparent standard of excellence—an excellence by which you, other members of your agency, and your service community can measure how good you actually are.

The above eight metrics are to be applied when constructing or evaluating an existing shared vision. No measurable metrics = no viable vision.

Approaches

There are two ways to build a vision statement—from the top (boss) down or from the bottom (staff) up. The first approach produces a vision statement, while the latter creates a *shared* vision.

Approach A: Top Down

The "A" in this approach signifies *above* or from the chief down. For the past three decades many police management teams have created vision statements and worked hard on communicating them to their employees. They believe that vision comes best from the wisdom at the top of the agency.

Consider the following scenario: A meeting is convened so the top managers can develop a vision statement and plan for its distribution. The intent is sincere, and the content is always appealing. Each police management team affirms its uniqueness by declaring that it:

- Is committed to being a professional department.
- Believes in its people.
- Stands firm for quality.
- Cares for customers.
- Affirms honesty and integrity.
- Supports teams.
- Is innovative.

But there's a built-in problem—ownership and implementation!

Buy-in resides with those who create a vision and with them alone. A vision statement created by the chief for a police agency to endorse is not *owned* by the employees. An even more fundamental defect is that, in most cases, the vision statement is created by management for the rest of the organization to implement. Creating a vision statement is an ownership function. If you want to see ownership widely dispersed, then each person needs to struggle with articulating his or her own vision of who he or she is, where he or she wants to go, and what he or she truly believes in.

If you're a part of the vision, you're going to make it happen—implement it. Involvement in ideating a vision makes you a part of realizing it.

Point—If a police employee does not feel ownership in a vision, why would he or she feel obligated to make it happen? End point.

Approach B: Bottom Up

The bottom-up method for achieving a vision statement escapes the two dangerous pitfalls of the top-down—ownership and implementation. The operational word here is *shared*. Yes, Approach A will indeed give the department a vision statement. But it is Approach B that gives it a shared vision. (The words *shared* and *empowerment* are similar. We'll spend a lot of time dedicated to this vital leadership practice in a following chapter.)

Erecting a shared vision requires considerable time, energy, and inspiration. It's well worth it! Why? Because everyone acquires ownership in the final product. And if you sense ownership in a product, you're certainly more apt to want it to happen.

> To truly be a shared vision statement means that everyone has equal participation in its evolution.

If a police leader sincerely wants his or her department to reap the rewards of a shared vision, then the leader must:

- Listen carefully to all input.
- Link it to the fundamental purpose of police work.
- Make certain that all employees are equally mandated to participate (empowerment).
- Retain an open mind and reserve judgment until all views have surfaced.
- Encourage differing, even conflicting, viewpoints.
- Retain the responsibility for the ultimate departmental vision.

Examples

As promised, I give you examples of three vision statements. If tempted to take a shortcut by simply adopting all or a potion of them—don't do it! Cookie-cutter vision statements are devoid of flavor, calories, and energy. We'll flex the learning here by casting the examples into a structured exercise (see Structured Exercise 4-1).

Realization

I see a lot of police department vision statements today. You can find them on Web sites, walls of the police building, business cards, and more. They read, sound, and look really impressive. But are they actually serving any purpose except looking pretty and professional?

There are at least four methods for making certain that visions translate into reality. First, include them in part or in total in all pre-entry and in-service training programs. Replication works. Discussing current events (e.g., arrests, awards, changes) as examples of the vision in operation is helpful. If you want your vision statement to be a daily reality, then as a leader you've simply got to reinforce it. Again—*repetition works.*

Second, the vision statement should be made a *core* portion of all career assignments and promotional tests. If I were on your promotional oral board, my first question of you would be, "What values comprise your vision or mission statement?" My second, "What have you done in the past few days to promote your vision statement?"

STRUCTURED EXERCISE 4-1

Examine the three vision statements that follow. First, highlight all the values you can spot in each one. Second, look for any goals and record them. Third, write a single sentence that summarizes the expressed purpose of the agency. Compare your findings with others. Are there similarities? Are there any unique concepts or values? What else did you deduce from your research? Finally, either alone or as a member of a group, develop a vision statement for your work unit.

LOS ANGELES COUNTY SHERIFF'S DEPARTMENT

Our Mission
The quality of neighborhood life, its safety and welfare, comes from the commitment of each of its citizens. The **Los Angeles County Sheriff's Department** takes pride in its role as a citizen of the community, partners with its members in the delivery of quality law enforcement services. We dedicate our full-time efforts to the duties incumbent upon every community member. As we act, we are universal citizens deriving our authority from those we serve. We accept our law enforcement mission to serve our communities with the enduring belief that in so doing, we serve ourselves. As professionals, we view our responsibilities as a covenant of public trust, ever mindful that we must keep our promises. As we succeed, our effectiveness will be measured by the absence of crime and fear in our neighborhoods and by the level of community respect for our efforts. In accomplishing this all-important mission, we are guided by the following principles:

> To recognize that the primary purpose of our organization is not only the skillful

enforcement of the law, but the delivery of **humanitarian** services which promote community peace.

To understand that we must maintain a level of professional **competence** that ensures our safety and that of the public without compromising the constitutional guarantees of any person.

To base our decisions and actions on **ethical** as well as practical perspectives and to accept **responsibility** for the consequences.

To foster a collaborative relationship with the public in determining the best course in achieving **community order**.

To strive for **innovation**, yet remain **prudent** in sustaining our fiscal health through wise use of resources.

To never tire of our **duty**, never shrink from the difficult tasks and never lose sight of our own humanity.

Our Core Values
We shall be **service oriented** and perform our duties with the highest possible degree of personal and professional integrity.

Service Oriented Policing means

- *Protecting* life and property
- *Preventing* crime
- *Apprehending* criminals
- Always *acting lawfully*
- Being *fair and impartial* and treating people with dignity
- *Assisting the community* and its citizens in solving problems and maintaining the peace

We shall **treat every member** of the Department, both sworn and civilian, as **we would expect to be treated** if the positions were reversed.

We shall **not knowingly break the law** to enforce the law.

We shall be **fully accountable** for our own actions or failures and, when appropriate, for the actions or failures of our subordinates.

In considering the use of deadly force, we shall be guided by **reverence for human life.**

Individuals promoted or selected for special assignments shall have a history of **practicing these values.**

NEW YORK CITY POLICE DEPARTMENT

Mission

The MISSION of the **New York City Police Department** is to enhance the quality of life in our City by working in partnership with the community and in accordance with constitutional rights to enforce the laws, preserve the peace, reduce fear, and provide for a safe environment.

Values

In partnership with the community, we pledge to:

- Protect the lives and property of our fellow citizens and impartially enforce the law.
- Fight crime both by preventing it and by aggressively pursuing violators of the law.
- Maintain a higher standard of integrity than is generally expected of others because so much is expected of us.

- Value human life, respect the dignity of each individual and render our services with courtesy and civility.

PLANO, TEXAS, POLICE DEPARTMENT

Our Mission

The Plano Police Department is a value-driven organization that serves the community by:

- Protecting Life and Property
- Preventing Crime
- Enforcing the Laws
- Maintaining Order for All Citizens

As the Police Department serves our community, we emphasize:

- Voluntary Compliance
- Education of Citizens
- Partnership with Community
- Visual Presence in the Community
- Detection and Apprehension of Offenders

Our Values

We achieve that mission by:

- Integrity
- Fairness & Equity
- Personal Responsibility
- Customer Orientation
- Teamwork
- Planning & Problem Solving

Third, the leader should conduct an *annual* survey of community opinions about the values professed in the vision/mission statement. (The survey should also include questions on work performance, and I'll cover this in the final chapter.) Some questions might be, "Your department has made a commitment to making you feel more secure. How secure do you feel right now in your home? Do you have any ideas on how we can make you feel more secure?"

Finally, integrate your *vision statement* with your *employee performance appraisal system.* This is a profoundly practical decision based on the premise . . .

STRUCTURED EXERCISE 4-2

I am sure that there are other creative ways to make a shared vision operative in your agency. Round up some of your co-workers and brainstorm ideas on how a department's vision can be assimilated into the living fabric of your organizational culture. I'll be doing the same with the police leaders I know. Keep in mind that when it comes to a department's vision, it is never a question of what others will do but of what you will do.

What gets measured gets done.

It makes sense. If, for example, "service" is one of the values expressed in your vision statement, then it is not only reasonable but relevant that a police employee's attitude and behavior be assessed on this value. Let's face it, it doesn't make sense to salute and cheer a vision while there's no bottom-line payoff for making it happen.

STRATEGY

We must become the change we want to see.
—Gandhi

The twentieth century began by changing the old constancies, while the twenty-first century began with change as the only constant.

How well a police agency negotiates the hurdles of change is the key to its survival and success. Some change is external (e.g., Americans with Disabilities Act, homeland security, shifting demographics) and some is internal (e.g., organizational structure, management style, labor relations). Regardless of its source, any change should pose two questions:

- Does it challenge our vision?
- How does it affect our values?

Incessant and avalanching changes can modify a goal, which means reexamining and perhaps recasting it. In other cases, the changes may alter how the goal will be implemented. In both situations the police leader must think strategically . . . long term!

Strategic thinking is the basis for developing strategic plans and operational plans. It is a leadership quality for making better choices about how to implement departmental goals in the face of chronic and random changes.

When it comes to the subject of strategy (long term), it is typically attached to the word *planning* or strategic planning. It has been my experience, as well as that of the police leaders who employ it, that . . .

Thinking strategically is a lot more difficult than planning for it.

I'm not implying that strategic planning is quick and humdrum. It requires great effort. But the truly tough brain work resides in thinking and not planning strategy. We'll focus your leadership on thinking strategically because as you wrestle with change, it invariably

- Uncovers the causes versus symptoms of problems.
- Hammers conventional thinking.
- Depends more on intuition than on intellect.
- Seeks to anticipate.
- Points out more than one approach for accomplishing a goal.

To sharpen your strategic thinking ability, you must complete four steps.

Step 1. Insight

Recognizing insight in yourself or others begins with increased comprehension of the characteristics that most insightful police leaders share. Don't look for once-in-a-lifetime brilliant flashes! Real insight is a basic and abiding skill that continually guides the thinking of a winner. Most often, you'll find insightful police leaders engaged in the following behaviors.

- They prefer tackling problems that do not have precise answers, asking questions such as "In what ways can we improve our police services for our community?"
- They spend more time synthesizing information than gathering it, relishing the process of breaking information down into its component parts, then reconfiguring those parts to expose the essence of a problem.
- They can easily drop an approach to a problem that isn't working, turning from habitual methods of thinking and analyzing.
- They doggedly grapple with difficult problems over long periods of time, never feeling frustrated when the solution isn't readily apparent.
- They don't worry about asking questions that might display their ignorance. Such "dumb" questions cut to the heart of the matter and open a new path of thinking.
- They usually think up more ideas more rapidly than others in brainstorming sessions, because their disciplined but flexible minds thrive on such exercises.
- They picture situations and possibilities with vivid imagery that often colors their language when describing possible solutions in rich detail.
- They have made meditation a habit, not an occasional exercise, and set aside time each day for such activity.
- They read voraciously to satisfy a thirst for knowledge and the experience of others. They are mavens.
- They entertain new ideas enthusiastically.

Step 2. Creative Questions

The majority of us function daily with mental blinders that constrain our creativity. There are six in particular that limit our powers of imagination. They are as follows:

- **Resistance to and Avoidance of Change.** Many of us who cling to the status quo for safety are consciously or unconsciously blocking new insights.
- **Dependence on Rules and Conformance.** Some managers emphasize conformance over performance by enforcing strict adherence to rules, procedures, and structures.
- **Fear and Self-Doubt.** Some police leaders become immobilized by insecurity, lack of confidence, and fear of criticism.
- **Fixation on Logic and Hard Data.** Many leaders have more of a commitment to mechanics than to results. Some expect problems and solutions to fit snugly into neat compartments. This hampers their intuitive powers.
- **Black-and-White Viewpoints.** The maturity that comes with experience tends to change previously black-and-white judgments to varying shades of gray. Regrettably, some police managers hold to an either/or approach, which seriously reduces their options to a few oversimplified solutions.
- **Narrow-Minded Dedication to Practicality and Efficiency.** Some police managers refuse to consider wild alternatives and ideas. For them, every idea must fit into some logical scheme.

Step 3. Tuning In

Most of us seldom tap the full reserve of our knowledge and experience. When we encounter problems, we suffer anxiety because problems pose dangers as well as opportunities. In our anxiety, we forget to trust our most valuable intuitive resources. Insight, like great poetry, music, or art, arises from the quiet depths of the unconscious from a source that lies beneath words, deeds, thoughts, and figures.

It is from this source that you seek to blend your knowledge and your wisdom in order to build conceptual frameworks. A conceptual framework creates a state of mind that enables police leaders to move to the heart of the strategic issues facing their agencies while at the same time sidestepping mountains of minutiae and nonsensical ideas.

Step 4. Goal Setting

Setting goals and the change process are close pals. You contact one and you automatically engage the other. Here's how:

> **Goal: (n) a desired state of affairs that one attempts to achieve; deciding on a destination and then proceeding in that direction.**

By definition, then, a goal requires two efforts—seeing the change you want and then making it happen. Dreaming alone is just that—dreaming—no change. Action alone is purposeless—haphazard change or maybe none at all. Yes, grammatically a goal is a noun. But, in reality, a goal is a verb because it demands action, and action produces change.

Now that you have a grip on what a goal is, let's explore three fundamental characteristics that all police leaders must consider: (1) stated versus real; (2) one versus many; and (3) vague versus clear.

Stated, or Real, or Both?

A stated goal and a real goal may or may not be identical. For example, a police agency proclaims a goal of "Equal police service for all our community." But in *reality* the deployment of resources is biased in favor of the business community. Another example: An agency doesn't state anything about gang enforcement but has actually set a latent goal of fervently combating gang activity. One more example: A department professes a goal of "Reducing Part One crimes by 5%" and in reality means it.

It's not being deceitful, but it can be confusing when organizations state goals that are not real or have real goals that are not pronounced. What matters a lot, however, is that the police leaders know which is which and can *morally, logically, and politically* defend them.

One or More?

I have never met a person who has only one purpose in life. Also, I am unaware of any organization that has exclusively one goal. Imagine Intel exclaiming, "Our only goal is to make a lot of dough," or a police agency stating, "Our only purpose is to hook and book."

Okay. Clearly all police organizations contain multiple goals. Typically a few dominate and influence others and that creates a "hierarchy" of goals or a system of priorities. Having interoperable priorities increases clarity, and that's next.

Vague or Clear?

For several centuries there was a furious debate over goals being vague (flexible) or clear (precise). The latter won. Why? In his brilliantly insightful book, *The One Thing You Need to Know*, Marcus Buckingham presented solid scientific evidence that humankind has five major fears that produce five critical needs. Look at the following list. Which in your opinion is foremost?

Fears		Needs
Death	→	Security
Outsider	→	Community
Future	→	Clarity
Chaos	→	Authority
Insignificance	→	Respect

It may come as a surprise, but the answer is *clarity*. After your integrity, if you do nothing else as a leader, be clear. Clarity reduces our anxiety about our future. An effective leader doesn't have to be passionate, charming, brilliant, or highly verbal; she or he must be clear. Our need for clarity, when met, is the most likely to engender within us confidence, persistence, resilience, creativity, and followership.

The *great* clarifiers are leaders who make us certain about: (1) who we really serve; (2) what our core strengths are; (3) what in reality is being measured—the score card; and overtly set an example for us to follow.

STRUCTURED EXERCISE 4-3

You can administer the following "clarifier awareness scale" in two ways. First, according to your perception of your leading. Second, merely switch the words in your mind to that of your supervisor. (It's best applied in both ways.)

THE "4" POINTS OF CLARITY

Are you (Is your boss) clarifying for your team? Use a number from 1 to 7; 7 is high.

1. Who do you serve? (Who do you really serve?) _____

2. What is your core strength? (Traffic, gangs, drugs, terrorism, safety, or . . .).

Do you tell your staff clearly where your core strength lies, and thus centered, will they do everything in their power to make it happen? What is your number?

_____

3. What is your core score? Do you sort through all the metrics and pick one (e.g., reduction of Part One crimes) that they have the strengths to impact—and daily broadcast it? What is your number?

_____

4. What actions are you taking? For one, I will be guided by the clarity of what you do. I need to see examples. I need to see you walk your talk. Do you clearly set the example? Your number? _____

To sum up—if you are really intent on leading others, you've got to:

- **Show them clearly who they serve.**
- **Show them their core strengths.**
- **Show them the score card.**
- **Show them what actions must be taken.**

They will reward you by following your leadership toward a better future for you, them, your department, and your community.

CULTURE

Organizational culture will eat strategy for breakfast every day.
—*Charles "Red" Scott*

You can create a compelling vision of where you want to go along with a superb strategy for getting there, but if your department's culture says, "No way," then it just won't happen. As "Red" exclaimed, if your agency's work culture is not in alignment with your hopes and plans, then it'll easily and rapidly devour them.

While tough to change, an organizational culture certainly can. It is not wired into our human DNA. Culture is nested in our values, not genes, and as those values and police leaders change and adapt, so too can culture. In other words, your strategy can escape culture at the breakfast table, but only through careful and clever planning.

STRUCTURED EXERCISE 4-4

This is a simple but powerful exercise to help you understand the significance of goal setting.

- Imagine learning that you have to retire in one year. List three things you'd like to accomplish during this last year.
- Assume 11 months have passed and you have one month left. Again, list three things you would like to do.
- Make a new list assuming you have one week left and another assuming that you have only 48 hours left.
- Examine what you've written. If your list includes activities you're not currently

pursuing, what's stopping you from pursuing them now? *Get on track!*

(*Note:* This exercise can be easily modified to focus on your personal life. Merely assume that you have one year to live. List three things you'd want to do within the year and so on to 48 hours.)

Goal setting sets the stage for the development of more precise operational objectives. This subject and "MBO" (managing by objectives) await you in upcoming chapters.

Fortunately there is a process that can help police leaders avoid the devastating experience of seeing their vision and strategy being gobbled up by entrenched no-change diners. In a word—it's *empowerment.* The full benefits and dynamics of this vital process await us in two chapters. A few pages ago you were exposed to it when you read about the bottom-up approach for conceiving a department's vision of a preferred future.

If you truly trust your staff and really delegate to them the right to participate in decisions that affect them, then you're an empowering leader and likely to avoid the breakfast table. Empowerment is not a democratic process. You retain at all times your responsibility and authority for the ultimate decisions.

In its simplest form, empowerment means listening very carefully to the ideas, needs, wants, and desires of your police employees and then deciding what's best for them, your department, and most of all the community.

PROSPECTION

Prospection (pro-spek-shen): The act of looking forward in time or considering the future.

In his inspiring must-read book, *Stumbling on Happiness,* Daniel Gilbert informs us how and why we are different from all other animal life. We can and frequently (typically two hours per day) think about the *future.* With our knowledge, needs, hopes, feelings, and memory, we imagine what is around the corner for us. But Gilbert warns us that while our imagination is a powerful tool that allows us to conjure up images from inner space, it has two shortcomings.

Imagination (that faculty that helps us to view the future) first has to cope with misremembering the past and, second, mispreviewing the present, which causes you and me to misimagine the future.

We must remember that as we imagine our future, there is a whole lot missing, and the things that are missing matter.

Congenital naysayers are among the greatest stumbling blocks to imagining the future. They want the facts, just the facts. Steven Samples, in *The Contrarian's Guide to Leadership,* writes that our imagination may be, in the end, every bit as important as vision! What's neat about one's imagination is you do not have to exclusively rely on your own. As a police leader you should tap into the ideas of the creative geniuses who work for you. After all, they're being paid to think, so help them earn their salary. Samples concludes that if you're incapable of imagining the future or incapable of engaging the fresh ideas of your staff, your followers are better off without you.

Many police managers are mesmerized by hard numbers, focus on concrete reality, and accept nothing else. Imagination is for them the soft stuff, guesswork, and lacks substance. Of course proven facts are important, but relying on them exclusively misses the messages that our guts transmit. We see managers striving to be rigorously objective at all times. It is the leader, however, who accepts and applies the vagaries of subjective experience. The accuracy of a leader's vision is more intuitive than empirical.

Imagination leads to new insights, which elevate our ability to predict and thus anticipate changes and trends. We do not want mystical, magical, crystal ball leaders guiding our police organizations. Nonetheless, we hope for police leaders who have a keen capacity for imagining incoming challenges and opportunities.

TEN TRENDS

Most of us view the future as a happening that is always stealing from us our security, breaking promises, changing the rules, creating all kinds of problems. Nevertheless, it is the future that holds our greatest leverage. The past is on record, and if we are alert, we can learn from it. Things occur only in one place—the present. Usually, we respond to those things.

It is in the incoming future, and only there, where a police leader has the time to prepare for the present! Strange, isn't it?

When imagining the future, you can look at it as *content* or *process.* The "content futurists" concentrate on data about the future. The "process futurists" focus on how to think about such new and unusual data.

The 10 trends you'll encounter now are the product of the imaginations of over 1,000 police managers I have been blessed to meet and train with over the past five years. Some of the trends we'll cover you may be feeling and experiencing right now. One of the most critical leadership skills needed during times of uncertainty and turbulence is anticipation. Reliable anticipation is the outcome of reliable trend identification. Some anticipation can be analytical, but the most important aspect of trend forecasting is our unpredictable, exciting, at times wrong, frequently right—imagination.

Trend 1. Flat World

Thomas Friedman, in *The World Is Flat: A Brief History of the Twenty-First Century,* points out that broadband connectivity around the world, undersea cables, omnipresence of computers, explosion of software, e-mail, and search engines have created a platform where intellectual work can be delivered from anywhere. Imagine criminal case preparations being completed in Bangalore, India. Right now some USA attorneys and CPAs are using their services.

Globalization is shrinking and flattening the world while empowering companies and police departments to participate in open-sourcing, outsourcing, offshoring, insourcing, in-forming, and more. We've entered an era of cheap, easier, and friction-free technology that is literally transforming every aspect of business (police, too), every aspect of life, and every aspect of society.

The flatters' "flanking technologies" have been around (e.g., e-mail, Web browsers) for nearly two decades. They're taking hold now because there is a growing cadre of police leaders using them, and organizational cultures are shifting away from vertical command and control to connecting and collaborating horizontally (this is the "agile" organization that's covered in a future chapter). Do you use or do you know any police manager using Bluetooth, an Iridium satellite telephone and living in a WiFi city? I do. And they are a player in our flattened world.

Trend 2. Higher Tech

When you write about "richer communications" today, within minutes (even nanoseconds) you're obsolete. Today, intelligent terminals connect with intelligent networks that are wired and wireless, local and global. Together, they empower police personnel and machines to communicate and share information in an increasingly rich variety of forms: voice, handwriting, video data, print, and image. Networks that never sleep can find you and deliver a message; hold videoconferences across the nation or the world; or identify, locate, and apprehend criminals who operate outside national borders.

The power of technology is indeed bringing police data banks together and giving them access to each other and to the information they want and need, anytime, anywhere—in ever new and useful ways. Around the world, police agencies now recognize (see Trend 4) that their professional futures are linked to their communication and information infrastructures.

More less-than-lethal weapons are available. Uniforms with wireless sensors to monitor life signs and measure stress levels along with pinhole cameras are being tested. We now have hand-held portable devices that see through walls and clothing and "bugs" that can be surreptitiously placed on individuals. Our Global Positioning Systems (GPS) are capable of locating us within less than three feet of our position. Clearly there are a lot of hardware gadgets in the offing.

Before moving on, it's fit that we mention the most ubiquitous of all electronic technology. They even surpass the omnipresence of the personal computer. They can do everything except wash your laundry, and that's probably next in their array of capabilities. You're right—it's the much loved and damned cell phone. The jury is out right now on the issue of whether it does more harm than good. Some police agencies have a policy on the use of cell phones while on duty. Eventually all agencies will have rules about cell phones.

Trend 3. Lower Touch

We are experiencing a trend now of *everyone being in touch and nobody being touched*. It's necessary to think and act high-tech. After all, no one wants to be a hit-and-run victim on the information superhighway. Regretfully, in our quest for more advanced communications technology, we are missing high-touch thinking and acting. We are a nation on a chaotic upward-and-onward race involving making everything wireless, compressing bits, increasing fiber-optic bandwidth—making our future digital. There seems to be a collective faith that technology guarantees us a cyber-utopia of robot cops.

E-mail has its functionality, but clearly it's not a way to build teams, create enthusiasm, or elevate understanding and mutual trust. We see an out-of-control higher-tech trend that is causing lower touch and thus undermining community-oriented policing.

Already police technology—the computer, cell phone, and hundreds of electronic messages—is preventing managers and supervisors from interfacing with their staff. As a consequence, police leaders must carefully and wisely apply the invading technology to areas in which it helps both productivity and people. *Leadership by e-mail just won't work;* being digital is not leadership.

Add deployment to technology, and it makes sense that a lot of police employees do not feel engaged, lack a sense of individualism, and approach police work as merely a job. The three-day/twelve-hour and four-day/ten-hour allocation plans are a two-edged sword. One side is loved by the officers in that they can spend more time elsewhere and commute less. Another side is detested by police leadership because it reduces face-to-face communications, trust, and teamwork. I have frequently heard from supervisors who rated the performance of their staff when they did not actually observe their work.

Some favorable news: Some police leaders have decided to combat this malady by pushing aside their computer, jumping over mounds of paperwork, and being physically present in the field of operations (not merely wandering through roll call with a smile). Some agencies have adopted policies that all watch commanders will be in the field at least 50% of their duty time. Here's the kicker. So far the results have shown they enjoy it, and the line officers appreciate it.

Trend 4. A 9/11 Partnership

While the subject is somewhat unpleasant, the police managers and I brainstormed 9/11 for any potential benefits. Surprisingly we found several (e.g., new jobs, new technology, increased patriotism, and more).

Our federal system of governance separates our nation's police into national, state, and local subsystems. They recognize the need to cooperate and support one another. Shared computer-based criminal justice information is one example. Unfortunately, much of the desire for closer and full cooperation has been lip service. But 9/11 has changed latent parochialism into a real partnership.

The hurricanes that earlier this decade devastated New Orleans and threatened Houston with a similar fate underscored the lessons learned after 9/11—all of American law enforcement must act as one to be effective in coping with major disasters. To be effective all levels of policing must be seamless. The terrorists love it when egos and politics scramble a united police front. Yet another benefit has emerged. Is the emotion of "I'm afraid to fly because of international terrorism" any different from "I'm afraid to walk in my neighborhood because of local gangs (terrorists)?" The source is different, but the emotion is identical—the terrorists have intimidated me. Our newly formed international police partnership has discovered a lot of similar interoperable patterns and tactics between international terrorists and local gangs (which are actually national and international). This point is demonstrated in the recently established joint regional centers for anti-terrorism. Their mission includes an anti-gang component!

Well, 9/11 can be thanked for making our law enforcement system synergistic, stronger, and more capable in stopping criminals here and abroad.

Trend 5. Pension Envy

When it comes to local government (that's where the majority of policing occurs), usually the largest percentage of the budget is allocated to the police and sheriff's departments. These are essential services, but we cannot ignore the fact that the cost of cops is high and growing. This is both good and bad news for our police officers. It's good that many of the personnel are earning a fine income with an enviable benefits package. The bad news is that many taxpayers are beginning to voice reservations about both the number and compensation of the police employees: Granted, they're important, *but* they're overpriced.

Across our nation many private pension programs have been modified, reduced, even eliminated. Private sector workers expecting a retirement of "X" are being told, "Tough luck, it'll be "X−50%." Simultaneously they discover that their taxes are being raised to pay for better police pensions. This countervailing set of circumstances is on a collision course—police pension systems versus private ballot boxes. Already some police leaders have made tough decisions about retirement packages. For example, newly hired employees receive the same pay but have to contribute more to their pension or simply receive a smaller benefit. All of this is occurring when most police departments are struggling to hire new employees.

It appears there is an increased likelihood that a greater percentage of a police officer's retirement (especially the medical benefit) will either be contributed by the officer, or be less at the point of retirement. Another aspect is the number of years needed to reach retirement. In some pension programs, at age 50 you can receive 80% of your salary. The bottom-line question is precisely the bottom-line dollar, or "as a taxpayer, how much am I willing to pay for my police?"

Trend 6. From Bureaucracy to Agility

Police leaders are confronting bureaucracy (the anatomy of an organization) and bashing it. From its inhibiting boundaries, boundarylessness and agility are evolving. *Boundarylessness* is a behavior definer, a way of getting police managers outside their organizational boxes and offices and working together faster. It also gets the police manager closer to the customers, the community and, most importantly, the work team. It positions them in front, in the lead. This behavior definer is encouraging police managers to cast aside thinking about teamwork and agility and actually practice it! They're finding that it eliminates barriers that slow the department down and detract from its success.

Boundarylessness will, if practiced, create an agile department, and an agile organization is:

- *Speedy:* Providing a very fast-paced reaction to emerging crime and social problems. Problem-oriented policing is a concrete example of boundarylessness and quick responses.
- *Teamwork driven:* Engaged in a highly focused endeavor to tear all the walls down and put teams from all police functions together in one room to bring new operations, tactics, and services to life.
- *Responsive:* Delivering quick community/customer intelligence means an advanced method for accurately knowing what people really want. It is a process that gives every police manager direct access to the customer. Community-oriented policing (COP) is one way to make this happen. There'll be much more on the subject of an agile organization in a future chapter.

Trend 7. Volunteers

In most police agencies today, if you work, you get paid. In some cases the reserve officers may be performing their duties without compensation. They may be hoping for eventual employment and/or just enjoying the excitement of police work. Related, but different, is the growing number of civilian volunteers. These people are willing to contribute their efforts to important causes. They can be observed serving in such capacities as

- Search and rescue
- Patrol
- Clerical/records
- Mechanics
- Training
- Pilots
- Clergy
- Counseling
- Data processing

People want to make a difference; they want purpose in life. We know of police organizations that are benefiting from thousands of hours of volunteer assistance. With more and more people living well beyond their retirement date, a reservoir of proven talent is building. And this talent seriously wants and, indeed, needs opportunities to be applied.

The prudent agencies are welcoming volunteers as prized workers. The dollar savings are tremendous; the work results are exemplary. Volunteers count. The San Bernardino, California Sheriff's Department has 3,000 officers and 3,000 volunteers.

Trend 8. Empowerment

We are convinced that the growing participation of police workers in decisions that affect them or their clientele will evolve into the mental muscle of a more full and rich empowerment. What we wrote earlier on this subject will steadily become a routine practice. Police unions won't cause it to happen. (In fact, they may resist it.) Preaching "humanism" won't promote it. The demand for better police services will cause it to happen.

Better police services depend on an empowered workforce. Police leaders realize that a committed and thinking workforce relies on being empowered to do their jobs.

Trend 9. From "Think Small, Act Big" to "Think Big, Act Small"

We admire big police organizations. Their scale, power, and expertise are awesome. Unfortunately, some devolve into thinking small and acting big. It is the smaller police departments that create excitement, while their larger counterparts, sometimes, just impress. We're defining "small" as police agencies with about 150 employees or fewer, *or* work units within a larger police agency that are encouraged to *act* small. In other words, several large-scale police and sheriff's agencies have reorganized in such a fashion that they're acting small and thinking big.

Small departments or small work units within a large department are uncluttered, simple, informal. They thrive on enthusiasm and bash bureaucracy. Small organizations win due to good ideas, regardless of their source. They need everyone, involve everyone, and reward or remove people based on their contribution to being successful. Small organizations set the bar high—increments and fractions don't interest them. We endorse the way in which small units communicate—with straightforward, convincing arguments rather than jargon-filled memos, "putting it in channels," "running it up the flagpole," and, worst of all, the polite deference to the small ideas that are too often sent from the big offices in big organizations.

The small organization or work unit's advantage is *speed* (see Trend 6)—which brings with it an urgency, an exhilaration, and a focus on what really counts. Speed is a vaccine against bureaucracy and lethargy.

Being "big" has certain advantages. First, it usually has ample resources to acquire big-ticket items such as computers, helicopters, single-print identification technology, remote video training, and so on. Second, "big" has a staying power when confronted by massive social problems such as terrorism, a natural disaster, or large-scale demonstrations.

Trend 10. Service Experience

The majority of people who have had a police contact evaluate it as either a neutral or negative experience. Why are we not hearing people exclaim that it was a highly positive experience or, in the jargon of business-speak, "a value-added service"?

The cutting-edge business organizations are endeavoring to engage their customers in an inherently personal way. If the private sector can create experiences that are memorable—and lasting—why can't our police departments? The answer is they can, and some are.

The method for providing a police "service experience" is customizing. When you customize an experience, you make it just right for an individual—providing exactly what he or she needs right now. When this occurs, the recipient is transformed. A customized experience on top of an efficient service results in a pro-police person. *Bingo!* This is what community-oriented policing (COP) is all about. COP is not service driven; it is customer driven.

Throughout this book, I have emphasized that *in theory*, COP is values-based. When *practiced*, however, it becomes values-added. Values are created and then added in four ways:

- *Origination:* work that generates value from something new
- *Execution:* work that generates value from something done
- *Correction:* work that generates value from something improved
- *Application:* work that generates value from something useful

Every activity of the police agency must be performed in order to anticipate and advance external change. The department can then fulfill its mission of actively making it happen. And that can be accomplished only through rigorous thinking and personal intuition about what police service really is.

STRUCTURED EXERCISE 4-5

To test your organization's vision IQ, we have designed an "opinionnaire" for you to complete.

1. Has your department consciously determined a vision for the organization?

1	2	3	4	5	6	7

None   Some   Considerable

EXAMPLES:

_____

_____

2. Do you know the specifics of your organization's vision?

1	2	3	4	5	6	7

No Knowledge   Some Awareness   Totally Informed

EXAMPLES:

_____

_____

3. Would most of the staff share the same vision of your organization's future direction?

1	2	3	4	5	6	7

No   Somewhat   Yes

Different Perspectives   Average Consensus   Complete Agreement

EXAMPLES:

_____

_____

4. Is your vision sufficiently clear that you and your colleagues can readily concur as to what new services or changes your agency should initiate?

1	2	3	4	5	6	7

No
Confused
EXAMPLES:

Somewhat
Fair Clarity

Yes
Perfectly Clear

5. Is your organization's vision statement used for making service and clientele choices?

1	2	3	4	5	6	7

No
None Stated
EXAMPLES:

Somewhat
Partial Use

Yes
Fully Applied

6. Are your vision deliberations held separately from your operational planning efforts?

1	2	3	4	5	6	7

No
Nonexistent
EXAMPLES:

Partially
Some Mixing

Yes
Completely Separate

7. Does your vision statement clearly determine what you plan, project, and budget (as opposed to your plans, projections, and budgets determining your vision)?

1	2	3	4	5	6	7

Totally
Full Use of Strategy

Sometimes
Strategy Has Some
Influence on Plans

None
Strategy Has
No Impact

EXAMPLES:

8. Are the assumptions *you* generate about the agency's vision used?

1	2	3	4	5	6	7

Ignored

Some Acceptance

Fully Included
(*Continued*)

STRUCTURED EXERCISE 4-5   (*Cont.*)

EXAMPLES:

_____

_____

9. Do your divisions have clearly stated operational plans?

1	2	3	4	5	6	7

No			Somewhat			Totally

EXAMPLES:

_____

_____

10. Do the divisional plans fully support your overall organizational vision?

1	2	3	4	5	6	7

No or by Accident			Somewhat Partial Intentional Support			Completely Full Intentional Support

EXAMPLES:

_____

_____

11. Is the total performance of your organization evaluated on both vision accomplishment and operating results?

1	2	3	4	5	6	7

No			Sometimes			Frequently

EXAMPLES:

_____

_____

12. My present level of understanding of the theory and practice of the department is

1	2	3	4	5	6	7

No			Sometimes Familiar			Highly Familiar

EXAMPLES:

_____

_____

How did you rate yourself and your department? If your total approached 80 points, you and your agency are to be congratulated!

Competency Checkpoints

- The four reasons a police agency experiences trouble are (1) no or poor vision, (2) no strategic plan and goals, (3) a negative culture, and (4) little imagination.
- The twentieth century began by changing the old constancies, while the twenty-first century began with change as the only constant.
- Vision ensures constancy of purpose while strategy copes with change.
- A vision statement emphasizes (1) purpose, (2) the future, (3) values, (4) principled decision making, (5) change, (6) conflict resolution, (7) overview, and (8) excellence.
- There are two methods for constructing a vision statement: (1) top-down and (2) bottom-up.
- To be functional, the building of a vision and vision statement must be a shared process.
- Strategic thinking involves four steps: (1) recognizing insight, (2) asking the creative questions, (3) tuning in, and (4) goal setting.
- The police agency that exists without goals will expend its future in the present.
- A goal is something we desire; police agencies have more than one, and "real" and "stated" goals are not necessarily the same.
- Culture will eat strategy for breakfast every time.
- Police managers rely on hard data and are suspicious of intuition. Police leaders acknowledge the facts but place enormous faith in their feelings about the facts.
- It is in the imagination of the future that police leaders are enabled to leverage it.

Flexing the Message

1. What police agency do you know of that is (or was) in a lot of trouble? In your opinion is (or was) it caused by one or more of the following: poor or bad leadership, no shared mission or vision, and/or no strategic plan or goals?
2. Does your agency have a mission or vision statement? If so, take a copy and highlight all the values you can find in it. Do you see these values actually functioning right now?
3. What are the stated goals of your department or bureau? If none are stated, then what do you think they are? Write them down, and see if your co-workers agree or disagree. Does your agency have a written strategic plan? If so, have you read it? Does it seem reasonable yet challenging? How much of it has been accomplished? If there is no plan, why not? What are the chances of the department building one?
4. Contact other police agencies that may have strategic plans. Ask for or borrow copies and compare them. (Some agencies have included their strategic plan on their Web page.) What are the similarities and differences? Which do you believe is the most compelling? Why?
5. Either in a group or individually, add three trends to the list of ten discussed in this chapter.
6. Which one of the ten trends is the most observable? Which one of the ten is the least detectable?

5

COMMUNICATIONS

Communications and trust are inseparable. Increased communications cause more trust within the workforce. Curtailed communications similarly reduce trust. The understanding of values, ethics, and vision depends on trust.

One becomes a leader when one is able to clearly communicate the department's vision in such a way that others want to make it a reality.

The difference between the right word and the almost right word is the difference between lightning and the lightning bug.
—Mark Twain

CHAPTER OUTLINE

1. The Four Main Reasons for Communications
   a. Meaning
   b. Trust
   c. Decisions
   d. Feedback
2. Formal Channels
   a. Compliance
   b. Discomfort
   c. Distance
3. Informal Channels
   a. Subformal
   b. Personal Task-Directed
   c. Personal Non-Task-Directed
4. Four Directions
   a. Downward
   b. Upward
   c. Horizontal
   d. Diagonal
5. Number of Messages
6. Kinds of Messages

Human communication has its own set of very unusual and counterintuitive rules. It is best defined as *mutual understanding*. The main problem in communication is translating what we mean into what we say and translating what we say into what we mean. The first challenge, therefore, is to learn to say what we mean; the second challenge is to learn to listen so that we understand what others mean.

Everything a police leader does involves communicating. Not a few things—everything!

For a vision statement to become a reality, communication must again take place. The most creative ideas or the finest community-oriented policing (COP) program cannot take form without communication.

THE FOUR MAIN REASONS FOR COMMUNICATIONS

*When I use the word, it means what I choose it to
mean—neither more nor less.*
—Humpty Dumpty, in Through the Looking Glass

Communication is information that flows throughout a police organization in order to bind it together. It directs the organization as to where and when to go, and it informs the organization about whether or not progress is being made. Communication makes it possible to have all of the organization's various parts moving toward its mission.

An agency's mission can be poorly communicated due to (1) the police manager holding a single meeting or issuing a memo that hypes it, (2) the police manager spending a lot of time haranguing the personnel about it in speeches and written materials, and (3) the managerial and supervisory staff merely echoing the boss's excitement about a lot of new words.

Police employees will not support a mission/vision statement without credible communications. If credibility is lacking, the hearts and minds of the troops are marginalized.

Police leaders who experience the vision becoming a reality for the community "walk the talk." They become a visual and communicating symbol of the department's vision.

> **At this point, we need to reintroduce Rule 150. This rule is based on the revolutionary scientific studies of British anthropologist Robin Dunbar. He discovered that there are limitations built into us either by learning or by the design of our nervous systems. He demonstrated that our channel capacity for effectively interacting with others is 150 people. This assumes an interaction in which people build the kind of relationships that go with knowing who others are and how they relate to one another.[1]**

For a communications statement to take hold, there must be (1) meaning in it, (2) trust in the meaning, (3) decisions that reflect on it, and (4) feedback that ensures compliance.

Meaning

All police organizations need shared meanings and interpretations of reality because they facilitate coordinated efforts. *Meaning* surpasses what is typically meant by *communications*. Meaning has little to do with facts or even knowing. Facts and knowing pertain to technique and tactics.

"Thinking" is much closer to what I mean by *meaning*; this is not a subtle difference. Thinking prepares you for what ought to be done. Depending on facts without thinking may seem all right, but in the long run it is dangerous because it lacks reason. The distinctive quality of police leadership is that the "know-why" occurs before the "know-how." The police manager says, "Do it." The police leader says, "Do it, and here's why."

Police leaders engage primarily in a mental process known as *problem solving*. Problem solving includes a problem, a method, and a solution based on the former two factors. When neither the problem nor the method, let alone the solution, exist, a creative mental process is required. There's no rule, manual, or guru to consult. It's up to the leader to uncover the real problem. Creativity reveals a hidden problem—one that requires attention from start to finish. *The highest type of discovery always centers on problem finding!*

Trust

By the very nature of their work schedule, police personnel experience blockages in their information channels. Police employees work on different shifts and in separated work units. This severely complicates "getting the word around," especially getting the word around *accurately*.

When communication suffers, so does trust. Communication and trust are linked; when one goes up, so does the other. Try it—you'll find that it works. Reduce your communications and openness with a co-worker, family member, or friend, and see what occurs: Mutual trust is reduced. Enhance communication, and the opposite happens: Mutual trust is elevated—simple but true, and vitally important to the success of a police agency. Moreover, a police leader must raise *both* to raise one.

Face it—how can the values, ethics, and vision of a police organization be comprehended without the police leaders communicating it? Additionally, how can the values, ethics, and vision of a police agency be implemented without mutual trust? The response to both questions is . . . They can't. As a leader you must communicate (speak, write, listen, and provide feedback). Also, you must trust (yourself, others, the situation). Sometimes it isn't easy, but whoever said leadership was easy? (Clearly, it was not a leader!)

The key to trust is trustworthiness. Being trusted is the best guarantee of maintaining the climate of effective communication. As with all natural processes, there are no shortcuts, no quick fixes.

STRUCTURED EXERCISE 5-1

HOW ARE WE DOING WITH COMMUNICATION AND TRUST?

On an individual basis, self-administer the following questionnaire. Circle the number you believe to be most accurate.

1. How open am I with my thoughts?

1	2	3	4	5	6	7

Very closed   Very open

2. How open with me about their thoughts are my co-workers/peers?

1	2	3	4	5	6	7

Very closed   Very open

3. How open with me about his or her thoughts is my boss?

1	2	3	4	5	6	7

Very closed   Very open

4. How open with me about their thoughts are those whom I manage/supervise?

1	2	3	4	5	6	7

Very closed   Very open

5. How trusting am I of my co-workers/peers?

1	2	3	4	5	6	7

No trust   Total trust

6. How trusting am I of my boss?

1	2	3	4	5	6	7

No trust   Total trust

(Continued)

STRUCTURED EXERCISE 5-1   (Cont.)

7. How trusting am I of those whom I manage/supervise?

1	2	3	4	5	6	7

No trust   Total trust

8. How trustworthy am I?

1	2	3	4	5	6	7

Not at all   Completely
                                                                        trustworthy

Now add the numbers. If the score is 56 or more, you're a fortunate person. If it is less than 17, you'd best do a career assessment.

Divide into groups and compare your results on a per-question basis. Conclude your discussion with a set of recommendations on what can be done to elevate the candor and quality of communications and to enhance mutual trust.

Decisions

Departmental decision-making mechanisms function in direct relationship to departmental communication systems. While most police leaders would attest to the necessity of effective communications, most of them would also concur that "effective" communication is tough to achieve.

Successful police leaders examine the quality of organizational communications to be certain that what is being generated at the top reaches the bottom in the same context as intended. They make certain that the same is true for information (feedback) that is initiated at the bottom, or from outside the organization, and moves to the top. They ensure the information is not impeded at some juncture or changed. Too often, for whatever reason, there are those who would "shield the boss." Accurate decisions depend on open and accurate communications.

Feedback

Feedback is the breakfast of champions! In other words, winning leaders demand feedback. Without feedback, police managers are saddled with unnecessary uncertainty and excessive risks. Ironically, while most police managers readily acknowledge the importance of feedback, few ardently seek it. If a manager does not push hard for feedback, it is unlikely to occur—that is, until the reason for it becomes so compelling that it is a crisis.

Securing feedback means, on occasion, bridging around the chain of command and soliciting ideas and information. It means managing by wandering around (MBWA) out of the office and interacting with the police employees. It means being open and not "killing the messenger." It means, above all else, not being content with only one feedback loop. No feedback is the breakfast of losers!

FORMAL CHANNELS

It is the province of knowledge to speak and the privilege of wisdom to listen.
—*Oliver Wendell Holmes*

All organizations have formal communication channels as a response to their size and the limited information-handling capacity of individuals. The formal channels comply with the organization's recognized *official* structure and transmit messages that communicate issues of policy. Hence, one typically sees formal orders and directives, reports, official correspondence, standard operating procedures, and so on. Those persons who emphasize going through channels are doing so in adherence to the unity-of-command principle within the *formal* hierarchy.

Compliance

Rigid compliance with formal channels can be harmful, mainly in terms of time, creativity, and experience. First, it takes a long time for a formal message from a police manager in one division to pass to a manager in another division. Second, formal messages are on the record and thus restrain the free flow of thought. Third, in practice, a formal communications system cannot cover all informational needs. Informational needs change quite rapidly, whereas the formal channels change only with considerable time and effort.

Police managers who rely solely on formal written or recorded communications will find themselves creating a feeling of mistrust, a suspicion that the documentation is being used for some other purpose.

There are obviously times when written formal communications are most appropriate. Everyone gets the same message; written messages alleviate confusion on complicated issues; specific inquiries receive specific replies; and so on. On the other hand, formal communications take time and require a formal response. They prevent the give-and-take and clarifications that occur with personal interaction.

Discomfort

Most employees at every organizational level are sensitive to the uncomfortable feelings that arise in response to some memoranda, especially those that appear to have an ominous hidden agenda. Chiefs themselves are not immune to this discomfort when communications with their bosses seem to be primarily formalized. For employees at the lower end, it is likely to be worse, especially if they receive a questionable memo at the close of the work shift. It is even more so at the workweek's end. Many an officer has left work with the feeling that his or her job is in jeopardy. That discomfort grows until the "boss" can be contacted for clarification.

Distance

Unnecessary formal communications will create morale problems. They distance leaders from their staff, creating an ivory-tower effect. They frustrate the process of feedback; communications initiated for one purpose at times turn to other productive subjects. They slow down the time between decisions and actions. They cause return memoranda to be prepared, which may not provide the desired information. There is also a tendency for people not to be as candid about critical input in written reports as they are in informal communications.

INFORMAL CHANNELS

> *He who answers before listening—that is his folly and his shame.*
> *—Proverbs 18:13*

While some managers consider formal communication channels the best way to send information necessary to the functioning of the police organization, this practice is no longer as popular as it was in the past. Police leaders recognize informal and personal communications as a supportive and frequently necessary process for effective functioning.

The more restricted the formal channels, the greater the growth of informal ones.

Although the informal system seeks to fill the gaps in the formal one, the managers can severely curtail the development of the former simply by directing employees not to communicate with each other, by physically separating people, or by requiring prior clearance for any communication outside a certain division. In doing so trust and teamwork crash.

There are three kinds of informal communication channels. The first two are task- and goal-oriented; the third is devoted to personal interests.

Subformal

Subformal channels move messages that arise from the informal power structure that exists in every police organization. Every member of the department must know and observe informal standards and procedures about what to communicate and to whom. Such practices are seldom written down and must be acquired by experience and example, a situation that causes difficulties for newcomers.

Subformal communications consist of two types: those that flow along formal channels but not as formal communications and those that flow along strictly informal channels. Both types have the definite advantage of not being official—they can be withdrawn or changed without an official record being made.

Almost all new ideas are first proposed and tried as subformal communications.

Formal channels are usually vertical, following the paths of the formal authority structure. Thus most of the gap-filling subformal lines of communication are horizontal, connecting peers and bosses. Subformal communications also supply a way for employees to speak freely with their leaders.

Subformal channels are particularly useful in the following types of situations:

- The greater the degree of interoperability among activities (e.g., patrol and detectives) within the department, the greater the number and use of subformal channels.
- The more uncertainty about department objectives, the greater the number and use of subformal channels.
- When a police agency is operating under the pressure of time, it will use subformal channels.
- Closely cooperating sections rely primarily on subformal communications. Conversely, if the divisions of a police organization are in competition, they tend to communicate only formally.
- Subformal communication channels are used more often if employees have predictable rather than uncertain relationships with each other.

Personal Task-Directed

Personal task-directed communications are those in which employees reveal their attitude toward the activities of their organization. While personal, this communication is also targeted toward the goals or activities of the organization. It possesses the following characteristics:

- Personal task-directed channels are nearly always used for informing rather than for directing.
- Before people act on the basis of information received through personal channels, they usually verify that information through either subformal or formal channels.
- The channels transmit messages with considerable speed because there are no formal mechanisms to impede the flow of information.
- Because personal task-directed messages are transmitted by employees acting as individuals, they do not bear the weight of the position generating them. (They differ from subformal messages, which are transmitted by individuals acting in their assigned capacity—but not for the official record!)

Personal Non-Task-Directed

This form of communication does not contain information related to the job. Paradoxically, this channel may on occasion handle information far more valuable to the achievement of organizational goals than any other channel, including the formal ones. An example of this type of communication is a manager learning from an employee of growing job dissatisfaction.

How are these channels used?

- Non-task-directed channels provide a way for people to satisfy their social needs.
- These channels provide a way for individuals to reveal their feelings about things that make them happy.
- Non-task-directed channels frequently supply useful feedback normally comprised of unexpected information not obtainable in any other way.
- Personal non-task-directed channels offer the best medium for people to become adjusted to the organizational culture (unwritten standards, group values, and "the way we do things here" are conveniently expressed through non-task-directed channels).

FOUR DIRECTIONS

History repeats itself because no one listened the first time.
—*Anonymous*

Traditionally, communication flow was viewed as being exclusively downward and identical with the pattern of authority. Now we appreciate that a message can flow in one of four directions: downward, upward, laterally (horizontally), and diagonally.

Downward
Communications from a leader to her or his staff are of five types:

- Specific task directives: *job instructions*
- Information to produce an understanding of the task and its relation to other organizational tasks: *job rationale*
- Information concerning organizational *procedures and practices*
- *Feedback* to personnel about their performance
- Information to instill a sense of mission: *indoctrination of goals*

Job instruction is most often given first priority in police organizations. Instructions about the job of police employee are communicated through direct orders from the police manager, training sessions, training manuals, and written directives. The objective is to ensure the reliable performance of every person in the organization.

Less attention is given to the second type of message, *job rationale*. This information provides employees with a full understanding of their position and its relation to similar positions in the same organization. Many police personnel know *what* they are to do but not *why*. Withholding information on the rationale of the job can reduce the loyalty of the work team. The benefits of giving more information on job understanding are: If people know the reasons for their assignment, they will often carry out their job more effectively; and if they understand what their job is about in relation to the overall mission of the department, they are more likely to identify with its goals.

Regarding the third type, information about *organizational procedures and practices* supplies a prescription of the role requirements of the employee.

For the fourth type, *evaluative feedback* is necessary to ensure that the agency is operating properly. Feedback to employees about how well they are doing their job, however, is often neglected or poorly handled, even in police organizations in which the management calls for penetrating evaluation.

The final type of downward-directed information emphasizes departmental *goals*.

Upward
Communications about or from the staff upward to management are of five types:

- *Information* about their *performance* and *grievances*
- *Information* about the *performance* and *grievances* of others
- *Feedback* regarding organizational *practices* and *policies*

- *Feedback* concerning *what* needs to be done and *how* to do it
- *Requests for clarification* of the goals and specific activities

For a variety of reasons, there are great barriers to free upward communication. First, the most prominent obstacle is the structure itself. Simply stated, bureaucracies tend to inhibit upward informal communications. Thus a tremendous amount of important information never reaches the upper-level decision centers. Second, managers are less in the habit of listening to their staffs than of talking to them. Third, because information fed up the line is often used for control purposes, a leader's staff is not likely to give him or her information that will lead to decisions that adversely affect them. They tell the manager not only what they think *the manager wants to hear* but also what they *want the manager to know.*

Horizontal

Communications between people at the same organizational level are basically of four types:

- *Information* necessary to provide task *coordination*
- *Information* for identifying and defining *common problems* to be solved through cooperation
- *Feedback* from co-workers that fulfills *social needs*
- *Information* needed to provide *social* (not organizational) *control* for a group so that it can maintain members' compliance with its standards and values

Horizontal communication is difficult. A working balance must be found between communications among co-workers. Unrestricted horizontal communications can detract from maximum efficiency because too much irrelevant information may be transmitted. Alternatively, efficiency suffers if employees receive all their instructions from the person above them, thus blocking teamwork.

The type and amount of information that should be circulated on a horizontal basis is best determined by answering the questions, Who needs to know, and why? A disastrous hang-up in horizontal communication occurs when police managers overvalue peer communication and neglect those below and above them (for example, when lieutenants talk only to lieutenants and captains only to captains).

Diagonal

An example of diagonal communications occurs when the patrol watch commander speaks directly to a criminal investigator about a job-related issue or personal matter. It happens all the time. The agile and high-performing agencies thrive on it. While similar to horizontal communications, there are differences that should be noted. Diagonal communications guarantee:

- Enhanced *teamwork*
- Promotion of *improvement*
- Immediate *feedback*
- *Speed* in operations
- *Agility* in changing tasks and goals

NUMBER OF MESSAGES

> *The words* silent *and* listen *contain the same letters.*
>
> —*Anonymous*

Communication is expensive! Every message involves time for deciding what to send, time for composing, costs of sending the message (which may consist of time, money, or both), and time for interpreting the message. Consider how much time you devote to your e-mail!

We all have a saturation point regarding the amount of information we can adequately handle in a given time period. If overloaded, many people are unable to effectively either comprehend the information or use it. The methods used by a police organization to collect, select, and transmit information impacts its success.

The frequency of messages in a police organization is determined by seven conditions:

- The total *number* of members in the organization
- The *direction* of the message (downward, upward, horizontal, or diagonal)
- The *regulations* controlling when and to whom messages are sent
- The degree of *teamwork* in the organization's activities
- The *speed* with which relevant changes occur in the external environment
- The *search* patterns and procedures used by the organization to investigate its environment
- The amount of and reliance on *e-mail*

High message volume frequently results in harmful overloading. Police managers can react to this situation in the following ways. First, they can slow down their handling of messages without changing the organization's network structure or transmission rules. (This action, however, will cause the police department to slow its reaction to events and will thereby lessen its output.) Second, police managers can change the transmission procedures so that their staff screens out more information before sending messages. (This reaction will also reduce the quantity of the department's output.)

Third, they can create more channels in the network to accommodate the same quantity of messages in the same time period. (This reaction will provide more opportunities for message distortion and will be more expensive.) Fourth, they can delegate tasks within the organization so that those units with the highest message traffic are grouped together within the overall communications system. (This action can reduce the quality of messages sent through higher levels in the network and will facilitate the coordination of effort.) Finally, managers can do the really wise thing—have more face-to-face staff meetings.

KINDS OF MESSAGES

> *Conversation: a vocal competition in which the one who is catching his breath is called the listener.*
>
> —*Anonymous*

Messages vary in content and delivery media. There are reports, statements, inquiries, questions, accounts, comments, notes, records, recommendations, rejoinders, instructions, and so on. Each message may have a different purpose and may thus lead to a different response. Messages can be transmitted either formally or informally in one of three ways:

- Written (text)
- Oral (spoken)
- Nonverbal (subtle)

Written Messages

There are six types of written messages: routine report, memorandum, inquiry, query, proposal, and decision.

1. *Routine Report.* A routine report is a message that supplies information as part of a standard operation. A report can be generated in two ways. First, it can be time-triggered—that is, called for at set time intervals. For example, a police manager could be required to send weekly reports on the work activities of employees. Second, it can be event-triggered—that is, called for when certain tasks are completed. For example, a report is to be sent when a case is finished or when certain training has been provided to a manager's staff.

2. *Memorandum.* A memorandum also furnishes information, but not as part of a routine procedure. A memorandum can be (1) a *statement of fact,* submitted in response to a request for assistance in evaluating a problem or to prepare plans for action; (2) *statement that is event-triggered,* released when circumstances have changed in an unpredicted manner, calling for some initiative by the sender to alert others to the change so that an action plan can be developed; or (3) a *comment,* made in response to some other statement or information or to give a different interpretation of data.

3. *Inquiry.* An inquiry is a message requesting information to aid in evaluating a given problem, usually before making recommendations for action. The response to such a request would be a memorandum, which would include a statement with the necessary information and an analysis of the data.

4. *Query.* A query is a message defining the characteristics of a problem and asking for instructions or plans about courses of resolution. A query is often made by an employee concerning problems not fully discussed in standing regulations, either because of the novelty of the situation or because of ambiguities or inconsistencies in procedures.

5. *Proposal.* A proposal describes a course of action the writer feels should be taken. It can be the result of several exchanges of queries, inquiries, reports, and memoranda. It may be generated by employees on their own initiative or at the instigation of a manager, or it may be created by a manager seeking to test the reactions of peers or staff.

6. *Decision.* A decision states the action to be taken. This message may be of two kinds: (1) a decision that provides direction on how to handle not only the specific events that caused the discussion before the decision but also similar events in the future, or (2) a decision on an ad hoc problem, which does not formally affect future procedures. A decision can take a number of forms. It may start with a request to review the reasons for making a decision to resolve certain problems. It may continue by outlining alternative courses of action and explaining the reasons for the rejection of some. The decision may go on to

specify what has been decided and how the decision is to be implemented; and it may then express what feedback is expected to keep the decision maker informed of progress in implementation.

A written message is formal, one-way (sender to receiver), and is more prone to being misunderstood and impersonal. Written messages alone contain a lot of downsides as far as securing understanding and delivering intended cordiality.

There are two ways to transmit a written message: hard copy and e-mail.

Hard Copy

What follows applies to e-mail messages as well. A fundamental rule to follow is to carefully plan what you want to convey to the sender. Here are some quick and proven methods for doing so.

TAB Your Thoughts

- Think about the situation. Why am I writing this?
- Action. What do I want to see done?
- Benefit. Who will benefit?

Three Cs

- Clarity. Is it easy to read and understand?
- Completeness. Does it cover the key points?
- Conciseness. Is it brief and focused?

Headliners

- **Use bold print.**
- Use short paragraphs highlighting each point.
- Use bullets.
- Use charts and graphs when appropriate.

Speak It in Writing

- Write as you speak.
- Use contractions.
- Ask questions.
- Personalize by using pronouns.
- Use short, uncomplicated sentences—no trivia.
- Avoid clichés and hype.

  Warning!
- Double-check your grammar and spelling—the "spell check" in your computer catches most but not all errors. For example, it can't tell the difference between "public relations" and "pubic relations."

E-Mail

"Happy Birthday . . .," etc. This note was on your desk when you arrived at work this morning. It was personally signed by your boss. *Stop!* How do you feel? What do you think? Compare this to the same birthday greeting in typewritten text from your boss.

Stop! How do you feel? What do you think? Now imagine that you opened your e-mail, and the same greeting appeared in an e-mail message. *Stop!* How do you feel? What do you think?

The e-mail movement has morphed into e-mail mania. It has produced more clutter, confusion, and conflict than it has understanding. Police managers are arriving at work to find hundreds of messages awaiting them. A few are important, a few are of some interest, and the rest are outright junk mail or spam. They are a complete waste of precious time.

Electronic capabilities have expanded so rapidly that new gadgets with hyper-cyber capabilities appear even before we can adjust to the impact of present technology. Many of us who are still struggling to master a programmable DVD player are now being bombarded by a vast array of Internet services.

Even though these technological advances seek to control information and bring order to the workplace, in many instances they have done just the opposite. The electronic gurus promised to reduce our paperwork and lessen our workloads; instead, this technology generated more information that must still be printed and—even more challenging—*assimilated*. Since computers entered office systems, studies show that paper utilization has increased dramatically and workweeks have lengthened.

The harder we work, the less time we have, and that can make us tired, frustrated, morose, anxious, or all of them combined. Equally dysfunctional is the impersonal nature of the hardware as it starts to displace personal needs brought into the workplace.

Here are five e-mail dos and don'ts.

1. Do use the above recommendations on written messages.
2. Do inform recipients when your e-mail doesn't require a reply.
3. Do verify whether important e-mail has been received by asking the person to acknowledge it.
4. Don't use e-mail to replace telephone or personal contacts.
5. Don't send a message to your entire list unless the message applies to everyone on it.

   Warning!

   - *Don't send any message that you would not want to see in the newspaper or tacked to the front door of your home.*

Oral Messages

What happens when two or more people talk? That is really the basic question here, because that's the context in which most persuasion takes place. We know that people talk back and forth. They listen. They interrupt. They move their hands. They try to connect.

Oral messages can be conveyed in three ways: meetings (face to face), telephone conversations (ear to ear), and telecommunications (electronic visual image to electronic visual image).

Meetings

A meeting is a discussion involving two or more persons. Meetings have six purposes:

1. To provide a vehicle for exchanges to take place quickly
2. To provide a job environment in which members are stimulated to new ideas by the rapid exchange of views

3. To lessen the degree of semantic difficulties through face-to-face interaction
4. To get the members attending the meeting committed more strongly to given plans or procedures than they would be otherwise
5. To increase teamwork and individual empowerment
6. To explain why things are happening and answer questions

There are two types of meetings: *routine meetings,* such as those of permanent committees, and *ad hoc meetings,* those called to discuss particular issues. The distinction between a routine and an ad hoc meeting is similar to that between a routine report and a memorandum. Like a routine report, a routine meeting can be either time- or event-triggered, while an ad hoc meeting may either be event-triggered or called in regard to a request to consider a particular problem. A meeting can also result from the issuance of any one or several of the messages listed earlier: a report, a memorandum, an inquiry for further information, a request for instructions, a proposal, or a decision.

Most employees hate meetings. Why? Most respond with, "They're a waste of time. Sometimes it seems that the only accomplishment is the decision on when to have another meeting." Here are some suggestions on how to make meetings more appealing and productive.

1. Use your team to build an agenda with time frames, and rigorously stick to them.
2. Based on the agenda items, determine who should be invited, and make certain they participate.
3. Start with successes. Have everyone report on one achievement, good news, something positive.
4. If you're the team leader, keep your big mouth shut until everyone else has contributed.
5. Make assignments; allocate them evenly among the participants. Establish feedback dates.
6. Keep a summary record of what was covered and decided.
7. Close the meeting positively by reviewing what was covered and then thank each person for his or her participation.

STRUCTURED EXERCISE 5-2

MEETING CHECKLIST

The way a leader conducts a meeting can make or break it for the participants. Use the following checklist to help you evaluate how effective your meetings are. The more "yes" responses, the better the meeting.

Before

_____ 1. I prepared an agenda for the meeting.

_____ 2. I distributed an agenda to participants in advance of the meeting.

_____ 3. I set a starting and ending time for the meeting.

_____ 4. I prepared visuals and/or handouts.

_____ 5. I assigned segments of the program to team members.

_____ 6. I appointed a member to be the recorder of the meeting.

_____ 7. I arranged for all needed equipment and supplies.

During

_____ 1. I stuck to the agenda.

_____ 2. I obtained participation from all members.

_____ 3. I kept blabbermouths and domineers under control.

_____ 4. I distributed assignments equitably.

_____ 5. I refrained from expressing my ideas until members expressed theirs.

_____ 6. I encouraged questions from the participants.

_____ 7. I encouraged others to answer questions asked by team members.

_____ 8. I summarized key points at the end of the meeting.

_____ 9. I verified members' understanding of their assignments before adjourning.

_____ 10. I concluded the meeting with a motivational statement or a call for action.

After

_____ 1. I distributed minutes of the meeting to all participants and others who may be affected.

_____ 2. I followed through on assignments made.

_____ 3. I gathered feedback from participants about the meeting.

Telephone Conversations

Most of the remarks made concerning meetings are relevant to telephone communications. The distinction made earlier between routine and ad hoc communications may be useful here. The following are, however, some noteworthy differences between these two types of oral messages: (1) A telephone conversation is generally confined to two participants, and (2) it lacks certain unique characteristics of interaction that take place in a face-to-face exchange.

If it is really important to influence someone, do it in person!

Telecommunications

Advanced technology is being used in police work for teleconferencing, teletraining, and more. Basically, we have combined the visual strengths of the television with the audio strengths of the telephone. Cable and microwave satellite dishes are giving us instant "electronic face-to-face" communications.

Nonverbal Messages

Our nonverbal communication accounts for *more than 50% of the total message*. Tone of voice—the *way* we say things—makes up 35% of the message. The actual words we say account for less than 10% of the total message. There are two forms of nonverbal communications: meta-talk and body-talk. The first deals with messages hidden in our speech pattern (conversational rhythm). The second is body language.

Meta-Talk Messages

Linguistics or "metamessages" is the study of how to prevent our normal ways of speaking from causing misunderstanding. Despite good intentions and good character all around, we frequently find ourselves caught in miscommunication. Varied cultural backgrounds can be especially troublesome.

When we use words to communicate, we automatically attach to them our emotions about relationships, values, attitudes, needs, and so on. The emotional message thus becomes the *metamessage*. And metamessages are what we respond to most strongly.

Metamessages and conversational rhythms are not fluff but rather the very substance of communication. The three main ones are:

1. *Pacing and Pausing.* The pace of the conversation and the amount of pauses have an enormous influence on the conversation. Being a fast talker and jumping into pauses can be effective in one situation and not another.
2. *Loudness.* Getting louder can show importance, excitement, and anger. Speaking softly can show respect, fatigue, and embarrassment.
3. *Pitch and Intonation.* The music of talk, or intonation, comes from the mixing of pacing, pausing, loudness, and pitch changes. Changing the pitch on a word can totally change the meaning of the message spoken. I worked for a police chief who, when informed of mistakes, would respond with the word "Great!" The lack of pause, the loudness of the utterance, and the sharpness of the pitch all indicated the exact opposite of "great."

In summary, different conversational styles can be the basis of confusion and miscommunication.

Body-Talk Messages

Some of the most meaningful understanding is transmitted neither verbally nor in writing, and without words. A loud siren at an intersection tells you something without words. A manager teaching a group of officers doesn't need words to tell when the trainees are bored. The size of a person's office and desk and the clothes people wear also send messages to others. The best-known nonverbal communication is *body language*. Body language includes gestures, facial configurations, and other movements of the body. A snarling face, for example, says something different from a smile. Hand motions, facial expressions, and similar body language can communicate emotions or temperaments such as aggression, fear, arrogance, joy, and anger.

When two people talk, they don't just fall into physical and aural harmony. They also engage in what is called *motor mimicry*. For example, if you smile or frown at people, they'll smile or frown back, although only in muscular changes so fleeting that they can only be captured with electronic sensors. We imitate each other's emotions as a way of expressing support and caring and even more basically as a way of communicating with each other. Emotion is contagious.

We normally think of the expression on our face as the reflection of an inner state. I feel happy, so I smile. I feel sad, so I frown. Emotion goes "inside-out." Emotional contagion, though, indicates that the opposite is also true. If I can make you frown, I can make you sad. If I can make you smile, I can make you happy. Emotion, in this sense, goes "outside-in."

Remember the lyrics, "When you're smiling, the whole world smiles with you"? Is it conceivable that as a leader, "When you're smiling, the whole department smiles with you"? Try it if you're not doing so already; there's solid research to support the smile and other forms of positive unspoken clues.

Unfortunately, many people have stereotyped certain body movements. The folded arms across one's chest, we're told, denote a defensive or combative attitude. With me, however, it shows that my lower back aches. Assumptions about body gestures are dangerous. Nonverbal cues may vary from person to person. They're not as simple as "red light, green light." First, you have to know the person before you're able to infer judgments about his or her body movements. Rather than spend a lot of time reading pop psychology on the subject of kinesthetics, start reading the person. Body language is very individualistic, as are our perceptions of it.

ARTFUL LISTENING

The average person suffers from three delusions: (1) that he is a good driver, (2) that he has a good sense of humor, and (3) that he is a good listener. Most people, however, including many leaders, are terrible listeners; they actually think talking is more important than listening. But contrarian leaders know it is better to listen first and talk later. And when they listen, they do so artfully.

—Steven Samples, Ph.D., President, University of Southern California

Please reread the quotations that open each section. I'll tell you why later.

The key to influencing another person is first to gain an understanding of that person. As a leader, you must know your staff in order to influence them. Most of us want other people to open their minds to our message. Wanting to understand other people requires that we open our minds to them.

True leaders are artful listeners not because it makes people feel good (which it does), but rather because artful listening is an excellent means of acquiring new ideas and gathering and assessing information.

When a police leader listens attentively without rushing to judgment, he or she will often get a fresh perspective that will help inspire independent thought. This kind of leader listens carefully to the staff (especially those in the inner circle).

The really artful listener is able to understand and appreciate what is being said without conveying to the speaker that he agrees or not and when to stop listening.

My guess is that the number of truly effective police leaders who have not developed good listening skills is quite small. For the vast majority of us who aspire to excellence in leadership, artful listening isn't just an asset—it's a *necessity*.

Seek to Understand

When we seek to understand, we are applying the principle of empathy. *Empathy* is a Greek word. The "em-" part of *empathy* means "in." The "-pathy" part comes from *pathos*, which means "feeling" or "suffering." Empathy is not sympathy. Sympathy is a form of agreement, a form of judgment. We have empathy, then, when we place ourselves within the other person, so to speak, to experience his or her feelings as he or she experiences them.

Seek to Be Understood

Once we understand, we can proceed with the second step of the interaction: seeking to be understood. But now it is much more likely that we will actually be understood, because the other person's drive to be understood has been satisfied.

- To understand another person, we must be willing to be open to their thoughts.
- When we are open, we give people room to release their fixed positions and consider alternatives.
- Seeking first to understand lets us act from a position of knowledge.
- By seeking to understand, we gain influence in the relationship.
- Seeking first to understand leads people to discover other options.

When we seek to understand people, they become less defensive about their positions. They become more open to the question, How can we *both* get what we want? As they get their position out of the way, they begin to see their values more clearly so that they can use them as guidelines for creating and evaluating other options.

Empathetic listening is particularly important under three conditions:

- When the interaction has a strong emotional component
- When we are not sure that we understand
- When we are not sure that the other person feels confident we understand

Under other circumstances, empathetic responses can be counterproductive. We don't need to reflect our understanding, nor would it be appreciated, when someone asks us what time it is.

Seek to Be Open While Structured

As a leader you have the right and responsibility to talk with anyone. You can and should talk informally to employees freely, giving and receiving ideas and recommendations about police operations and priorities. Here's the inherent danger . . . you may accidentally undercut the authority of your line supervisors by intentionally or accidentally agreeing with someone's opinion.

The route to avoid this situation is via *structured decision making*. All employees should be encouraged to talk with everyone in the agency with the explicit rule that any and all commitments, allocations, and decisions be made strictly through the chain of command.

Open communication only works if the other part of the bargain, structured decision making, is strictly and faithfully adhered to.

Now the reason I asked you to reread the quotations is that all except the first one directly reference the importance of artful listening. Now the real question: Are you an artful listener? If so, great! If not, it's time to become one!

A CROSS-GENERATIONAL WORKFORCE

To be effective with other human beings we must know them as individuals—
their unique background, personality, preferences, and style.
—*Ron Zemke, Claire Raines, Bob Filipczak*

A lot of conventional wisdom, random research, and newfound experts nowadays refute the above quote. They argue that we should approach, understand, and relate to people of different generations as unique and separate groups—in essence, stereotyping them as "traditionalists" (born before 1945), "Boomers" (1946–1964), "Xers" (1965–1976), and "Nexters" or "Generation Y" (1977 or later). Once they are catalogued by age, you know how to recruit, retain, motivate, and reward them. This is flat out *wrong* and actually blocks teamwork and hinders performance.

STRUCTURED EXERCISE 5-3

This "awareness" exercise will point out how well you're doing as an empathetic listener. If you discover areas where you need improvement, work on them—now. Realizing there is room for improvement is the first step toward building more effective communications and trust between you and those with whom you work.

On a scale of 1 (never) to 7 (always), rate yourself on the frequency of each of the following good listening skills.

_____ I maintain appropriate eye contact.

_____ I focus my attention on what my co-worker is saying rather than on what I'm going to say next.

_____ I listen for feelings as well as facts.

_____ I avoid letting my mind wander during a conversation.

_____ I tune in instead of tune out when difficult or controversial issues come up.

_____ I think first, then respond.

_____ I think of questions to ask and ask them.

How do you feel about the results? Do you detect needed areas of skill building? If so, what specifically are you going to do?

If you are interested in acquiring feedback and validation of your results, then take the next step. Ask three people (e.g., a friend, a family member, and a co-worker) to complete the scale with you in mind. Compare their thinking about your listening ability with yours. Any surprises? Now what do you plan to do?

Granted, there are some general characteristics that can be reliably ascribed to each generation. When viewed in totality, one can spot the barriers or "gaps" that may occur between the generations. An excellent coverage of the multigenerational workplace and how to anticipate and bridge the gaps is provided by Ron Zemke, Claire Raines, and Bob Filipczak in *Generations at Work*.

I remain convinced that the rubber meets the road with you, the leader, getting to know the values, needs, hopes, and strengths of each member of your team. According to the words above, Zemke and his colleagues agree with me. After all, I doubt you're approaching your family as a group of people who all share the same values, ideals, purposes, and talents. Like myself, you're acknowledging and appreciating their uniqueness, similarities and differences, strengths and weaknesses—their individuality. To be an effective leader you *must* do the same in the workplace.

Obviously, getting to know someone's character and competency takes considerable time, careful observation, and trained intuition. One way to accelerate this process is applying Structured Exercise 5-4. You will learn a lot about yourself and your staff. It facilitates communication, understanding, and appreciation for one another's style and talents.

STRUCTURED EXERCISE 5-4

EMPLOYEE EXPECTATIONS

When an employee accepts a job (new employment, transfer, or promotion), there is an unwritten *psychological contract* established based on a set of beliefs both parties have about what each is entitled to receive and required to give in the employee/employer relationship. One large-scale study of exit interviews revealed that 75% of the people quit their jobs because their expectations had not been met *and* these same people had not told their supervisors what those expectations were!

As a leader you have a choice: Are you going to discover what your employees' expectations are *and* whether or not they are being met? Or are you going to assume you know?

The following job expectation survey can be conducted in several ways. First, you can administer it anonymously and use the group statistics as indicators of problem areas. Second, and better still, you can apply it on a one-to-one basis in a counseling-coaching session. Are your interactions basically positive and supportive? Do you feel as if you're a welcomed team member? Third, you can, *and should*, self-administer it looking at the job environment you are involved in creating for your team members.

You're likely to find that the mere act of asking someone about his or her job expectations is as valuable as actually having them met.

We'll use the *Likert scale* of: (1) very low; (2) low; (3) slightly low; (4) average; (5) slightly high; (6) high; (7) very high. Ask each respondent to circle the appropriate number.

1. **Culture.** This expectation covers your people relationships and general workplace ethic. Are your interactions basically positive and supportive? Do you feel as if you're a team member?

| 1 | 2 | 3 | 4 | 5 | 6 | 7 |

2. *Voice.* This deals with your feeling about being involved and heard in your job. Is anyone interested in what you're saying? Are you being listened to?

   1   2   3   4   5   6   7

3. *Empowerment.* Here we deal with your participation in decisions that affect you and how much responsibility is, in fact, being delegated to you. Are you being empowered?

   1   2   3   4   5   6   7

4. *Career Paths.* How much of a career growth factor is there in your job? Can you see future opportunities to extend and expand your talents and skills?

   1   2   3   4   5   6   7

5. *Purpose.* Does your work, the tasks you perform, seem important? Does your role connect into a broader mission that has merit and significance?

   1   2   3   4   5   6   7

6. *Job/Personal Balance.* Does your organization recognize that you value both your job and your personal/family life? While you are committed to your work, do you have a strong allegiance to your family and a need for leisure time?

   1   2   3   4   5   6   7

7. *Recognition.* Are you loved and appreciated for your individuality? Are you known by name and treated as a distinct human being?

   1   2   3   4   5   6   7

8. *Security.* How secure are you in the long-term retention of your job? Do you believe that you have reasonable job protection and appeal rights?

   1   2   3   4   5   6   7

9. *Clarity.* How clear are you about your organization's vision and values? Are you clear about what is expected of you?

   1   2   3   4   5   6   7

10. *Compensation.* This expectation includes pay, overtime, retirement, vacation, sick leave, medical/dental insurance, and other perks. Is your overall compensation package appropriate and fair?

    1   2   3   4   5   6   7

NEXT

After you've circled the numbers and reflected on their meaning, it is time to evaluate what actions can be taken to better meet your job expectations or the expectations of those who are your direct reports. It involves communication, initiation, and adjustment.

Communication. To whom do you need to communicate your expectations so that they can be evaluated and possibly fulfilled? This step depends on understanding and clarification.

Initiation. What actions can you take to meet your own expectations? This step depends on your self-determination to meet your needs.

Adjustment. What changes or reductions in your expectations should be made to assure your contentment? This step depends on your self-realization that not all of your expectations can or will be fulfilled.

COMMUNICATION PROBLEMS IN THE INFORMATION AGE

The twentieth century has been labeled "A Century of Infotech." It is now predicted that the twenty-first century will be known as "A Century of Biotechnology." (In our opinion, the former will be known as "infotech.")

The phrase *information age* has come to denote the explosion of information and computing technology and its impact on society. Whereas the industrial age manufactured things, the information age generates "information"—and a lot of it! As a dominant economic trend, it should last until around 2030. Then slowly the economics of biotechnology will supersede it.

Just how we got here so fast—from Marconi's first tentative radio transmission to live photos of Mars broadcast over the Internet (1997)—is a story experts are still struggling to comprehend. In hindsight, what appears to have happened is that several diverse forms of communications and information processing (radio, telephone, computing, and TV), each following its own technological track, emerged from stuttering starts, built up speed, and then converged suddenly into a kind of Grand Central Terminal known as the World Wide Web (1990).

Along the way, vital components began to shrink: The vacuum tube (1904) became the transistor (1947); the transistor led to the microchip (1958); the microchip married the phone and gave birth to the modem (1978). Soon enough, sounds, photos, movies, and conversations would be ground down into the smallest components of all: 1s and 0s. Was the digital revolution inevitable? In our brave new wired world, it certainly seems that way.

We now rely on a number of sophisticated electronic media to carry our information. In addition to the more common media (the telephone and Internet), we have closed-circuit television, voice-activated computers, xerographic reproduction, and a host of other electronic devices that we can use in conjunction with speech or paper to create more effective communication. Electronic mail (e-mail) and fax machines are now commonplace technologies. The cellular phone further expands our communications capacity. (In mentioning cell phones, how many adults do you know who do not have one?)

Information alone does not answer bigger questions. From a social point of view, information has not brought people any closer to understanding the deeper, significant questions of life and morality. From that perspective, learning from information becomes merely functional, not enlightening. Additionally, while such technology as e-mail and fax capabilities has enhanced the movement of information, there is no substitute for face-to-face communication. We see e-mail junkies who'll e-mail you rather than walk a few feet or use the telephone to communicate with you in person. We're getting tons of information with only a few pounds of understanding.

Obviously, e-mail and other communication technologies provide several advantages for police leaders, but they must not supplant the human contact so vital to those we lead.

If you want me to follow you, I need you in front of me while providing an example of what is expected of me. An e-mail message or teleconferencing just won't do it.

Competency Checkpoints

- Communication is mutual understanding.
- Without credible communications, the likelihood of people pursuing a mission/vision statement is very low.
- Leaders communicate in order to foster meaning, build trust, underpin decisions, and get feedback.
- Communication follows multiple channels that are both formal and informal; both are essential in healthy organizations. The police leader is the key person in developing and maintaining effective communications.
- Rigid compliance with formal channels can be harmful. Formal channels are often too slow, and they can impede creativity and experience because they often restrict the free flow of thought.
- Informal communication channels can also effectively plug gaps in formal channels.
- Communication flows downward, upward, horizontally, and diagonally. Each direction serves to inform, and each has a specific purpose.
- The number of messages being conveyed in a police agency has a marked significance in terms of performance; too many and too few are dysfunctional.
- The kinds of messages are (1) written, (2) oral, and (3) nonverbal.
- An important function of communication is listening, and listening can be learned.
- Telecommunications and information technology offer police organizations numerous benefits, but there are some significant downsides attached to the high-tech.

Flexing the Message

1. Write down the names of three people whom you know at work or elsewhere who impress you as good communicators. Why did you select these people? What in particular are they capable of doing that causes them to communicate effectively with you? What have you learned and can you learn from their strength in communication?
2. Select two work-related subjects that you are confused about or have questions about. Who is able to provide the answers that you are interested in? What steps can you take to secure this information?
3. In which direction (e.g., upward) is it easiest for you to gain mutual understanding in your organization? Alternatively, which is the toughest? Why is one so easy and the other so difficult? What part do you have in the "ease" or the "difficulty"?
4. Spend one day recording the nonverbal messages that you hear (meta-talk) and see (body-talk). Put a star next to those that *really* stood out. Put a plus next to all of them that were of a positive nature, a minus next to those that were negative, and a circle next to the neutral ones. Study your list carefully. What do you find? Anything that surprises you? How can you apply your findings to become a more successful communicator?
5. Write down the names of three people (at work or elsewhere) whom *you know* who impress you as active (empathetic) listeners. Why did you select these people?

What in particular are they capable of doing that causes them to listen empatheti-cally? What have you learned and can you learn from them? Are any of the names that you listed in question 1 the same as those you listed here? If so, think about it. Does it have a message for you?

Note

1. Dunbar's theories have been described in a number of places. The best is probably R. I. M. Dunbar, "Neocortex Size as a Constraint on Group Six in Primates," *Journal of Human Evolution* (1992), vol. 20, pp. 469–493.

   There are hundreds of case studies about the successful application of his theory. The most convincing is about Gore Associates (Gore-Tex fabric, Glide dental floss, etc.). The late founder, "Bill" Gore, discovered that things get clumsy at 150 employees. So no plant was built or configured to accommodate more than 150 workers.

   There are several medium- to large-scale police agencies that have either intentionally or accidentally applied Rule 150 to their organizational structures. Most of the agencies have dispersed their employees into smaller work units with a rationale of "geographical stations," in essence, creating physical plants within the communities that comprise the area of governance.

CHAPTER

6 EMPOWERMENT

Second only to your decision about your own character is your decision about empowering others.

Community-Oriented Policing and Problem Solving (COPPS) is the vehicle for delivering law enforcement services. Leadership is the driver. And empowerment is the lubricant that makes COPPS function smoothly.

When you truly establish the conditions for empowerment, control is not lost: it is simply transformed into self-control.

—Steven Covey

CHAPTER OUTLINE

1. We Don't Act on What We Know
   a. Really Opening Up
   b. Ducking
   c. Believing
   d. Risky
   e. Misunderstanding
   f. All or None

2. The "E" Formula
   a. T = Trust
   b. D = Delegation
   c. P = Participation
   d. C = Capitalization

3. How Do I Know?
   a. Event-Triggered: "By Exception"
   b. Time-Triggered: "By Milestones"

4. When Not to Empower

5. Team Leadership = Teamwork
   a. Team Leadership
   b. Teamwork

6. Competency Checkpoints

7. Flexing the Message

Today's management buzz-word is *empowerment*. It is alleged to be the cure-all for job dissatisfaction, low morale, employee inefficiency, poor performance, and risk avoidance. Everyone seems to be hailing its virtues and scorning any detractors.

Empowering people without replacing the *discipline* and order that come out of a command-and-control bureaucracy produces chaos. We have to learn how to disperse power, so *self-control* can largely replace imposed, top-down command discipline. That immerses us in the area of culture: replacing the bureaucracy with aspirations, values, and visions.

Empowerment works! The advantages far exceed any downside. My *concern* is for those who seek to wave a magic wand and have it happen effortlessly. My *hope* is for those sworn and civilian supervisors who choose to nurture and carefully unleash the full potential of their staff.

The word *power* (the root of *empowerment*) is related to the French term *poudre*. What does this term suggest to you? Perhaps you can see in it the word *powder*, as in gunpowder. There's a *lot* of power in gunpowder. Similarly, there's a lot of power in empowerment. Power sharing motivates people to get with it, get involved, get the job done, give high performance, and give top-quality services—and that is what Community-Oriented Policing and Problem Solving (COPPS) is all about.

COPPS depends on power sharing or empowerment. *Power* is our capacity to think, act, make changes, and get results. If power within a police organization is limited to those in management, the organization's capacity for being successful is automatically curtailed. COPPS becomes a paper tiger. Conversely, if all the personnel—sworn and civilian alike—are empowered, the full potential or capacity of the agency is unleashed to provide total, high-quality police services.

Please stop here and complete Structured Exercise 6-1.

STRUCTURED EXERCISE 6-1

EMPOWERMENT: INVOLVEMENT, INDEPENDENCE, AND INNOVATION

Instructions: Following are 27 statements about your job environment. If you feel the statement is true or mostly true of your job environment, mark a T. Conversely, if you believe the statement is false or mostly false, mark an F.

1. The work is really challenging. _____

2. Few employees have any important responsibilities. _____

3. Doing things in a different way is valued. _____

4. There's not much group spirit. _____

5. There is a fresh, novel atmosphere about the place. _____

6. Employees have a great deal of freedom to do as they like. _____

7. New and different ideas are always being tried out. _____

8. A lot of people seem to be just putting in time. _____

9. This place would be one of the first to try out a new idea. _____

10. Employees are encouraged to make their own decisions. _____

11. People seem to take pride in the organization. _____

12. People can use their own initiative to do things. _____

13. People put quite a lot of effort into what they do. _____

14. Variety and change are not particularly important. _____

15. The same methods have been used for quite a long time. _____

16. Supervisors encourage employees to rely on themselves when a problem arises. _____

17. Few people ever volunteer. _____

18. Employees generally do not try to be unique and different. _____

19. It is quite a lively place. _____

20. Employees are encouraged to learn things, even if they are not directly related to the job. _____

21. It's hard to get people to do their work. _____

22. New approaches to things are rarely tried. _____

23. The work is usually very interesting. _____

24. Things tend to stay just about the same. _____

25. Supervisors meet with employees regularly to discuss their future work goals. _____

26. Things always seem to be changing. _____

27. Employees function fairly independently of supervisors. _____

Scoring: This awareness is comprised of three dimensions: involvement, independence, and innovation (I^3). We believe that a high I^3 score for you means high empowerment. The lower the I^3 score, the greater the likelihood that you're not experiencing much, if any, empowerment at work.

- Give yourself one point each if you've marked the following statements as follows: 1 = T; 4 = F; 8 = F; 11 = T; 13 = T; 17 = F; 19 = T; 21 = F; and 23 = T. Your score for involvement is _____.

- Give yourself one point each if you've marked the following statements as follows: 2 = F; 6 = T; 10 = T; 12 = T; 16 = T; 18 = F; 20 = T; 25 = T; and 27 = T. Your score for independence is _____.

- Following the same pattern: 3 = T; 5 = T; 7 = T; 9 = T; 14 = F; 15 = F; 22 = F; 24 = F; and 26 = T. Now add up your score for innovation: _____.

If your scores were 0 to 3, that particular dimension is very low; 4 or 5 is below average; 6 is average; 7 is above average; 8 is well above average; and 9 is very high.

Obviously, I'm hoping that you're looking at scores from 6 on up. An understanding of your job environment can help you deal with both the positive and negative aspects of your work. This information may help you in improving the various aspects of empowerment.

WE DON'T ACT ON WHAT WE KNOW

Every society has a concept of the need to balance dominance with submission. And every society has a word for leader.
—*Michael Josephson*

What is beguiling about empowerment is that we already know that it works. The books have been written, the experiments have been conducted, and the results are in.

We know, intellectually and empirically, that empowerment is a team leadership strategy for creating high-performance workplaces. Virtually every police organization showcases the success it has had with empowerment, quality improvement efforts, community-efficient operations, and superior customer service.

> **So what's the problem? The problem is that despite this load of knowledge and evidence, there has been disturbingly little fundamental change in the way police departments manage themselves.**

Even the agencies that are out telling their stories about COPPS and empowered police personnel have enormous difficulty in capitalizing on their experience. *This overall problem is comprised of barriers that involve the following attitudes.*

Really Opening Up

Empowerment is enabling decision making in others. Since empowerment is cutting-edge stuff today, most police managers and supervisors are espousing its magic. In actual practice, however, they are averse to really opening up and sharing their decision-making authority.

Ducking

When you empower your staff, you share with them successes and failures. Everyone is in the same boat. You can't sign on only for the victories and duck the failures. There are some people who do not want to be empowered! They do not, or cannot, make the commitment to be held accountable.

Believing

Empowerment necessitates a strong belief in the integrity of the employees' work ethic. If a leader does not truly believe that the police employees want to do a good job and enjoy their work, then empowering them should *not* occur.

Risky

Empowering others is risky when you lack faith in their ability to make the right decision. A police manager would be foolish to chance a set of "no-brainer" decisions in order to be recognized as an empowerer. (Taking a risk and being a fool are not synonymous.)

Misunderstanding

A few moments ago, you read that "empowerment is enabling decision making in others." Those being empowered could erroneously assume that they own the ultimate decision, that the manager abdicated the rights and responsibilities of his or her rank. Empowerment is *not* giving away the decision; it is permitting those who are affected by it to input their ideas and aspirations.

All or None

The "all or none" approach to empowerment can be mistakenly adopted by a police manager. Behind such thinking is equal treatment. While well intentioned, the underlying reasoning is faulty. If equality really counted, then all of us should have the same salary, same rewards, and so on. What really counts is being fair with everyone. Clearly, it is fair to empower those who are ready while denying it to those who are not.

THE "E" FORMULA

$$\frac{D + P + C}{T} = \text{Empowerment}$$

It's true; I am only one, but I am one. And the fact that I can't do everything
will not prevent me from doing what I can.
—*Edward Everett Hale*

The four ingredients "powering" empowerment are: participation; delegation; capitalization; and trust. The first three are dependent on the *foundational* value of trust. We'll go there next.

T = Trust

Trust is a *moral duty,* not a means to an end. It's a combination of integrity and competency. Empowerment is first and foremost a relationship. This relationship depends on trustworthiness. Without it there should be no empowerment. The trust relationship requires setting up a trust bank account (TBA) with the other person. Each trustworthy action on your part is a deposit, and each untrustworthy action is a withdrawal on your account.

A TBA starts with you. You can't simply build a TBA; you have to walk the path. You can't be trusted by other people if you haven't paid the price of trusting yourself. In other words, you must first trust in your own integrity and your own competency before others will. There are seven major deposits that build a TBA.

1. *Understanding the Person.* Understanding another person is the most important deposit you can make, and it is the key to every other deposit. You simply don't know what constitutes a deposit to another person until you understand that person.
2. *Little Things Mean a Lot.* Small kindnesses and courtesies are so important. Little affronts (micro-inequities), unkindnesses, and forms of disrespect make large withdrawals. In working relationships, the big things are the little things. The so-called little things can make or destroy teamwork in an organization. Little things often create either big deposits or big withdrawals.
3. *Clarifying Expectations.* Conflicting or vague expectations about your role at work or the objectives to be attained can ruin a working relationship. Expectations and goals can be implicit or explicit. It is important that they be discussed and clarified—get them on the table. Once understood, a TBA deposit is in the offing.
4. *Demonstrating Loyalty.* Being loyal (faithful) to those around you is relatively easy. But the best way to manifest integrity is to *be loyal to those who are not present.* When you defend those who are absent, you retain and build the trust of those present (a co-worker, your department, your community). When you defend those who are absent, you retain and build the trust of those present.

5. *Apologizing for "Withdrawals."* People with little internal security find the words "I'm sorry" very difficult. It makes them feel vulnerable—soft and weak. Their security is based on the opinions of other people, and they worry about what others might think. Sincere apologies make deposits. It is one thing to make a mistake, and quite another thing not to admit it. Most people will forgive mistakes of judgment. But people will not easily forgive the mistakes of the heart, ill intention, and bad motives.

There are three steps in apologizing: (1) describe what you did wrong; (2) say you're sorry; and (3) tell them you'll never do it again.

6. *Really Caring.* Coach Lou Holtz informs us that the first thing he convinces his players of is his care for them as individuals—not as a team, but as individual human beings. There are some managers who do not even recognize their staff on sight. Those who do often do not know their names. How can you as a leader expect people to care about their jobs, their department, or their community members if you could not care less about who they are and what they value? If you really care about them *and* they know it, they'll do anything to maintain that "deposit."

7. *Displaying Personal Integrity.* A lack of personal integrity will erase all the TBA deposits described above. Integrity includes honesty but goes well beyond it. Honesty is telling the truth or *conforming our words to reality.* For example, even if I say, "I'll be on time to roll call" and I fully intend to keep this promise, it is when I show up on time that I prove my integrity. Hence integrity is *conforming our reality to our words.* It is the follow-through on our promises.

The key to handling many people is how you treat the *one* you're dealing with right now. It is how you treat that person that speaks to your regard for others.

D = Delegation

Delegation of responsibility has been a central topic in leadership thinking through the ages. But today's demands on police employees to initiate far-reaching actions and think creatively propel the subject toward the top of the list. Proper delegation frees up the police organization to work faster and with less traditional hierarchy (e.g., strict adherence to chain of command, rules and regulations for everything, established routines, and so on). Delegation is required *now* more than ever before in meeting the challenges of managing police work successfully.

Yes, But ...

When you delegate, you are always delegating one thing for certain—uncertainty! In other words, will the person who now possesses the responsibility come through? Will the empowered person perform the task, and if so, will it be done correctly?

Is it any wonder why some police managers fearfully resist delegating? After all, when something goes sideways, they're accountable. They must answer for their decision to delegate. At the same time, how would police work ever get done if delegation did not occur? The "yes, but . . ." syndrome is often voiced like this: "Yes, but if I delegate this task, it may not get done—or at least not done to my satisfaction." This frequently causes us not to really "let go."

Effective delegation takes emotional courage as we inspire others to make decisions that might be in error and, in turn, cast doubt on our capabilities. This courage consists of patience, self-control, faith in the potential of others, and respect for individual differences. Effective delegation must be two-way: responsibility given, responsibility received.

Really Letting Go

The majority of police managers do *not* delegate enough. They think they do. They hand over tasks and pass out assignments routinely. But rarely does the officer really get motivated and become empowered with true ownership—and its parallel, the sense of being fully committed. Most studies agree that only about 5% of the managers truly delegate.

What goes wrong? First, there is a distinction between "letting go" and "really letting go." However, does really letting go mean chaos, confusion, and substandard performance? Perhaps, but not necessarily so. Steps can be taken to avoid the pitfalls of delegation, all the while ensuring that its advantages are secured for the police agency. Before reviewing these steps, it's important to consider the consequences of not really letting go.

- You sap your time.
- You get buried in trivia.
- You irritate your subordinates.
- Your subordinates lack initiative.
- Your subordinates either avoid your assistance or seek it too frequently.
- Your subordinates express dissatisfaction with their jobs.
- The work unit evidences confusion.
- The work unit is stagnant.
- The work unit experiences inept communication, which creates lowered mutual trust.

STRUCTURED EXERCISE 6-2

HOW DO I REALLY KNOW?

Are you really letting go? Here is a checklist of questions that will help you know if you are or not.

- Have you transmitted the overarching vision with clarity? Does the officer, through demonstrated behavior, clearly buy in?
- Is the person aware of the level of performance standards?
- Do you trust the person and have you conveyed it?

- Are you known for butting in at the last minute to handle a problem that someone is experiencing with an assignment?
- Do you hold your tongue on asking questions about someone's work efforts?
- Have you avoided excessive reporting?
- When the officer stops by, do you avoid giving direct orders or imply that such-and-such may be a better approach?

Who Benefits

A police officer/deputy sheriff is expected to produce a service—to get desired results. With each role we play in life (spouse, parent, friend, etc.), production expectations are attached. But when we are expected to work with and through people and systems to produce results, we become an indirect producer, a supervisor or manager. (Many of our other life roles involve working with and through people such as family and friends.)

We can (assuming no loss of efficiency) generate one hour of effort and produce one unit of results or police services.

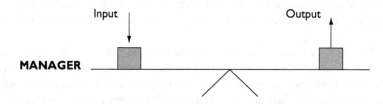

A team leader, on the other hand, can invest one hour of energy and create 10 or 50 or 100 units of services through effective delegation. Police leadership means shifting the fulcrum over to achieve 1:10 or 1:50 or 1:100. Effective leadership is effective delegation.

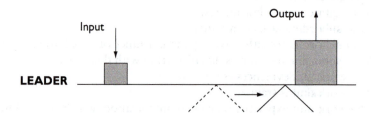

There are four parties that benefit from real delegation. First, there is the *community*—you and me. Empowered police employees are typically more skillful and dedicated. Hence we get better, less costly services. We, in turn, are more likely to respect and support our police department.

Second, the *organization* itself harvests the wealth of brain-power that exists within its sworn and civilian ranks. Everyone takes on the mantle of total commitment.

Third, *you* benefit as a leader/manager because you're

- Building commitment for getting the job done
- Increasing mutual trust between yourself and your officers
- Enhancing the officers' job skills and knowledge
- Encouraging a feeling of ownership
- Leveraging your power to provide high-quality police services
- Increasing your time for high-priority tasks

Fourth, *your staff* benefits by becoming more

- Committed to their work
- Trusting and trustworthy

- Professional growth oriented
- Accurate in operational decisions because they're being made where the action is
- Recognized as being competent
- Self-confident
- Capable of producing top-notch police work
- Satisfied with their job

Delegating is a skill that you learn, not a talent that you're born with. Any police leader who makes the effort can acquire the skill.

Four Types of Delegation

Delegation does not come in one style or shape. There are four ways to delegate: (1) stewardship, (2) gofer, (3) dump, and (4) micromanagement. Only one promotes empowerment—stewardship. The latter three either inhibit or prevent empowering employees.

1. *Stewardship.* Stewardship delegation concentrates on results instead of methods. It affords police personnel with a choice of method and, more importantly, makes them 100% responsible for results. Admittedly, it takes more time in the beginning, but it's time wisely invested. Stewardship delegation moves the production fulcrum way over, thereby *increasing your empowerment leverage.* This holds for both *growth* and *routine* activities. Stewardship delegation involves being committed to five expectations:

   Desired Results: Generate a mutual understanding of what needs to be accomplished, focusing on *what,* not how, and *results,* not methods. Spend time; visualize the needed outcome. Have the officer describe for you how the results will look and when they will be achieved.
   Guidelines: Carefully identify the boundaries within which the person must function. These should be as few and inflexible as possible. If you know of any land mines, be certain to reveal them. In other words, instruct your employee in what not to do but do tell him or her what to do. Keep the responsibility for his or her performance with him or her—*to do whatever is essential but within the guidelines.*
   Resources: Identify the various resources that the person can elicit to obtain the preferred outcomes.
   Accountability: Establish minimum standards that will be applied in evaluating the work effort and when the evaluation will occur.
   Consequences: Indicate what will happen, both positive and negative, as an outcome of the evaluation. This involves rewards and reprimands.

2. *Gofer.* Gofer delegation is highly routine assigned work wherein you merely go for this or go for that. You're not encouraged to think of the task as being part of *your job.* Indeed, you're probably not encouraged to think at all. It's a put-down and a turn-off for police employees.

3. *Dump.* Dump delegation occurs when you give your staff all of your work. Those who engage in the dumping of their work on others are viewed as lazy and incompetent. Delegation dumpers rationalize that they are doing a great career service to others.

4. *Micromanagement.* Empowerment is resisted, often bashed, by managers who practice vertical command and control. Even though micromanagers may ask for employee input and delegate many tasks, the underlying assumption is that successful police managers are those who possess the *true* overarching picture of what the department should be doing and have the *ultimate* knowledge and responsibility for seeing that the job is done. This is a very "micro" way of viewing the manager's job. The micromanager believes that he or she

- Should have more technical expertise than any subordinate
- Should know at all times what is going on in the department
- Should be the primary (if not the *only*) person responsible for how the department is working
- Should be able to solve any problem that comes up (or at least solve it before a subordinate can)

The micromanagers are afraid that if they do not direct you each and every moment, the work won't be done. They look over your shoulder and constantly meddle in your work. How much does this type of delegation really accomplish? How many people is it possible to manage when you micromanage? The answers are, respectively, "not much" and "very few."

Bad or No Delegation

In an agency where the police employees are technically and professionally prepared to be empowered so as to handle complex and interdependent tasks, micromanaging or other dysfunctional types of delegation can cause the following problems:

- Information does not flow to the right places. If it does, it requires enormous energy and time to get it there.
- Responsiveness to incoming problems and opportunities is slowed drastically. Speed is sacrificed for the sake of someone's ego or feeling about job security.
- Coordination of interdependent tasks suffers. There may be overlapping efforts, unnecessary work, and gross inefficiency.
- Problems are suppressed to the extent that when they finally surface, they're tougher to solve.
- Employees become disillusioned and dissatisfied with their jobs. They become victim to the "care-less" syndrome. Simultaneously, they develop the "what's-in-it-for-me" syndrome.
- Advancement is slowed within the department. If others are not encouraged or helped to grow into police supervisors and police managers, the promotable pool of qualified talent is woefully curtailed. In many cases, micromanaging will force a department to open a promotional test to candidates from other police organizations. And morale plunges downward into the toilet.
- Managing triumphs to the detriment of leading. So much time is spent micromanaging that the manager does not have the time to provide leadership. Basically, the invading present blocks any endeavor to harness the future.

P = Participation

A few years ago a sheriff told one of us, "I'm a great believer in participative management. I'm going to manage, and you'd damn well better participate." How would you feel about working for such a person? Are you working for that person right now? (Are you that type of manager?) What's participation like in your organization?

Why Participation Pays Off

Why *encourage* others to participate in decisions that will or might affect their ability to do their job? Here are solid reasons that you will want to include in your thinking.

The best means for getting a good idea is to generate a lot of ideas because:

- It builds their faith in you that you really care about their welfare and workfare.
- Their inclusion in a decision-making process usually increases their commitment to its eventual implementation.
- Increased commitment often causes increased productivity.
- Participation is the springboard for teamwork.
- *Teamwork* leads to synergy, wherein the mental energy of a few people is multiplied into what hundreds are capable of contributing.

How do you get your people to bring the same motivation to work-related tasks that they do to their leisure activities? Part of the answer is participation. Although you can't give your team total freedom to decide, the more input they have in setting goals and devising their own methods, the more motivated they will be.

Misconceptions About Participation

Encouraging others to express their ideas, their needs, and their hopes about an issue or pending decision that affects them is what we mean by participation. We've heard some police managers voice irritation with, and resistance to, participation as follows: "We're not running a democratic vote here. I'll make the decision, and they're expected to get with it." In part, I agree. A police organization cannot be effective if the majority rules. Can you imagine a police lieutenant, during roll-call briefing, asking those working on her shift to vote on whether they want to patrol or stay in the station? The lieutenant is being paid to make that decision, and it's nonnegotiable!

My proposition is rather simple but extraordinarily compelling—when a decision is going to affect others, let them have a chance to express their ideas. Do you wonder why people reject an idea, a general order, a new policy? Often, it is because they had no input—"No one asked me!" Letting others participate in decisions that may affect them does not surrender your authority or responsibility for the ultimate decision.

Many years ago I worked for a police agency that commanded all uniformed personnel to wear a helmet when riding in a patrol car. The officers on my shift, as did others, found the helmet uncomfortable. We complained, but the response was that the chief had said, "Wear 'em." Most of us didn't and received verbal and, at times, written reprimands for violating his order. We were told that it was for "our own protection when traveling in a patrol car."

Our grumbling over the helmet finally ignited a near revolt. All of us (26) officers signed a memorandum asking to speak to the chief. He consented and came to roll call the following evening. He spoke convincingly about the importance of officer safety and concluded by saying, "My decision is in your best interest." The junior member of our shift stood and said, "Sir, this department has given me the best in training. I know when and how to use a shotgun, handgun, baton, and chemical Mace. You allow me to make the critical decision on when to use these potentially lethal weapons. Can't I also be allowed to make a far less important decision—when and where to wear my helmet?"

The chief thought for a moment and replied, "Sit down, officer. From here on, you and the others decide when, and if at all, you wear your helmets. Come to think of it—I don't even own one." It was his decision; we merely had an opportunity to input our concerns. Now that's participative management—and the sure indication of a *leader*.

C = Capitalization

Mediocre managers assume (or hope) that their staff will be motivated by the same things, driven by the same goals, desire the same kind of work relationships, and learn in roughly the same way. Their approach to managing is "plain old vanilla" for everyone. They set expectations in great detail. They coach their people on identifying their weaknesses and correcting them. They praise most often those employees who have worked hard to replace their natural work behavior. In short, they are convinced that it is their responsibility to *mold*, or transform, each employee into the ideal version of their job role.

Leaders discover what is unique about each person and capitalize on it.

Smart police managers know that the differences among police employees will far outweigh the similarities. The differences I'm referring to are not the obvious—race, gender, creed, or nationality. I'm referring to such human differences as how we think and learn, our degrees of patience and altruism, what drives and challenges us, and what are our birth talents, acquired expertise and values. The grand majority of these differences are *enduring* and *resistant to change*.

Here's my point. By far the best way to lead people in light of their vast array of differences is to identify exactly how each team member is unique. Then figure out how you can most effectively *incorporate* these differences into your action plan.

The more one listens to or observes successful leaders, the clearer it becomes: Leading is not about transformation; it is about *release*.

If you dedicate yourself to changing each member of your team into some predetermined, cookie-cutter job role, you will end up frustrated while annoying the hell out of the employee. Conversely, if you will tweak the job to accommodate the unique contributions, needs, and style of each police employee, you will create a win-win-win situation. Essentially, the person is empowered (Win #1) to do a better job for the department (Win #2). Your success as a leader depends almost entirely on your skill at releasing the strengths of your staff. Win #3 is for you. Capitalizing on each person's uniqueness saves you time. It makes each person more accountable. It builds a stronger team. Finally, you expose creativity and dispose of group thinking (the herd mentality).

Should you ignore individual weaknesses? No way. It is your job to spot them and then decide whether it is a matter of training or talent. If the former, the fix is relatively easy. If the latter, then you'll have to manage around this weakness and neutralize it by: (1) finding the person a work partner who has a countervailing strength; or (2) rearrange the person's working world so that his or her weakness is no longer in play.

The chief responsibility of a leader is not to set standards, measure performance, or build high-performing teams. Each of these is valuable. But these are outcomes, not a starting point. The starting point is your decision on how each employee's talents and abilities can be released and converted into performance.

HOW DO I KNOW?

Trust, but verify.
—*Ronald Reagan*

There is a critical aspect of this question about "knowing." It goes like this: "How do I know that they've accepted responsibility for what I have given them?" In other words . . .

Are those whom you've empowered fulfilling their assigned responsibilities?

Controls are among the most important techniques for successful empowerment. On the surface, this seems like a contradiction. Doesn't empowerment mean giving up control? Isn't the whole point to let your staff handle tasks on their own, make decisions independently? How can you, as a responsible police leader, control without either doing the job yourself or breathing down the neck of your team (micromanaging) to see that it's done right?

Empowerment never means relinquishing control. Actually, controls enhance the process of empowerment in two ways. They give leaders the confidence to give up the actual "doing" to a team member. It also helps them to hand over the work without giving up the responsibilities.

Basically, there are two types of control: (1) event-triggered and (2) time-triggered.

Event-Triggered: "By Exception"
The exception principle is one of the fundamental rules of management. It means that only *significant* changes from the expected method of operation or results will be brought to your attention.

To make the exception principle effective when empowering, you need to set up objectives, plans, and standards that give your staff latitude to make decisions on unexpected events and changes.

The main thing is that you and your subordinates have achieved a common understanding of what *is* an exception.

The advantages of management by exception are:

- It focuses your attention on major rather than minor factors.
- It keeps you from wasting your time reviewing tasks that are running smoothly.
- It encourages your team members' self-direction by giving them the latitude to handle their work within the reporting limits.
- It directs both your attention and that of your staff toward results.

Time-Triggered: "By Milestones"

Controls have costs. The question you should ask yourself is, "Are the costs of the controls I've imposed justified by the resulting benefits?" If a simple reporting system can prevent a major problem, obviously the benefits justify the cost.

If a detailed and expensive reporting process results in a negligible increase in police service quality, the cost of the controls probably outweighs the benefit. Your job is to balance costs and benefits.

Set your degree of control where the benefits justify the cost and effort. Some of the factors to weigh are:

- How much time and effort will the controls require? (Does the control of evidence demand more or less rigor than fleet maintenance?)
- What mistakes and potential trouble will controls help to prevent? (Does the control of a narcotics unit demand more or less precision than routine patrol?)
- What is the probability of errors and oversights occurring? (Does the control of the budget require more or less accuracy than in-service training?)
- What could have a disastrous impact on the department? (Does the control of internal affairs call for more or less control than a records unit?)

Time-triggered reporting can be set for specified milestones, established dates, or both. The type of reporting can vary from on-site observations to written reports, meetings, telephone updates, and conversations.

WHEN NOT TO EMPOWER

If you are conscious of what is happening in a group, you will recognize emerging situations long before they have gotten out of hand.
—Tao Te Ching

If any one of the five following conditions exists within the work team or an individual employee, then don't empower the team or the employee. Rather than delegate, it's best you micromanage; rather than participate, it's best you command. If you do empower, you'll be taking a dangerous risk.

1. Those being empowered are not well trained in doing their jobs.
2. You doubt their commitment.

3. You do not understand the values and needs of each employee.
4. There is no conduit for open and candid feedback.
5. For some reason you *don't* trust the person.

If one or more of the above conditions exist, *forget* empowerment.

TEAM LEADERSHIP = TEAMWORK

We fought as a team without standout stars. We were like a machine.
—St. C. Carwood Lipton, 506th Regiment, 101st Airborne,
WWII, a member of the Band of Brothers

A leader's decision to empower her or his staff both sets the stage and serves as a stimulus for: (1) COPPS; (2) team leadership; and (3) teamwork.

All of the chapters in Part One have a common goal—to encourage, build, and nurture a community-oriented policing and problem-solving (COPPS) law enforcement organization. (See Chapter 8.) All of the chapters in Part Two are intended to make COPPS efficient and effective in its daily operations and performance.

More on COPPS later; right now we'll take on the two key outcomes of empowerment.

- Team leadership
- Teamwork

Team Leadership

Team leadership and leadership are not identical. Leadership per se was covered in Chapter 1. You may recall it is the individual who has the capacity to command others due to his or her character and competency. It is not the sole property of a person wearing a star, bar, or stripes. It can occur anywhere at any time among rank and file, civilians, volunteers, and reserves. For those who remain convinced a captain's bars denote leadership, you are sadly confused. Yes, all police managers have bars and stars; a few have *earned the honor* of leading others by their trust, worthiness, and clarity of vision.

It is becoming less frequent that the person sitting at the top of the pyramid is the sole manager/leader. Rather, we see a group of managers strategizing together, reaching decisions by consensus, coordinating implementation, and generally performing many—if not all—of the functions previously performed by a single person. Through this team leadership at the top, these police agencies are seeking ways of better using all the talent and intelligence of their managers.

Creating a competent team of police managers is a new quality of leadership and a demanding one. It may be a discipline in its own right.

The current concept of *individual leadership* does not leave much room for that of *team leadership*. We need a way to hold on to the initiative, accountability, and use of team leadership and to abandon the inevitable baggage of personal superiority and self-centeredness.

For the past 30 years or more we've heard the clarion call of police managers to their staff, "Behave as a team. Teamwork is vital. T.E.A.M. assures our department that Together Everyone Achieves Much!" Super; I fully concur. *But* here is the rub. Many commanders, while shouting for more teamwork from the line employees, are *not* themselves performing as a team. The staff feels, "Hey, what you expect of us, you should expect of yourselves." The ideas, practices, and benefits expressed in the next section apply here.

Teamwork

The strongest teams are forged out of the notion of *interdependence.* "Interdependency" is a tongue-twisting, dry word. But it takes heart when you realize it means . . .

> **I need you, and I rely on you, and I value you because I can't do this as well as I want to alone.**

Once you've achieved teamwork within your staff, here is what it will produce for the department:

- Superior decisions
- More accurate problem solving in complex situations
- Improved coordination
- Better implementation
- Higher-quality services
- Individual development
- Expanded individual feedback
- Increased job satisfaction
- Improved performance as a result of all of the above

Earlier we reviewed Rule 150 as far as communications and understanding were concerned. Now we'll take a second look at it as it applies to size. It asserts that there is a peril to bigness. Organizations should be kept under 150 people. Crossing the 150-person line is a small change that can make a big difference.

> **For similar reasons, teams should be kept under 15. With larger groups you lose teamwork.**

Teamwork depends on the team leader and all of the team members knowing one another. They share a common relationship. They trust and depend on one another. They live up to one another's expectations. They share a collective commitment to team, over individual, success.

Teamwork depends on empowerment. It also depends on knowing one another. This means frequent face-to-face communications. With more than 15 on the team, it is very tough to achieve teamwork. A weekly meeting won't do it. A ten-minute pep talk at the beginning of the work shift won't do it. Teamwork does not merely evolve by somebody knowing someone. Teamwork occurs when you know others well enough that you comprehend and appreciate their skills, abilities, passions, and weaknesses.

Structured Exercise 6-3 has a variety of useful applications. If it's not relevant at this point, it will be at some time in the future.

STRUCTURED EXERCISE 6-3

TEAM-BUILDING EVALUATION

The following questionnaire should be used during a workshop, after a team meeting, and periodically in the work setting. The findings serve as evaluative feedback on how the team process is progressing. This information can then be fed forward into the team development practices.

WORK-GROUP EFFECTIVENESS INVENTORY

Work Group: _____

Date: _____

Circle one number for each statement:

	Strongly Disagree	Disagree	Undecided	Agree	Strongly Agree
1. I have been speaking frankly here about the things that have been uppermost in my mind.	1	2	3	4	5
2. The other members of this team have been speaking frankly about the things that have been uppermost in their minds.	1	2	3	4	5
3. I have been careful to speak directly and to the point.	1	2	3	4	5
4. The other members of this team have been speaking directly and to the point.	1	2	3	4	5
5. I have been listening carefully to the other members of this team, and I have been paying special attention to those who have expressed strong agreement or disagreement.	1	2	3	4	5
6. The other members of this team have been listening carefully to me and to each other, and they have been paying special attention to strongly expressed views.	1	2	3	4	5

(Continued)

STRUCTURED EXERCISE 6-3   (*Cont.*)

7. I have been asking for and receiving constructive feedback regarding my influence on the team.

    1   2   3   4   5

8. I have been providing constructive feedback to those who have requested it—to help them keep track of their influence on me and the other team members.

    1   2   3   4   5

9. Decisions regarding our team's operating procedures and organization have been changed rapidly whenever more useful structures or procedures have been discovered.

    1   2   3   4   5

10. Everyone on the team has been helping the team keep track of its effectiveness.

    1   2   3   4   5

11. We have been helping our team keep track of its own effectiveness.

    1   2   3   4   5

12. Our team's internal organization and procedures have been adjusted when necessary to keep pace with changing conditions or new requirements.

    1   2   3   4   5

13. All members of this team understand the team's goals.

    1   2   3   4   5

14. Each member of our team understands how he or she can contribute to the team's effectiveness in reaching its goals.

    1   2   3   4   5

15. Each of us is aware of the potential contribution of the other team members.

    1   2   3   4   5

16. We recognize each other's problems and help each other to make a maximum contribution.

    1   2   3   4   5

17. As a team, we pay attention to our own decision-making and problem-solving processes.

    1   2   3   4   5

Competency Checkpoints

- The second most important decision you are obligated to make is about empowering your staff.
- Empowerment makes COPPS operable.
- While there is concrete evidence that empowerment works, many police managers refuse to deploy it.
- The "E" formula consists of trust, delegation, participation, and capitalization.
- *Trust* is a unique amalgam of integrity and competency.
- *Delegation* is a transaction of responsibility given and responsibility received.
- *Participation* means encouraging your staff to express themselves on decisions that will affect them.
- *Capitalization* involves the identification and release of individual strengths into your action plan.
- Empowering people without a time- or event-triggered feedback loop is stupid and dangerous.
- There are five reasons not to empower a police employee, ranging from poor training to a lack of trust.
- Without team leadership, teamwork is likely to fail.

Flexing the Message

1. Revisit Structured Exercise 6-1. Think about your scores. What are you experiencing and feeling in your work that caused your scores?
2. In analyzing the "E" formula, ask yourself: Which component is the strongest (e.g., participation) and which one is the weakest (e.g., delegation)?
3. We presented four different types of delegation. Have you seen or experienced a fifth type? If so, what did it look like?
4. Think about your staff. Are you able to discern their individual strengths and weaknesses? Make a list for each police employee.
5. Describe the event- or time-triggered feedback mechanisms that ensure you that those you've empowered are fulfilling their responsibilities.
6. Of the five reasons not to empower someone, which one(s) have you actually experienced?
7. What is the difference between "team leadership" and "teamwork"?

7 | VITALITY

Our vitality depends on our wellness, and our wellness depends on how we deal with stress.

Stress is the nonspecific response to a demand for change. How it affects us depends on our response to it.

> *Generally, it seems to me vitality and endurance are fundamental qualities of leadership, though they may wane before leadership capacity does.*
> —*Chester I. Barnard*

CHAPTER OUTLINE

1. Vitality, Wellness, and Stress
   a. Stress
   b. Wellness
2. Stress and Police Leaders
3. Stress: What Is It?
   a. Medical Research
   b. Megachanges, Leading, and Stress
4. Stressors: Sources and Types
   a. The Three Sources of Stress
   b. The Four Types of Stress
5. Stress Management for Vitality
   a. Step 1. Affixing Responsibility
   b. Step 2. Reliable Data
   c. Step 3. Strategies for Wellness and Vitality
6. Competency Checkpoints
7. Flexing the Message

VITALITY, WELLNESS, AND STRESS

Life is 10 percent what you make it and 90 percent how you take it.
—Irving Berlin

The respected and successful business executive Chester I. Barnard pointed out that fundamental qualities of leadership are vitality and endurance. In other words, *you've got to be not only fit enough to run the race but to finish it as well.* Your vitality hinges on your wellness. And your wellness is tied to managing your stress. If you're managing your stress, then you're most likely to be well or healthy. Together, stress management and sound health assure you of the enormous amount of vitality it takes to lead others.

Vitality and endurance are important for three reasons:

- *Acquisition* They both promote and permit the unremitting acquisition of exceptional experience and knowledge that, in general, underlies extraordinary personal capacity for leadership.
- *Attraction* Vitality is usually an element in personal attractiveness or force that is a great aid to persuasiveness. It is sometimes even a compelling characteristic.
- *Tenacity* Leadership often involves prolonged periods of work and extreme tension without relief. Failure to endure may mean permanent inability to lead. Maintaining confidence depends partly on uninterrupted leadership.

Stress

The pressures of daily life—jobs, relationships, money, raising children, and terrorism—have become such constant companions that many of us function with growing sensations of change, anxiety, or turmoil. For many of us it has become so unflagging that we accept it as a normal part of life. It doesn't go away; it goes to work inside the body. How we cope with it is crucial for our health and the health of others.

All of us have been, are now, and will continue to be stressed. Some of us can control stress, the *nonspecific response to a demand for change,* better than others. Some people can anticipate it in some situations; others are surprised by it. How we cope with stress—and police management is associated with many things that cause stress—determines how we behave, think, and feel. Too much stress is clearly not good; ironically, neither is too little stress. Unless stress is harnessed and converted into a "steady state," over time, it will make us ill—perhaps very ill.

Stress, the demand for change, can either arrive from an external source or be generated from within. The main thing is to recognize that everyone is destined to be stressed.

First, it is critical that you be aware of being stressed. Scientifically documented signs and events can disclose when you are being stressed, and to what extent or degree.

Second, proven techniques exist for not only coping with *distress* (the injurious type) but also, more important, converting it into *eustress* (the favorable type). Relaxation exercises are one method for controlling stress. Police managers can either cope with and thus master stress, or allow it to wear on them. In other words, it's not so much what you eat but what's eating you.

> What saps our vitality isn't the stress so much as it is the *perception* of stress. Someone who doesn't see the world "out there" as a threat can coexist with the environment free of the damage created by the stress response. In many ways, the most important thing you can do to experience a world without entropy or fatigue is to nurture the knowledge that the world is you.

Wellness

Wellness is learned! Police leaders who are vital (healthy) teach themselves to be so. They realize that stress doesn't have to make people sick; giving up their inner adaptability to stress does. Bluntly, we have a choice—am I going to react to change with a positive "can do" spirit, or am I going to "cave in" to depression and emotional numbness?

Stress can be an invisible *threat* (lowered vitality) or a *treat* (elevated vitality). It is your choice. A choice for wellness.

> *The height of human wisdom is to bring our tempers down*
> *to our circumstances and to make a calm within, under the weight*
> *of the greatest storm without.*
> —Daniel Defoe

STRESS AND POLICE LEADERS

> *The main thing in life is not to get balance between our work and personal life*
> *but balance within our work and life.*
> —James Autry

There seems to be a "stress fad" in police organizations today. Granted, police work can be a stressful occupation. But so are many other stressful occupations: business managers, city managers, supervising nurses, construction foremen, and investment bankers all experience stress in their daily activities. What counts is that we know when stress has become too much or too little, and that we maintain a stress-wellness program.

Life is largely (certainly more so in the case of the police leader) a constant process of adaptation to the "spice of life" that is change. The prescription for health and happiness is to gain a successful adaptation to ever-changing circumstances and to remember that the penalties for failure to adjust to change are illness (physical and mental) and unhappiness. Paradoxically, the very same stressful event or level of stress that may make one person ill can be a motivating experience for someone else. It is through the *general adaptation syndrome* (GAS) that the various internal organs—especially the endocrine glands and the nervous system—help us to adapt to the constant changes that occur in and around us and to navigate a reasonably steady course toward a meaningful purpose.

As a police leader, then, you should understand the following:

- Stress in daily life is natural, pervasive, unavoidable, and thus to be expected.
- Depending on how you cope with stressful events, the experience of stress can be positive (healthy and happy) or negative (sick and unhappy).
- Because people differ in a variety of ways, each person's means and success in coping with stressful incidents will vary.
- Police managers are subjected to megachanges. As a result, they typically experience high levels of stress (change).

STRESS: WHAT IS IT?

There is more to life than increasing its speed.
—*Gandhi*

Stress is reflected in the rate of all the wear and tear caused by life. Although stress cannot be avoided for your whole life, a great deal can be learned about how to keep its damaging side effect, distress, to a minimum. For instance, it is just beginning to be seen that many common diseases are largely due to errors in the adaptive response to stress, not to direct damage by germs, poisons, or life experiences. In this sense, many nervous and emotional disturbances (high blood pressure; gastric and duodenal ulcers; and certain types of sexual, immunologic, cardiovascular, and renal dysfunction) appear to be diseases of adaptation.

Medical Research

Stress causes certain changes in the structure and chemical composition of the body. Some of these changes are merely signs of damage, while others are indications of the body's adaptive reactions (its mechanism of defense against stress).

The nervous system and the endocrine (or hormonal) system play particularly important parts in maintaining resistance to stress. They help keep the structure and function of the body steady, despite exposure to stressor agents (e.g., tension, wounds, infections, and poisons). This steady state is defined as *homeostasis*.

Whenever you experience a stress, there are three phases to your response: (1) the stressful event, (2) your inner appraisal of it, (3) your body's reaction. What makes the stress response so difficult to handle is that once it begins, the mind has no control over it.

In totally inappropriate situations, such as sitting in a traffic jam or being criticized at work, the stress response can be triggered with no hope that its intended purpose—fighting or running away—can be carried out.

Megachanges, Leading, and Stress

Anyone in a management role must expect increased change and thus increased stress. The accelerating rate of change is a reality. Planning for change—not just for the sake of change but also for survival—is more than a new discipline; it's a whole new philosophy. If we are to better manage situations of stress, we must place more emphasis on better self-management and the decisions we must make to enhance our personal growth and development.

Hans Selye, who made the public aware of stress over 70 years ago, and a host of management consultants and practitioners advise us that managing produces considerably more than the typical amount of job stress, and if a manager wisely approaches stress, he or she can respond in such a way that *stress* is transformed into *eustress*, which is pleasant or curative, rather than *distress*, which is unpleasant and potentially disease producing.

STRESSORS: SOURCES AND TYPES

> *For as many causes as exist for stress, there are almost as many techniques, practices, and treatments for dealing with it.*
> —*Harvard Medical School*

Humans can withstand extraordinary stresses from the environment, but if we are pushed too far, our stress response turns on our own bodies and begins to create breakdowns, both mentally and physically. In war, which is a state of extremely heightened, continual stress, every front-line soldier will eventually go into shell shock or battle fatigue if kept under fire too long; both syndromes are signs from the body that it is exceeding its own coping mechanisms.

We are affected by three types of stress: personal, environmental, and organizational. The first source is within us; the latter two are external. Most often they present their demands for change in combination with one another. Let's explore the sources in more detail and then look at the four types of stress they produce for us.

The Three Sources of Stress

Personal

A list of all the possible personal or inner stressors would be impossible here. They can range from a sexual disorder, to grief over the loss of a loved one, to a fear of flying. Those that are related to management fall into one of three categories: emotions, values, and power base.

The majority of us have received absolutely no training in how to deal with our own emotions. At best, we have probably been given some advice on what to do during emotional periods—for example, we have been told "there is nothing to fear but fear itself" when we are feeling frightened. Such advice is rarely helpful in overcoming the effects of the emotion. There are six very potent emotions that you should be able to recognize and deal with: depression, anxiety, guilt, failure, anger, and disapproval. More will be said about these six emotions later when we discuss stress-reduction methods.

Environmental

The environmental stressors are technological, economic, and political. For example, computers are causing numerous and profound technological changes for police leaders (many offices have interactive terminals). Economically, computers require large capital outlays and maintenance. Politically, they imply power. Noise and air pollution in the work setting are also stressful. Insufficient workspace elevates tension. (We could continue, but we believe you know other examples because you are probably experiencing some of them right now.)

Organizational

Five pervasive stressors within an organizational setting are:

- **Lack of predictability**
- **Lack of outlets for frustration**
- **Problem personalities**
- **Lack of control**
- **Lack of time**

Most of us do not like surprises—even favorable ones. We strive for certainty, and being unable to predict incoming demands for change is highly stressful.

The greater the *lack of predictability*, the *less control* we feel. And no one wants to be "out of control"—it's stressful.

When we experience *no outlet* at work *for our frustration* over a lack of predictability and control, distress is likely. Our outlet valve is usually with friends and family, which can result in higher degrees of distress.

The element of *time pressure* alters behavior, attitudes, and physiological responses. So subjective time can be an incredibly powerful force. It's no accident that the word *deadline* contains the word *dead*. A deadline implies a threat: "If you don't meet this limit, you're finished." The threat may be subtle or blatant, but it is almost always present. If it were not, we would not feel anxious under time pressure. Sometimes we expose the threat more clearly in phrases such as "I'm under the gun" or "His time is up" (which may sound like a neutral phrase until you remember that we apply it to people who are about to die).

Finally, certain types of *personalities* commonly act as stressors. Police managers often cannot avoid these personalities—indeed, their agencies may be plagued with more than their fair share of them, and they may also be in the manager's primary social groups. However, whenever feasible, managers should minimize their exposure to them. Who are these problem personalities? (Some introspection may be helpful here; ask yourself if you are one of those defined.)

- *Type A behavior* This type is aggressive; enjoys competition for its own sake; is usually in a hurry, impatient, and tense; and concentrates on his or her own self-interest.
- *The Worrier* This type often rehearses disaster scenarios; is dependent and fatalistic; and is frequently in pain.
- *The Guilt-Tripper* This type suffers from an overdose of conscience and rear-view-mirror thinking; he or she is cynical, contrite at all costs, and humble to a fault.

- *The Perfectionist* This type believes that everything can be done better, faster, cheaper; he or she ignores successes and focuses on failures.
- *The Winner* This type is addicted to winning and being number one at all costs; he or she does nothing just for fun, creates competitive situations, and belittles the loser.
- *The WSM* (the Whining, Sniveling, Malcontent) The WSM proactively seeks opportunities to carp, complain, and voice displeasure. Conversely, WSMs are never available to correct any of the reasons for their constant woes.

The Four Types of Stress

Let us graphically review what we have covered thus far and preview what remains. Figure 7-1 depicts the four major dimensions that comprise stress or change:

1. *Hyperstress:* overloaded with change
2. *Hypostress:* underloaded with change
3. *Eustress:* favorable or positive changes
4. *Distress:* unfavorable or negative changes

Our coping mechanisms are divided into two basic categories: the subconscious and the conscious. Space does not permit adequate treatment of the subconscious mechanisms, but essentially the subconscious coping techniques are developed during our formative years, when we learn to rely automatically on one or more of them. The conscious coping techniques are those that one can practice, test, nurture, and sustain to reduce stress. In essence, you can choose to convert distress into eustress.

FIGURE 7-1 Coping With Stress

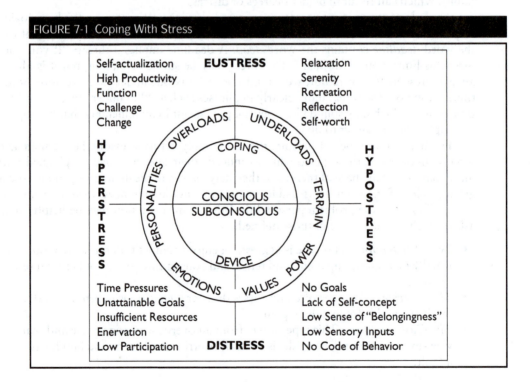

STRUCTURED EXERCISE 7-1

STRESS DETECTORS

We now present four questionnaires to give you an opportunity to assess your own stress level. The questionnaires should be self-administered (1) once a year, (2) at the time of major changes in your life, or (3) when you notice certain telltale signs of mounting tension or uneasiness in yourself or members of your department. The scales probe for hyperstress (eustress and distress). Hypostress cannot be dealt with effectively in the pages allotted for this subject, but the vast majority of police managers are not, fortunately, suffering from this form of stress. The data presented following these instruments include a table of percentiles against which you can evaluate your scores.

Stress Detector 1: Episodic, Work-Related Stress Evaluation

Listed below are many organizational events that have been found to stimulate stress reactions in individual organization members. The scale value of each event reflects the degree of disruption it causes in the average person's life (i.e., it represents the average amount, severity, or duration of personal adjustment required to restore equilibrium after experiencing the event). Generally, the higher the score, the greater the probability of a significant health change in the near future. However, since individuals vary in their tolerance for stress, the total score should be taken as a rough guide only.

For each of the following events you have experienced during the past 12 months, transfer its average value to the corresponding line in the "My Score" column. If you have experienced an event more than once within the past 12 months, you may record its value only twice. Then add all entries in the "My Score" column to obtain your total episodic, work-related stress score; record this number below.

Event (last 12 months)	Average Value	My Score
1. Being moved against my will to a new job	83	_____
2. Being moved to a less important job	78	_____
3. Experiencing a decrease in status	67	_____
4. Being disciplined/reprimanded by my chief/supervisor	67	_____
5. Having my request to transfer to a better assignment denied	66	_____
6. Receiving sudden and major change in my tasks	60	_____
7. Experiencing the cancellation of an important assignment I was involved in	60	_____
8. Encountering major or frequent changes, or both, in departmental policies or procedures	58	_____
9. Being promoted at a slower pace than planned	57	_____
10. Voluntary reassignment to a new position (not a promotion)	53	_____
11. Forthcoming retirement	48	_____
12. Experiencing a major reorganization in my unit	47	_____

(Continued)

STRUCTURED EXERCISE 7-1 *(Cont.)*

Event (last 12 months)	Average Value	My Score
13. Experiencing a sudden reduction in the number of positive recognitions for my work accomplishments	47	_____
14. Confronting a major change (increase or decrease) in the technology affecting my job (computers, new weapons)	46	_____
15. Providing a major briefing (not roll call) or formal presentation	46	_____
16. Encountering a significant deterioration in environmental conditions such as lighting, noise, temperature, space, and filth	45	_____
17. Being assigned a new chief or supervisor	45	_____
18. Maintaining a significant decrease in the pace of my assigned tasks	44	_____
19. Maintaining a significant increase in the pace of my assigned tasks	44	_____
20. Adjusting to a significant physical relocation of my workplace	30	_____
21. Acquiring an increase in status	30	_____
22. Being required to work considerable overtime	29	_____
23. Experiencing the transfer, resignation, termination, or retirement of a close co-worker	24	_____
24. Being promoted or advanced at a faster rate than I had hoped for	24	_____
25. Being assigned new subordinates	23	_____
26. Receiving a major change in my work schedule	23	_____
27. Acquiring new co-workers (peers)	20	_____
28. Receiving an increase in the number of positive strokes for my accomplishments	20	_____
29. Experiencing a significant improvement in environmental conditions such as lighting, noise, temperature, and space	18	_____
30. Adjusting to a minor physical relocation of my workplace	−3	_____
Total episodic, work-related stress score:		_____

List below, in order, the corresponding item numbers of the three events you personally felt to be the most stressful.

1. _____

2. _____

3. _____

Now compare your score with those listed in the "Percentile Scores" table at the end of this exercise.

Stress Detector 2: Episodic, Non-Work-Related Stress Evaluation

The following list describes many events in life that have been found to produce individual stress reactions. Follow the same instructions as for Stress Detector 1.

Event	Average Value	My Score
Death of a significant partner (e.g., spouse)	100	_____
Divorce from a significant partner	73	_____
Marital/partner separation	65	_____
Jail term	63	_____
Death of close family member	63	_____
Personal injury or illness	53	_____
Marriage	50	_____
Fired from work	47	_____
Marital reconciliation	45	_____
Retirement	45	_____
Change in family member's health	44	_____
Pregnancy	40	_____
Sex difficulties	39	_____
Addition to family	39	_____
Business readjustment	39	_____
Change in financial status	38	_____
Death of close friend	37	_____
Change to different line of work	36	_____
Change in number of marital arguments	35	_____
Mortgage or loan over $200,000	31	_____
Foreclosure of mortgage or loan	30	_____
Change in work responsibilities	29	_____
Son or daughter leaving home	29	_____
Trouble with in-laws	29	_____
Outstanding personal achievement	28	_____
Spouse/significant partner begins or stops work	26	_____
Starting or finishing school	26	_____
Change in living conditions	25	_____
Revision of personal habits	24	_____

(Continued)

STRUCTURED EXERCISE 7-1 *(Cont.)*

Event	Average Value	My Score
Trouble with boss	23	_____
Change in work hours or conditions	20	_____
Change in residence	20	_____
Change in schools	20	_____
Change in recreational habits	19	_____
Change in religious/church activities	19	_____
Change in social activities	18	_____
Mortgage or loan under $200,000	17	_____
Change in sleeping habits	16	_____
Change in number of family gatherings	15	_____
Change in eating habits	15	_____
Vacation	13	_____
Christmas season	12	_____
Minor violation of the law	11	_____
Total episodic, non-work-related stress score:		_____

Source: Kenneth R. Pelletier, *Mind as Healer, Mind as Slayer.* Copyright © 1977 by Kenneth R. Pelletier. Used by permission of Delacorte Press/Seymour Lawrence, a division of Bantam Doubleday Dell Publishing Group, Inc.

Again, how does your score compare to those listed in the "Percentile Scores" at the end of the exercise?

Stress Detector 3: Long-Term, Work-Related Stress Evaluation

Stressful day-to-day conditions such as those listed below often exist at work. Indicate the relative frequency with which you experience each of the stressors listed below according to the following frequency scale:

1 = Never

2 = Infrequently

3 = Occasionally

4 = Frequently

5 = Always

Frequency	Condition
_____	1. I am unsure about what is required of me.
_____	2. My peers appear confused about what my role is.

Frequency	Condition
_____	3. I frequently oppose the viewpoint of my chief/supervisors.
_____	4. The demands of others for my time are excessive.
_____	5. I lack confidence in the chief/sheriff.
_____	6. My chief/supervisor expects me to interrupt my assigned work for new priorities.
_____	7. Conflict exists between my unit and other coordinating units.
_____	8. I get feedback only when my work is in error.
_____	9. Decisions or changes that concern me are frequently made without discussing them with me.
_____	10. I am expected to endorse the policies of the chief/supervisor without being informed of their rationale.
_____	11. I must attend too many meetings.
_____	12. I am careful about what I say in meetings.
_____	13. I have too much to do and insufficient time in which to complete it.
_____	14. I do not have sufficient work to do.
_____	15. I feel overqualified for the assignment I have.
_____	16. I feel underqualified for the assignment I have.
_____	17. The police personnel I supervise are trained in an area that is different from mine.
_____	18. I must go to other units (bureaus) to get my job done.
_____	19. I have unresolved disagreements with my fellow managers.
_____	20. I do not receive emotional support from my fellow workers.
_____	21. I spend most of my time dealing with emergencies rather than completing assigned projects.
_____	22. I do not have the correct amount of interaction (too much or too little) with others (supervisors, peers, staff).
_____	23. I do not receive the correct amount of supervision (too much or too little).
_____	24. I do not have the chance to use my professional knowledge and management skills.
_____	25. I do not receive meaningful police work assignments.
_____	*Total*

Now list any ongoing sources of stress you experience at work that are not included in the evaluation form.

26. _____

27. _____

28. _____

(*Continued*)

STRUCTURED EXERCISE 7-1 (*Cont.*)

List below, in order, the corresponding item numbers of the three conditions in the evaluation form or on your list that are the most stressful for you personally.

1. _____

2. _____

3. _____

Now, turn to the "Percentile Scores" table at the end of this exercise.

Listed below are several long-term, potentially stressful conditions of life at home and in our society generally. Indicate how stressful each is for you personally by writing the appropriate response number from the following scale. Then add all numbers in the "Severity" column and write the result in the "Total" blank.

1 = Not stressful

2 = Somewhat stressful

3 = Moderately stressful

4 = Very stressful

5 = Extremely stressful

Severity	Condition
_____	1. Possibility of natural disaster (earthquake, major fire, flood, etc.)
_____	2. Hazardous waste and materials (radon gas, asbestos, etc.)
_____	3. Morals in our community (homosexuality, pornography, divorce, abortion, etc.)
_____	4. A reduction in our standard of life (reduced income, inflation, etc.)
_____	5. Noise pollution (traffic, aircraft, neighbors, etc.)
_____	6. The threat of being a victim of a crime
_____	7. Personal, long-term illness
_____	8. Family or close friend with chronic illness
_____	9. Sustained depression
_____	10. Personal drug abuse (alcoholism, caffeine, tranquilizers, etc.)
_____	11. A family member or close friend with a drug problem
_____	12. Traffic congestion (gridlock, etc.)
_____	13. The national debt and interest rates
_____	14. Continuing dispute with a loved one
_____	15. Concern over a financially comfortable retirement
_____	16. A growing sense of my own mortality
_____	*Total*

Now list any ongoing, non-work-related sources of stress you experience that are not included in the evaluation form.

17. _____

18. _____

19. _____

To summarize, episodic stress both on and off the job causes disruption, triggers a chain reaction, and requires a certain amount of personal adjustment. The more often we trigger the stress response with any kind of change event, the more likely it is that we will become ill. Although specific kinds of stress usually cannot be linked to specific diseases, with excessive stress our latent tendencies to become ill or psychologically distressed are more likely to become manifest.

The "Percentile Scores" table that follows shows the scores for each of the four evaluations as reflected by the results of 2,000 managers who have participated in training workshops. As an example of using the table, consider the entry of 159 in the "Episodic, Work-Related Stress Evaluation" column. This score represents the 20th percentile; it means that 20 percent of the 2,000 scores on this evaluation have been 159 or lower and that 80 percent of the scores have been over 159.

After completing the evaluations and determining your total scores, your next step is to make Xs in the table to indicate where each of your scores falls and then connect these four Xs with a line to show how your scores compare with those of the larger population.

Percentile Scores for Stress Evaluations

Percentile	Episodic, Work-Related Stress Evaluation	Episodic, Non-Work-Related Stress Evaluation	Chronic, Work-Related Stress Evaluation	Chronic, Non-Work-Related Stress Evaluation
90	512	327	76	44
80	480	254	71	40
70	394	206	67	37
60	330	170	64	35
50	280	142	61	33
40	232	120	58	31
30	195	93	55	28
20	159	64	50	26
10	129	37	43	22

STRESS MANAGEMENT FOR VITALITY

No one can do us any harm without our consent, and our chosen response is the key determiner of our life—that we are a product of our decisions, not our conditions.

—*Stephen Covey*

Now that you have learned about sources of stress, effects, and our own stress levels, you can begin to consider stress management and your desire for vitality. Remember that *a healthy and happy police manager is in much better shape to be an effective one.* People who work harder on their work than on themselves tend to burn out.

The vitality we're talking about is a function of our deep inner life. It is joyful living. It's found in the center of life, not in an escape from it. If your time (self) management plan was carefully thought out, your life should be reinforcing the habits of the heart that create harmony. These habits are:

- Our ability to live, love, learn, and fulfill a purpose
- The development and maintenance of human relationships
- Appreciation and gratitude for what we have
- Forgiving others and apologizing for our mistakes
- Learning to listen to and live by a conscience that is connected to principles

If you're in need of vitality (wellness), rely on the habits noted above, all the while recognizing that there will be challenges. Our expectations set up our challenges: no expectations, no challenges; a lot of expectations, a lot of challenges. The earlier quotation from Defoe indicated that our expectations are within our control. He was not implying that we lower our expectations but rather that we ensure that they are tied realistically to our habits.

Step 1. Affixing Responsibility

Twenty-four centuries ago in Greece, Hippocrates, the father of medicine, told his disciples that disease is not only suffering (*pathos*), but also work (*ponos*)—that is, disease is the fight of the body to restore itself to normal. This is an important point, and one that, although constantly reinforced during the intervening centuries, is not generally acknowledged even today.

Disease is not a mere surrender to attack; it is also a fight for health. *Unless there is fight, there is no disease.* Or to state it another way, our health is our *responsibility,* and we must work at it!

Step 2. Reliable Data

While medical science continues to develop new means to keep us alive, we nullify such efforts by refusing to slow down, relax, and consume less. Alas, the American way of life is killing people at an early age. The United States is twenty-fifth among countries in the world for male longevity and nineteenth for female longevity. (The longest life expectancy in the industrialized world is that in Japan.)[1] It appears that it is our lifestyle, as well as a fear of old age, that is killing us before we reach our longevity potential.

An undisciplined, random, fast-paced existence is dangerous to our wellness. It is essential that we be aware of our varying levels of change. The previous two sections on general and specific stress signs afford us the opportunity to measure our life-change units. In knowing ourselves, we can, if we choose, know our stress; and in knowing our stress factors, we are in a position to take accurate and positive action. In other words, by assuming the responsibility for our own health, we automatically create the need for reliable data about it.

Step 3. Strategies for Wellness and Vitality

It seems that the majority of us have a particular stress-reduction program that we want others to use. What works for one person, however, may not work for another. Jogging, for example, may be helpful stress therapy for one police manager, while another may find it harmful to the knees. Hence a stress-management and wellness program must be *custom designed* to meet the specific requirements of the individual.

My review of the literature on wellness and the successful adaptation to the accelerated pace of change leads me to propose five "wellness strategies." A police leader will select tactics from one or more of these strategies and *act on them*.

Wellness Strategy 1: Supportive Relationships

- Build supportive structures in your home that include sacred times, family rituals, and protected settings for recuperation. Build supportive structures within yourself to deal with discomfort, work, personal needs, and the like.
- "No person is an island." This statement is a tried-and-true axiom in terms of mental health and coping with stressors. We all need people, especially helpful people, who will give support when we are depressed, anxious, unhappy, angry, or simply distressed. Whom do you turn to at midnight when you are experiencing a strong sense of impending failure?
- Such thinking as "Oh, I can handle that myself" or "Dealing with this problem alone will make me stronger" is not only erroneous, it can also be dangerous to the point of injury.
- In establishing a supportive relationship, you should remember two things: (1) A supportive relationship requires cultivation; if unattended, it may dissolve; and (2) be certain that the relationship is reciprocal—that is, that there is both giving and taking.
- Finally, it takes *positive strokes* to give emotionally healthy people a sense of well-being. Without supportive relationships there would be no chance of receiving such affirmations.

Wellness Strategy 2: Mental Discipline

- *Step 1:* Learning to reduce the complexity and the number of tasks that confront you will reduce stress. You will cope more effectively when you handle problems one by one, on a priority system, and in manageable installments. As some people are prone to display on their car bumpers or office walls, "One day at a time."
- *Step 2:* Reducing the time pressures on yourself will lessen stress. We have a natural reflex for reducing time pressures when we are faced with overwhelming stress, but many of us fight nature's automatic mental stress-control mechanism. The old adage, "Who's going to know the difference in 100 years?" seems proper here.
- *Step 3:* Mind-focusing exercises are very helpful ways of reducing mental stress. Various meditative methods have been developed and promoted to help people unload tensions by focusing their minds on neutral thoughts, such as a

mantra or deep breathing (a deep-breathing exercise concludes this chapter). In effect, meditation allows you to put down your mental burdens several times a day, to rest your mind for 20 minutes, and then to pick up your burdens once again with renewed mental energy. It has been found that people who practice meditation or mind-focusing respond better to stress, and they seem to recover much more rapidly from the effects of stress than do nonmeditators.

STRUCTURED EXERCISE 7-2

A RELAXED STATE

The way to reduce physical stress is relatively simple. The principle underlying physical stress control is that it is impossible for anyone to exist in two contradictory states simultaneously. You cannot be short and tall at the same time. You cannot be pregnant and not pregnant concurrently. Vigor and fatigue cannot coexist. Similarly, it is impossible to be stressed and physically relaxed at the same time. If you know how to find a state of physical relaxation and how to sustain it, you will be better able to prevent the occurrence of physical stress overload and you will be able to control excessive tension once it has occurred.

The stress-control formula is once again useful here. You need to learn how to focus on physically relaxed states and how to rehearse physical relaxation responses until they can be achieved easily and quickly, and then learn when and how to implement the physical relaxation response at a time preceding or during a stressful event.

Focusing on a physically relaxed state is achieved by three means: First, use diaphragmatic breathing in slow, 4-second "in" and 4-second "out" excursions to assist the relaxation process. Lie down on a flat surface, facing up, and place your hand on your stomach. When you breathe in, your stomach should slowly rise, and the diaphragm, acting like a piston, moves out of the chest cavity to suck air into your lungs. At the same time, the diaphragm descends into the abdominal cavity, pushing your intestines down and forward—the cause of your rising stomach. Exhale slowly, and your stomach falls; your rib cage should be quite still. Breathing to a count of four on each inhalation and exhalation is a restful breathing pattern.

Second, you must learn to relax your muscles and blood vessels. When your blood vessels are relaxed, your hands feel warm. When the blood vessels in your body are tense, your hands feel cold and clammy. You can increase the warmth of your hand by focusing on the sensations in your hand as it rests on the arm of the chair. You can feel the texture of the arm of the chair upon which your hand rests. Whatever the room temperature may be, your hand can feel the sensations of airy coolness as well as of warmth. If you wish to intensify the warmth, simply keep "warmth" in a relaxed focus in your mind. Imagine lying on a sunny beach with the sun beating down on your hand. Imagine your body filling up with warmth from the toes on up.

To relax your muscles, you can take the hand that is gently resting on the arm of the chair and tense all your fingers without pressing them into the chair. Your hand will feel as if it is hovering just above the arm of the chair. Tense muscles make your limbs feel light. Now relax your arm, wrist, and fingers. The limb will feel heavy as it lies on the arm of the chair.

Third, starting from the top of your head and proceeding through every muscle and joint in your body down to your toes, contract each muscle to feel the sensation of tension—the lightness—and then feel the weight and heaviness associated with muscular relaxation.

You must now learn to rehearse warming your hands, relaxing your muscles and joints, and breathing slowly with your diaphragm. Take about 20 minutes to do so. Do not watch the clock—just guess at a time span of roughly 20 minutes, and rehearse the relaxation of your breathing, blood vessels, and muscles.

While relaxing your body, you may wish to relax your mind simultaneously by using a mind-focusing exercise such as that described above. Breathe in cycles of three breaths, repeating in your mind:

Breath 1: Give up caring
Breath 2: Heavy and warm
Breath 3: Breathe and relax

As distractions enter your consciousness, do not let them trouble you, even if they throw you off your pattern temporarily. Simply resume your slow, three-breath cycle of

Breath 1: Give up caring
Breath 2: Heavy and warm
Breath 3: Breathe and relax

When you have rehearsed these relaxation exercises for a period of several days, you can begin to implement them in your daily life.

Wellness Strategy 3: Otherness

- *Step 1:* Develop the skills to read the signs of distress, anger, and depression in yourself and others.
- *Step 2:* Develop listening skills. Most police managers who are concerned about doing or solving something forget how powerful and helpful it is to just be a concerned and active listener.
- *Step 3:* Tend to the people issues that are associated with changes. Remember that because change is the cause of stress, there needs to be more than just preparation for the change. There must also be aftercare, which concerns such things as listening for and understanding the processes that unfold in individuals and groups after significant changes. This is not working harder, but smarter.
- *Step 4:* Put issues into words. Words are structures in themselves. Sometimes issues need to be written down, particularly when you are working to build supportive structures for yourself or your family. Problems that are terribly difficult to manage, and that hang over your head for weeks or even for years, may surprisingly dissolve once they have been cast into words.

Wellness Strategy 4: Anger Management

The word *anger* is one letter short of becoming *danger*. Reverend Billy Graham gave us this wisdom, "Hot heads and cold hearts never solved anything." When you feel aggravated and hostile, it will hurt you, hurt others, and hurt relationships, all of which police leadership depends on. When anger enters the workplace, teamwork exits. Consider how much more you suffer from your anger than for those very things for which you choose to be angry about.

Everyone gets angry from time to time. It's a normal human response to unfair treatment and other injustices, and it's a common reaction to frustration and criticism, whether justified or not. But normal anger is one thing, excessive hostility quite another. Some people get angry without provocation, others react excessively to minor adversity, and still others experience inappropriately intense or prolonged anger to legitimate triggers.

Outbursts of anger are never pretty, and they can damage us and make us ill—very ill. The incidence of heart disease, strokes, and hypertension is shockingly high for those who have "intermittent explosive disorder" (IED). IED is an explosive outburst of rage. A recent survey reported that 5% of the population has it. Hypothetically, if you work for an organization that employs 100 people, 5 of them might have IED. IED is anger with a capital A.

What to do? First identify the stuff that bugs you. Then look for the warning signs of building tension. Second, when you recognize those signals, immediately intercede to relieve tension before it escalates to the flash point. The above three wellness strategies as well as the one that follows are very helpful in defusing emotional anger.

There is always professional help and medication. However, I'm convinced Seneca has the best advice, "The greatest remedy for anger is delay." By pausing, you engage that "space" we explored in the first chapter. In doing so, you take control of your conditions by exercising your freedom choice.

STRUCTURED EXERCISE 7-3

HOW SORE AM I?

Answer true or false to each of these questions:

1. At times I feel like swearing. _____
2. At times I feel like smashing things. _____
3. Often I can't understand why I've been so irritable and grouchy. _____
4. At times I feel like picking a fistfight with someone. _____
5. I easily become impatient with people. _____
6. I am often said to be hotheaded. _____
7. I am often so annoyed when someone tries to get ahead of me in a line of people that I speak to the person about it. _____
8. At times I have had to be rough with people who were rude or annoying. _____
9. I am often sorry because I am so irritable and grouchy. _____
10. It makes me angry to have people hurry me. _____
11. I am very stubborn. _____
12. Sometimes I get so angry and upset I don't know what comes over me. _____
13. I have gotten angry and broken furniture or dishes when I was drinking. _____
14. I have become so angry with someone that I have felt as if I would explode. _____
15. I've been so angry at times that I've hurt someone in a physical fight. _____
16. I almost never lose self-control. _____

For questions 1–15 each "true" scores 1 point; for question 16 "false" scores 1 point. The higher your total, the higher your anger level.

Wellness Strategy 5: Happiness

If you were arrested for being happy, would there be enough evidence to convict you? Think about it! Is there enough evidence?

> *Happiness can't buy money.*
> —*Turk's Bar, Dana Point, CA*

While happiness can't buy money, I believe it has a lot to do with leadership (happiness, that is—not money!). Although I cannot scientifically document the validity of the observation that follows, I can attest to watching at least 10,000 police managers and supervisors in police training courses, team building workshops, assessment centers, and consulting. Now here is what I saw—those who evidenced leadership qualities were usually happier than those who did not possess those qualities. Hence, I have two hypotheses: (1) Leaders choose to be happy, and (2) those who opt to be happy are destined to experience fewer problems with the downsides of stress.

The Merriam-Webster dictionary defines happiness as "a state of well-being and contentment: joy; a pleasurable satisfaction." You and I experience our own state of happiness or that of others by feeling optimism versus pessimism; positiveness versus negativeness; gratitude versus ungratefulness; smiles versus frowns; encouraging words versus discouraging words; and hope versus surrender. In terms of these traits, whom would you prefer to follow?

Like our car, we have a reverse and forward gear. Unlike our car, we do not have a neutral. When we opt for a forward gear, we're selecting happiness, and when we choose the reverse gear, it's the opposing set of emotions. Remember, there is no neutral; we're in one direction or the other. The good news—the really good news—is we get to select the gear!

Abraham Lincoln commented about one of his cabinet members, "Well, I guess he's about as happy as he wants to be." Are you as happy as you want to be? If you are, then you're making quality decisions about your life every day. If not, then you've got the right and ability to do so. The greatest birth gift we have is the power to choose.

STRUCTURED EXERCISE 7-4

TEST YOUR HAPPINESS

Read the following five statements. Then use a 1–7 scale to rate your level of agreement.

1	2	3	4	5	6	7
Not at All True		Moderately True			Absolutely True	

1. In most ways my life is close to my ideal.

2. The conditions of my life are excellent.

3. I am satisfied with my life.

4. So far I have gotten the important things I want in life.

5. If I could life my life over, I would change almost nothing.

Total Score:

31 to 35	You are extremely satisfied with your life
26 to 30	Very satisfied
21 to 25	Slightly satisfied
20	Neutral point
15 to 19	Slightly dissatisfied
10 to 14	Dissatisfied
5 to 9	Extremely dissatisfied
4 to 5	Sign up with a shrink
1 to 4	You're probably depressed

Whether "happy" or "unhappy" with your test score, you can forward gear by adhering to University of Pennsylvania psychologist Martin Seligman's findings about joyful folks: (1) They fully enjoy what pleases them; (2) they build and maintain several close interpersonal relationships; and (3) they commit and do noble purposes. A seminal researcher on this subject, David Lykken, concluded, "It's clear that we can change our happiness levels widely—up and down."

In 1998 a small but very influential crew of psychologists met to form a new field of psychology. It sought to refocus psychology away from pathology (abnormality, mental illness) and toward positive emotions (happiness, optimism, healthy thoughts). Seldom has a scientific field been brought so quickly and deliberately to life. A small sampling of scientific findings produced by the school of positive follow.

> *Wealth?* Once your basic needs are met, additional income does little to raise happiness. (Is this why many officers avoid overtime?)
> *Education?* Sorry, no correlation to happiness.
> *Youth?* Surprise, no correlation. In fact, older people are typically happier.
> *Marriage?* Usually married people are happier.
> *Friends?* Yes, yes, a high positive correlation.
> *Contributing?* Again, a strong correlation for those helping others.

A couple of caveats. First, happiness is not a static state. At times, the positive people feel blue and the negative folks feel joy. Second, our genetics provide us with a "set-point." We're born with a predisposition for or against happiness. Bluntly, we are naturally wired to be as "happy as we want to be." Third, and most important, our set-point can be drastically shifted upward or downward by our *circumstances* and our *choices*. Incidentally, just knowing that we have the freedom of choice elevates our hope, which boosts our happiness and which combats the negative tugs caused by excessive stress.

STRUCTURED EXERCISE 7-5

BUILDING YOUR WELLNESS STRATEGY

There are some tabloids that report on events such as "Eighty-Year-Old Mother Gives Birth to Twins." You'll find them at newsstands and markets. Recently, I spotted a front-page headline, "The Ultimate Secret to Stress Reduction." For 50 cents how could I go wrong? Here is what I learned.

A fellow in Canton, Ohio, buys an enormous amount of Jell-O. When he is distressed, he puts it into his bathtub, gets in, and lies there until it sets. He assures readers that it works. His worries are removed; no more troubles; aches and pains gone. Well, I didn't try it. It made for amusing reading, though. Who knows? It probably did help him. The lesson from this scenario is simply, What works for one person may not work for another.

Wellness programs must be custom designed. What works for me may not help you. Nonetheless, you must identify and stick to those highways that avoid the barriers of distress and lead to success. At this point, construct your own unique wellness program. Good luck!

To build a wellness strategy, you must first answer the following questions:

1. What major stressor do you currently face? What creates anxiety or discomfort for you? (For example, "I have too much to do.")

_____

_____

2. What are the major attributes or components of the situation? Break the major problem down into smaller parts or problems. (For example, "I said 'yes' to too many things." "I have deadlines approaching." "I don't have all the resources I need to fulfill all my commitments right now.")

_____

_____

_____

_____

3. What are the subcomponents of each of those smaller problems? Divide them into yet smaller parts. (For example, "I have the following deadlines approaching: a report due, a large amount of reading to do, a family obligation, an important presentation, a need to spend some personal time with someone I care about, a committee meeting that requires preparation.")

Attribute 1: _____

_____

Attribute 2: _____

_____

Attribute 3: _____

_____

And so on: _____

_____

4. What actions can I take that will affect any of these subcomponents? (For example, "I can engage the person I care about in helping me prepare for the presentation. I can write a shorter report than I originally intended. I can carry the reading material with me wherever I go.")

_____

_____

_____

5. What actions have I taken in the past that have helped me cope successfully with similar stressful circumstances? (For example, "I have found someone else to share some of my

(Continued)

STRUCTURED EXERCISE 7-5   (*Cont.*)

tasks. I have gotten some reading done while waiting, riding, and eating. I have prepared only key elements for the committee meeting.")

_____

_____

_____

6. What small thing should I feel good about as I think about how I have coped or will cope with this major stressor? (For example, "I have accomplished a lot when the pressure has been on in the past. I have been able to use what time I had to prepare to the best advantage.")

_____

_____

_____

Repeat this process each time you face major stressors. The six specific questions may not be as important to you as (1) breaking the problem down into incremental parts and then breaking those parts down again, and (2) identifying actions that can be done and that have been done in the past that have been successful in coping with components of the stressor.

Answers

Some of the answers to the preceding questions reside in the seven coping strategies. The most important answers, however, are housed within you. Each one of us must develop and (on occasion) use a stress management program. Being prepared for incoming stressors is like preparing for incoming artillery rounds.

On the lines that follow, think through and write down what you do to cope with excessive stress. When you review the guidelines you've written, ask yourself: (1) Are they healthy? (2) Do they really work for me? and (3) What else might I do to put joy and success in my life?

_____

_____

_____

_____

_____

_____

_____

_____

_____

_____

The following admonition is a fitting encouragement to the vital subject of vitality.

Success

To laugh often and much; to win the respect of intelligent people and affection of children; to earn the appreciation of honest critics and endure the betrayal of false friends; to appreciate beauty, to find the best in others; to leave the world a bit better, whether by a healthy child, a garden patch or a redeemed social condition; to know even one life has breathed easier because you have lived. This is to have succeeded.

—*Ralph Waldo Emerson*

Wellness Strategy 6: "Altruistic Egoism"

Hans Selye coined the expression, articulated the philosophy, and advanced the practice of altruistic egoism, which basically means looking out for yourself, but in an altogether different frame of reference than you might initially suspect. Selye went on to reveal that this "selfism" is to be developed in the context of making yourself necessary to others. Eliciting the support and goodwill of others is a key ingredient in the practice of altruistic egoism.[2]

"Earn thy neighbor's love." This motto, unlike love on command, is compatible with natural human structure; although it is based on altruistic egoism, it could hardly be attacked as unethical. Who would blame anyone who wants to ensure his or her own homeostasis and happiness by accumulating the treasure of other people's benevolence toward her or him? Yet this makes a person virtually unassailable, for nobody wants to attack and destroy those on whom he or she depends.

Competency Checkpoints

- Leadership depends on vitality and endurance.
- Stress management means responding and adapting to demands for change.
- There are three sources of stress: (1) personal, (2) environmental, and (3) organizational.
- There are four types of stress: (1) hyperstress (too much), (2) hypostress (too little), (3) eustress (positive change), and (4) distress (negative change).
- The steps for managing stress are: (1) first acknowledge that you are responsible for dealing with it; (2) obtain reliable facts about its causes and consequences; (3) finally, build a strategy for sustaining your wellness and vigor.
- All wellness strategies should be custom designed and operable.

Flexing the Message

1. Think of the five most successful people you know. Now, think of the five happiest. How many made both lists? Most people think of success in terms of possessions and achievements while happiness is a state of mind, and though it's common to think that success will bring happiness, it's often not the case.

Think about what the people on your happy list have in common. I'll bet they have much better than average relationships, especially with their spouses and children. Of course, other factors besides good relationships tend to produce happiness, like good health, enjoying one's work, and having fun. Still, if we had to choose the one thing most essential to a good life, it's good relationships. Do you agree? What does "good relationships" have to do with one's vitality as a leader?

2. What we call "stress" today used to be called "temptations." And when we called them temptations, we knew we were expected to resist, overcome, and never give in. Can you imagine expecting forgiveness by declaring to your boss or family that you lied or cheated because you were "tempted"? What stressors did you list earlier in Structured Exercise 7-1 that could be considered as temptations? Does it make any difference to you if they are viewed as temptations as compared to stressors?

Notes

1. Centers for Disease Control and Prevention, "Health, United States, 1999," <http://www.cdc.gov/nchs/data/hus00.pdf> (March 19, 2007).
2. Hans Selye, *The Stress of Life* (New York: McGraw-Hill, 1976).

PART

II | MANAGEMENT

8 | TIME MANAGEMENT

With the building blocks of values, ethics, vision, communication, teamwork, and empowerment in place, we're now able to add the next one—managing our time. Community-oriented policing and problem policing demand of you one of your most precious resources—time. The core of what we'll cover here requires that you constantly "place first things first."

Either you're going to manage time, or time will manage you. Time management is self-management! Thus police leaders manage their time by managing themselves.

I would rather be ashes than dust, a spark burn-out in a brilliant blaze than be stifled in dry rot ... For man's chief purpose is to live, not to exist; I shall not waste my days trying to prolong them; I shall use my time.

—*Jack London*

CHAPTER OUTLINE

1. The Total You
2. Time-Bound Versus Timeless
   a. Time-Bound
   b. Timeless
   c. Who's in Control?
3. Time and Stress
4. If It's Worth Doing, It's Worth Doing Poorly
5. Four Generations of Time Management
   a. Time-Management Matrix
   b. Just Say No
   c. Underloads
6. On Becoming a Category B Police Leader
   a. Step 1. Your Mission Statement
   b. Step 2. Your Roles
   c. Step 3. Your Goals
   d. Step 4. Your Schedule

We all have a sense that time expands and contracts, seeming to drag one moment and race the next, but what is our constant, our absolute? I believe it is "me," our core sense of self. For example, if two men are sitting with the same beautiful girl, the time might drag for one because the girl is his sister, while it flies for the other if he is in love with her. This means that each of us has personal control over our sense of time. Consider all the subjective qualities we attach to time. We say things like:

"I don't have time for that."
"Time's up."
"Your time's running out."
"How the time flies!"
"I've got time on my hands."
"I love you so much, time stands still."

These statements do not say anything about time measured by the clock. The clock doesn't lie about how much *linear time* has elapsed "out there." But *subjective time*, the kind that exists only "in here," is a different matter. All the above statements reflect a state of self. If you're bored, time hangs heavy; if you're desperate, time's running out; if you're exhilarated, time flies; when you're in love, time stands still. In other words, whenever you take an attitude toward time, you are really saying something about *yourself*. Time, in effect, is a mirror.

Raise one of your hands and snap your fingers. The sound you just made was the present—your compelling, immediate "now." Everything that transpired prior to that snap is history, and everything after it is the future. This chapter will assist you as a leader to claim your time and harness it for what it's worth—your most valuable resource.

Time is an *inelastic* resource. The dictionary defines it as "the measured or measurable period during which an action, process, or condition exists or continues." As a unit of measure, an inch cannot be stretched or compacted. Similarly, as a unit of measure, time cannot be saved ("I'm going to save time") or lost ("I'm losing time"). If we fail to use it properly, however, we can certainly waste it. You don't lose it; actually, you voluntarily or accidentally give it away.

Time is your most precious resource—you have a limited amount of time to make more money, but you can't make more time. As a leader, when you give someone your time, you are giving them a "time byte" of your life that can never be returned.

Once you've finished this chapter, you'll be managing your time better by managing yourself better. If you truly intend to manage yourself (time), this process will require much more thought and effort than the mere number of pages in this chapter would suggest. You'll discover that much of what you will be doing depends on the successful accomplishment of the preceding seven chapters. If you have those well in mind, *you'll find the necessary steps for designing a self-management program to be richly rewarding and even fun.* Moreover, you'll be incrementally closer to what we earlier assumed you sought to become: an effective team leader.

THE TOTAL YOU

The most valuable time is your own.
—*Anonymous*

We gain control of time and events by understanding how they relate to us. The subject of Chapter 8 is the exercise of our independent and conscious will for becoming a leader, which automatically means a more effective person. We do not lead a compartmentalized life. The various roles that we play out in life (e.g., police lieutenant, son, husband, father, daughter, wife, mother, friend) definitely overlap and influence one another. If you spot a wise time manager at work, you'll probably discover that this person also prudently manages time as a parent, family member, sports participant, hobby enthusiast, and so on. Conversely, the worker who is managed by time, misses deadlines, is late to work, and unprepared to do the tasks probably acts the same way outside the office.

Your approach to time management must involve the total you. Dealing with your role of manager exclusively would be suboptimal, at best a long list of "to dos," many of which would never get done. Obviously, we'll concentrate on making your time at work more productive. At the same time, remember that when we use the term *mission,* **we mean your comprehensive mission in life— the total you.**

The importance of things can be measured by how much time we are willing to invest in them. The more *time* you give to something, the more you reveal its *value.* If you want to know your priorities, or someone else's, just look at how they invest their time.

How you spend your time depends on whether you're a leader or not. Leaders devote a lot of time to cultivating *relationships.* Words alone are *worthless*; relationships require time and focused attention.

TIME-BOUND VERSUS TIMELESS

A little sleep, a little slumber; a little folding of the hands to rest.
—*Proverbs 24.33*

We can choose whether to make time an enemy (time-bound) or an ally (timeless). It's possible to have actual experiences of timelessness, and when that happens, there is a shift from time-bound awareness to timeless awareness.

Time-Bound

Time-bound awareness is defined by

- External goals (approval from others, material possessions, salary, climbing the ladder of professional success)
- Deadlines and time pressure
- Self-image built up from past experiences
- Lessons learned from past hurts and failures
- Fear of change and of death
- Distraction by past and future (worries, regrets, anticipations, fantasies)
- Longing for security (never permanently achieved)
- Selfishness, limited point of view (typical motivation: "What's in it for me?")

Timeless

Timeless awareness is defined by

- Internal goals (happiness, self-acceptance, creativity, satisfaction that you are doing your best at all times)
- Freedom from time pressure, with the sense that time is abundant and open-ended
- Little thought of self-image, with action focused on the present moment
- Reliance on intuition and leaps of imagination
- Detachment from change and turmoil, with no fear of death
- Positive experiences of being
- Selflessness, altruism, and a sense of shared humanity (typical motivation: "Can I help?")
- Sense of personal immortality

Most of us do not manifest either extreme, yet in many ways our deepest traits and attitudes are based on how we relate to time and internalize it.

Who's in Control?

If we decide that chronological time, our time-bound clock, is the key to time management, time controls us. Conversely, if we see it as a timeless value to be experienced, we control it. From here on, this chapter combines the time-bound chronological with the timeless, with a definite emphasis on the latter. If you enjoy this chapter, time will fly; if you find it boring, time will drag. It all depends on whether *you* really want to manage *your* time or if *you* allow it to manage you.

STRUCTURED EXERCISE 8-1

TIMELESSNESS

Being able to identify with a reality that is not bounded by time is extremely important; otherwise there is no escape from the decay that time inevitably brings. You can catch a glimpse of timelessness with a simple mind-body exercise: Choose a time of day when you feel relaxed and unpressured. Sit quietly in a comfortable chair and take off your watch, placing it nearby so that you can easily refer to it without having to lift it or move your head very much. Now close your eyes and be aware of your breathing. Let your attention easily follow the stream of breath going in and out of your body. Imagine your whole body rising and falling with the flow of each breath. After a minute or two, you will be aware of warmth and relaxation pervading your muscles.

When you feel very settled and quiet inside, slowly open your eyes and peek at the second hand of your watch. What's it doing? Depending on how relaxed you are, the second hand will behave in different ways. For some people, it will have stopped entirely, and this effect will last anywhere from one to perhaps three seconds. For other people, the second hand will hesitate for half a second, then jump into its normal ticking. Still other people will perceive the second hand moving but at a slower pace than usual. Unless you have tried this little experiment, it seems very unlikely, but once you have had the experience of seeing a watch stop, you will never again doubt that time is a product of perception. Time does not exist apart from your awareness of it.

When this experience becomes a practice, the fears associated with change disappear; the fragmentation of eternity into seconds, hours, days, and years becomes secondary; and the perfection of every moment becomes primary.

TIME AND STRESS

Think about your earlier work on values and value systems. It should interest you to know that in the past few years more and more value is being given to time. Frequently, I see it ranked in the top ten values cited by a police manager. Also, I frequently see the word *leisure* in front of it. Does this surprise you? Not having enough time can be stressful, and so can having too much!

If you are under extreme time pressure (stress) at work, your body's reaction to the pressure is not automatic. Some people thrive under time pressure, using it to fuel their creativity and energy, while others are defeated by it, losing incentive and feeling a burden that, when lifted, will bring no satisfaction compared with the stress it creates.

Those who respond with creativity have learned not to identify with the time pressure; they have transcended it—at least partially—unlike those who feel constriction and stress. For them, identification with time has become overwhelming—they cannot escape the ticking of the internal clock, and their bodies cannot help but mirror their state of mind. In various subtle ways, our cells constantly adjust to our perception of time; a biologist would say that we have entrained, or locked in sequence, a series of processes embracing millions of related mind-body events.

IF IT'S WORTH DOING, IT'S WORTH DOING POORLY

> *The tyranny of the urgent will always outshout the essential nature*
> *of the important . . . if you let it.*
> —Charles R. Swindoll

Take a moment and reread the title of this section. This comment was made by a very successful person. Think about it. Before reading further, attempt to develop some type of a rationale for refuting or confirming "If it's worth doing, it's worth doing poorly."

Let me now add: To make the best use of your time, you have to make a habit of using it flat out. Conversely, do you not agree with the proposition that working hard is not necessarily the same as working smart? One more question: Are working hard and working fast synonymous?

Many of us prefer fast decisions to slowness, wrong ones to none at all. Perhaps some of you have heard a U.S. Marine Corps drill sergeant shout at the recruits, "Move! Move! Move!" The title of this section essentially means that if something is vitally important, make a decision quickly. It may cause less-than-perfect results (even poor results), but the fact remains that someone is taking on the problem. It's the quick and timely response, with the underlying knowledge that you're doing the best you can. Now the big *but*—slow decisions are usually better than fast ones. It has been demonstrated again and again that shared or *participative* decision making produces significantly better results. Further, shared decision making typically builds in a commitment on the part of those involved to implement it.

Fast or slow—which should it be? No doubt both approaches relate to your truly unpredictable commodity: time. Both have their place in police organizations. An emergency situation (robbery in progress) obviously requires fast decisions, a fast time frame. Many police leaders, however, tend to make all decisions fast, when in most cases there is ample time to involve those people in the decisions that are going to affect them. Getting one or two really good ideas normally requires, at first, getting a lot of ideas. Keep in focus the importance of "empowerment." Fast decisions impede the empowerment of people.

> I'm not against fast decisions. At times they're needed. What I am arguing
> for is flexibility. Sometimes fast, sometimes slow—it all depends on the situation.

FOUR GENERATIONS OF TIME MANAGEMENT

> *There is only one moment in time when it is essential to awaken.*
> *That moment is now.*
> —Buddha

There are four generations of time management. Each builds on the others. The first three conform to the axiom *Organize and execute around priorities.* The first generation is characterized by notes and checklists. It essentially recognizes the varying demands made on our time. The second generation is epitomized by calendars and appointment books. Here we see an endeavor to schedule ahead. The third generation portrays the more prevalent form of time management. It takes the above two and adds the dimension of prioritization. It focuses on values toward which time and energy are allocated. (The higher the priority of a value, the more time spent.) It is planning with a purpose. The emerging fourth generation recognizes that "time management" is misconstrued!

The challenge is not to manage time; after all, time by its very nature manages itself. Rather than concentrating on activities and time, the fourth generation emphasizes preserving and *enhancing* relationships and on getting *results* through teamwork.

Time-Management Matrix

The matrix shown in Figure 8-1 categorizes activities or things as fast/slow and critical/noncritical. Fast activities press us to respond now. Critical matters have to do with results and the fulfillment of our job duties.

Category A is both fast and critical. All of us operate on occasion in this area. Regrettably, some become habitual crisis persons. Push, push, faster, faster. These

FIGURE 8-1 Fourth-Generation Time-Management Matrix	

	Fast	Slow
Critical	**A** Activities: Crises (shots fired) Pressing problems (computers down) Deadline-driven projects (staff reports)	**B** Activities: Prevention of conflicts (value clarification) Relationship building (increasing trust) Recognizing new opportunities (imagination) Planning, recreation (energy building) Team building (synergy building)
Noncritical	**C** Activities: Interruptions, some calls (open door) Some mail, some reports (in-basket) Some meetings (roll call) Proximate, pressing matters (evaluation) Popular activities (Code 7)	**D** Activities: Trivia, busy work (emptying the wastebasket) Some mail (reading junk mail) Some phone calls (aimless conversations) Time wasters (studying your wristwatch) Pleasant activities (nurturing your garden)

people are frequently experienced as task-driven and aggressive. Unfortunately, they beat themselves up while tackling the crises (e.g., stress, burnout, overloads, always putting out fires). When exhausted, they often retreat to category D, with little attention paid to categories B and C. There are others who expend a lot of time in category C, believing that they're in category A. They are confronting crises all right, only the issues are relatively unimportant in terms of their mission. In fact, they are likely responding to the values and expectations of others. Those of us who spend most of our time in categories C and D basically lead *irresponsible* lives. Effective leaders stay away from categories C and D because, urgent or not, they aren't critical.

> **Category B is the crux of managing ourselves. It deals with things that do not require a fast response but are critical, such as building trust, enhancing candid communications, long-range planning, physical exercise, preparation, and renewal. These are high-leverage, capacity-expansion activities. Your effectiveness will grow measurably if you focus on them. They will make a tremendous, positive difference in your professional and personal lives.**

Just Say No

The only place to get time for category B in the beginning is from categories C and D. You can't ignore the urgent and important activities of category A, although they will shrink in size as you spend more time with prevention and preparation in category B. But the initial time for category B has to come out of C and D. You have to be tenacious to work in category B because categories A and C suck you in. To say "yes" to critical category B priorities, you have to learn to say "no" to other activities that sometimes seem to be urgent things. Just as we expect kids to "just say no to drugs," we adults must be equally capable of just saying "no" to time wasters.

It is not bad to be in category A. Police leaders will spend a significant amount of time in it. The main issue is why they're there. Is it due to urgency or importance? If urgency dominates, when importance disappears, the leader is apt to slip into category C. However, if it is because of importance that the leader is in category A, when urgency ceases, the leader will move to category B. Note that categories A and B describe what is important; it's only the time dimension that changes. The real problem occurs when a person is spending time in categories C and D.

Underloads

A lot is written about overloads, very little about underloads. An *underload* is too little demand on us for change. Routine work, thinking, and patterns of behavior can become very boring and unrewarding. For us, we'd rather burn out than rust out.

Too little change can be fatiguing to the point of being harmful. Low sensory inputs are physically and mentally disabling. Paradoxically, a police manager who is working harder is probably not working smarter. Underloads often look like overloads! Are you working very hard in your job? Do you feel challenged? Do you approach your workday with a willingness to experiment, shake up the routine? Are you exercising your imagination?

> **Overloads explode around you. Underloads, conversely, surreptitiously undermine your wellness.**

STRUCTURED EXERCISE 8-2

TIME-MANAGEMENT AWARENESS SCALE

In responding to the following statements, circle the number that indicates the frequency with which you do each activity. Assess your behavior as it is, not as you would like it to be. How useful this instrument will be to you depends on your ability to assess your own behavior accurately.

The first section of the instrument can be completed by anyone. The second section applies primarily to people currently serving in some kind of police management job. At the end, you will find the scoring key and an interpretation of your scores.

0 = Never

1 = Seldom

2 = Sometimes

3 = Usually

4 = Always

Section I

1. I don't read everything. I skim the material until I find what is important and then study it.	0	1	2	3	4
2. I use a time-management system.	0	1	2	3	4
3. I categorize and update files.	0	1	2	3	4
4. I prioritize the tasks I have to do during the day according to their importance and urgency.	0	1	2	3	4
5. I concentrate on only one important task at a time.	0	1	2	3	4
6. I make a list of short five- or ten-minute telephone calls.	0	1	2	3	4
7. I divide large projects into smaller, separate tasks.	0	1	2	3	4
8. I identify which of my tasks will produce the biggest results.	0	1	2	3	4
9. I do the most important tasks at my best time during the work period.	0	1	2	3	4
10. I reserve time during each day when I can work uninterrupted.	0	1	2	3	4
11. I don't procrastinate.	0	1	2	3	4
12. I note the use of my time.	0	1	2	3	4
13. I set deadlines for myself.	0	1	2	3	4
14. I do something productive whenever I am waiting.	0	1	2	3	4
15. I do redundant "busy work" at one set time during the day.	0	1	2	3	4
16. I complete at least one major task every day.	0	1	2	3	4

(*Continued*)

STRUCTURED EXERCISE 8-2   *(Cont.)*

17. I schedule leisure time carefully during the day.	0	1	2	3	4
18. I avoid negative energy.	0	1	2	3	4
19. I have clearly defined long-term goals that I work on.	0	1	2	3	4
20. I continually look for new ways to improve my use of time.	0	1	2	3	4

Section II

1. I hold routine meetings during the workday.	0	1	2	3	4
2. I hold all short meetings standing up.	0	1	2	3	4
3. I set a time limit at the outset of each meeting.	0	1	2	3	4
4. I cancel meetings that are not absolutely necessary.	0	1	2	3	4
5. I have a written agenda for every meeting.	0	1	2	3	4
6. I stick to the agenda for every meeting.	0	1	2	3	4
7. Someone is responsible for taking minutes and watching the time in every meeting.	0	1	2	3	4
8. I start all meetings on time.	0	1	2	3	4
9. I have minutes of meetings prepared immediately after the meeting and see that follow-up occurs promptly.	0	1	2	3	4
10. When my staff comes to me with a problem, I require that they suggest solutions.	0	1	2	3	4
11. I meet visitors outside the office or in the doorway.	0	1	2	3	4
12. I go to subordinates' offices when feasible so that I can control when I leave.	0	1	2	3	4
13. I leave at least one-fourth of my day free for unplanned occurrences.	0	1	2	3	4
14. I have someone else who can answer my calls and meet citizens at least some of the time.	0	1	2	3	4
15. I have one place in the department where I can work uninterrupted.	0	1	2	3	4
16. I act on every piece of paper I handle.	0	1	2	3	4
17. I keep my workplace clear of all materials except those I am working on.	0	1	2	3	4
18. I empower others.	0	1	2	3	4
19. I specify the amount of freedom I want others to take when I assign them a task.	0	1	2	3	4
20. I insist that others get credit for work they perform.	0	1	2	3	4

Scoring Key

Total Score	Interpretation
70 and above	You are a skilled and prudent user of time.
60–69	Most of the time, you are using time appropriately.
50–59	You have a hit-and-miss approach to time management.
40–49	You possess a random style with wasted effort.
39 and below	Time is using you!

ON BECOMING A CATEGORY B POLICE LEADER

> *Until you value yourself, you won't value your time. Until you value*
> *your time, you will not do anything with it.*
> —M. Scott Peck, M.D.

The objective of a category B leader is to manage employees' time effectively—from a center of sound principles, from a knowledge of the overall (career and personal) mission, with a focus on the "critical" as well as the "fast," and within the framework of maintaining a balance between increasing actual production and increasing this capability for producing. Category B organizing involves

- An individual mission statement
- The identification of roles
- Selection of your goals
- Weekly scheduling
- Time-trap avoidance
- Taking action and being flexible

Step 1. Your Mission Statement

When you read your agency's mission statement, or one from another police department, it is probably only idealistically interesting and does not appear to require a formidable set of tasks. Hold it! What you're reading is in reality a *values statement*. Moreover, if the people who represent the statement believe in it and act accordingly, you'll quickly understand where they intend to go. (Frequently, the statement will convey how they intend to get there.)

Now it's your turn. If you choose not to do what is required next, you've also chosen not to be a fourth-generation time manager.

First of all, return to Chapter 2 and write down on a separate sheet of paper the top six or seven values that you identified at that point. Using those values, create a one-page mission statement for yourself. (It is likely this will take three or four drafts before you are pleased with it.) Complete Structured Exercise 8-3.

STRUCTURED EXERCISE 8-3

YOUR PERSONAL MISSION
STATEMENT

As you change and grow, your perspective
and values may do likewise. It's important
that you keep your mission statement current and aligned with your values. Here
are some questions to help you:

- Is my mission statement based on proven
  principles that I currently believe in?

- Do I feel this represents the best
  within me?

- Do I feel direction, purpose, challenge,
  and motivation when I review this
  statement?

- Am I aware of the strategies and skills
  that will help me accomplish what I have
  written?

- What do I need to do now to be where
  I want to be tomorrow?

Keep in mind that you can never build
a life greater than its most noble purpose.
Your "constitution" can help you be your
best and perform your best each day.

To help you craft your mission statement, take a look at Derek Paulson, a hypothetical police lieutenant, age 33, married, with two children. Derek's core values are, in
rank order: (1) integrity, (2) spouse, (3) children, (4) parents, (5) police work, (6) house,
(7) financial security, and (8) physical and mental health. Here is what he might have
written:

<u>Mission Statement</u>

Derek J. Paulson
Age 33

My mission in life is to consistently demonstrate integrity in myself and with others
as follows:

- I will love and care for my wife, being certain that she is receiving top-priority time.
- I will serve as an example of responsible citizenship for my children. They will be
  daily recipients of my love and help.

(and so on)

All right, once you've finished your mission statement, you're ready to move to
identifying your various roles in life.

Step 2. Your Roles

The first step is to record your main roles. Write down what comes to mind immediately. You have a role as an individual. You may want to list one or more roles as a family member: a husband or wife, mother or father, son or daughter, a member of an
extended family of grandparents, aunts, uncles, and cousins. You certainly want to list
a few roles in your police job, indicating different areas in which you invest time and
energy on a regular basis. You may also have roles in church or community affairs.
(Your mission statement will coach you on what they are.)

You don't need to worry about defining the roles in a way that you will live with forever—just reflect on your upcoming week and write down how you see yourself spending your time. For example, Lieutenant Paulson might list the following seven roles:

1. Husband
2. Father
3. Son/brother
4. Police lieutenant, leader
5. Police lieutenant, manager
6. Self-growth/mental and physical
7. Investor

Note how Derek's values, mission statement, and roles are integrated, systematic, and logically compelling. Complete this step for yourself now and then proceed to the next.

Step 3. Your Goals

It's late Sunday afternoon and Lieutenant Paulson has set aside 30 minutes for managing himself during the ensuing week, which begins on Monday. Derek lists the following:

Role	Goals
Husband	Discuss vacation plans; review insurance; schedule a dinner and movie; ask about her job.
Father	Discuss schoolwork; play one group game; play one individual game; develop a new sport.
Son/brother	Phone parents; send photographs of family; write sister.
Police lieutenant/leader	Complete performance evaluations; counsel Officer Mead; meet with each officer for coffee (15 minutes each).
Police lieutenant/manager	Analyze called-for services; prepare a problem-oriented approach to a major need; assess assigned equipment.
Self-growth/mental and physical	Read assigned textbook chapters; read *Time* and 50 pages in a fiction book; 50 minutes of exercise five times; read national newspaper daily.
Investor	Paint interior of small bathroom (first coat); read *Money* magazine; assess CDs.

You're probably wondering how in the world Derek is going to accomplish all of these goals. At this point it is straightforward; all he has to do is schedule. It is now your turn to specify your goals for the next week. Stop here and do so.

Step 4. Your Schedule

Now you can look at the week ahead with your goals in mind and schedule time to achieve them. For example, if your goal is to telephone your parents, you may want to set aside a 15-minute block of time on Sunday to do it. Sunday is often the ideal time to do your weekly organizing.

If you set a goal to become physically fit through exercise, you may want to set aside an hour three or four days during the week, or possibly every day during the week, to accomplish that goal. There are some goals that you may only be able to accomplish during work hours, or some that you can only do on Saturday when your children are home. Do you now see some of the advantages of organizing the week instead of the day? Having identified roles and set goals, you can translate each goal to a specific day of the week, either as a priority item or, even better, as a specific appointment.

Let's return to our Lieutenant Paulson to illustrate what must be done at this juncture. To begin with, he has to (1) divide up the goals on a per day basis, and (2) at the same time assign them a priority. We'll cover Monday and Tuesday as examples of what you'll soon be doing.

It's time for us to integrate this step with those above. Turn to Structured Exercise 8-4 and fill in the blanks. (Remember to prioritize your goals before scheduling the specific activities.) For future time-management planning, you're welcome to copy and use the form or design one of your own. Obviously, the time frames will vary according to night or early morning shift work. One more reminder: Keep the category B activities prominent in your goal setting, prioritizing, and scheduling.

	Monday		Tuesday
Priorities:	Complete performance evaluations		Meet with officers
	Meet with sergeants		Assess equipment
	Analyze called/service		Counsel Mead
	Read assigned text		Read assigned text
	Exercise 50 minutes		Exercise 50 minutes
	Schoolwork		College class
0500–0600	Awaken 0530	0500–0600	Awaken 0530
0600–0700	Jog	0600–0700	Drive to work/audio tape
0700–0800	Drive to work/audio tape on current affairs	0700–0800	Lift weights
0800–0900	Briefings/roll call	0800–0900	Briefings/roll call
0900–1000	Meetings with sergeants	0900–1000	Meeting with officers
1000–1100	Performance evaluations	1000–1100	Meeting with officers
1100–1200	Performance evaluations	1100–1200	Review reports
1200–1300	Lunch/read text	1200–1300	Lunch/read text
1300–1400	Analyze called/services	1300–1400	Assess equipment
1400–1500	Field supervision	1400–1500	Counsel Mead
1500–1600	Field supervision	1500–1600	Field supervision
1600–1700	Report review	1600–1700	Report review
1700–1800	Drive home	1700–1800	Drive to college/dinner
1800–1900	Dinner	1800–1900	College course
1900–2000	Review schoolwork	1900–2000	College course
2000–2100	Games with children	2000–2100	College course
2100–2200	Alone time with wife	2100–2200	Drive home/wife

STRUCTURED EXERCISE 8-4

MANAGING PRIORITIES AND SCHEDULING

Weekly Worksheet

Week of: _____

Roles	Goals	Weekly Priorities	Sunday	Monday	Tuesday	Wednesday	Thursday	Friday	Saturday
				Today's Priorities				Today's Priorities	
			Appointments/Commitments			Appointments/Commitments			
			8	8	8	8	8	8	8
			9	9	9	9	9	9	9
			10	10	10	10	10	10	10
			11	11	11	11	11	11	11
			12	12	12	12	12	12	12
			1	1	1	1	1	1	1
			2	2	2	2	2	2	2
			3	3	3	3	3	3	3
			4	4	4	4	4	4	4
			5	5	5	5	5	5	5
			6	6	6	6	6	6	6
			7	7	7	7	7	7	7
			8	8	8	8	8	8	8
			Evening	Evening	Evening	Evening	Evening	Evening	Evening

Step 5. Time Trap Avoidance

Take a separate sheet of paper and respond to each of the following questions with a written "yes" or "no"—not "maybe" or "I don't know." You either are or are not experiencing one or more of the following situations. Consider your answers thoughtfully.

- Are there papers on your desk, other than reference materials, that you haven't looked through for a week or more?
- Have you forgotten an appointment or a specific date in the past two months?
- Do your newspapers and magazines pile up unread?
- Do things pile up in corners of closets or on the floor because you can't decide where to put them?
- In case of a tragedy, would your spouse be able to find your valuable papers and records?
- Do you want to get organized but everything is in such a mess you don't know where to start?

If you answered "yes" to any of the questions above, you're making one or more of the following mistakes.

Time Trap 1: Failure to Divide a Complex Problem into Manageable Segments

Forget about straightening up your life as a whole. Just work on the ten elements in your life that need to be put in order. Make a list of them. Divide the problems on your list into smaller units. If the problem is a physical one—a disorganized wall unit or a messy closet—stand in the doorway, visually check out the entire room, and list elements to work on. If the problem is a system or process, mentally run through it and break it down (e.g., frequently late for work).

Then rank the ten problems on the list on a scale of 1 to 7, according to how much they irritate you. A problem that creates serious tension is a 7; one that could wait until next year is a 1. Tackle the sevens first, and so on. Important: Work on solving only one small problem at a time.

Time Trap 2: Failure to Make Time to Organize

Set a specific time for tackling your organization problems. Write it in your appointment book as if it were a doctor's appointment. Be certain to make time every day to work on B priorities. To do this, you must give yourself at least one hour of *screened/prime time* every day to work on top-priority goals.

Time Trap 3: Failure to Deal with Paper

There are only four things that you can do with a piece of paper: (1) toss it, (2) refer it (pass it along to someone else), (3) act on it, or (4) file it. Each piece of paper requires its own small decision. The worst mistake is picking up a piece of paper, staring at it, and putting it down again because you don't know how to handle it.

To sort the papers, you need: A wastebasket—and file folders marked Category B, Category A, To File, Home. Divide the papers according to what holds interest for you and what doesn't. Toss the "no interest" pile.

Time Trap 4: Failure to Follow Up
Don't assume you'll remember what you have to do in the future. Even if you could remember, why would you want to clutter up your mind? Record it on your schedule so that you'll be alerted to the need for following up on an activity.

Time Trap 5: Failure to Set Priorities
Establishing priorities means that you evaluate your goals and place them in rank order from first to last. Without priorities you, in essence, have lost the ability to attain your goals logically.

Time Trap 6: Failure to Plan Ahead
If you're working on a complex project, it is extremely important to pace yourself over the weeks or months you have to complete it. On a single sheet, list the starting and deadline dates for each component. Then enter each starting and deadline date on your daily calendar. When you reach that date, you can then put that job or its components on your daily list. On a simple project, list the components and then enter each of them in your daily calendar on the appropriate date. On that date, enter it on your daily list.

Time Trap 7: Failure to Make Use of Delegation
Many of us were raised to feel that it is wrong to delegate to others. Necessary attitude change: "My time is worth too much to waste it doing things others can or should do."

Time Trap 8: Failure to Consolidate
Return all phone calls during a specific time period rather than responding to each one as you get it. Consolidate and prioritize all callbacks. Make written notes and questions before you call. Combine errands. When you're out grocery shopping, also get your shoes and the broken lamp fixed. Consolidate movement.

Time Trap 9: Failure to Control E-Mail
Do not look at e-mail first thing. Instead, use the first hours of your work shift to focus on your most pressing tasks. Your mind is sharpest in those hours and completing important responsibilities early creates a sense of accomplishment that gives you self-discipline throughout the rest of your workday.

Step 6: Action and Being Flexible
With category B, weekly organizing becomes more of a response to daily adaptations of prioritizing activities and adjusting to emergent circumstances, relationships, and experiences in a systematic way. As mentioned above, you can analyze each incoming day and fine-tune your schedule as appropriate. (Your after-work travel home or elsewhere is often a convenient time to review the immediate past and confirm your schedule for tomorrow.) You're now organizing and executing around your goals and priorities. While you cannot manage time, you certainly can manage yourself—if you want to.

The six steps are summarized in Figure 8–2.

You will never "find" time for anything. If you want time, you must make it.

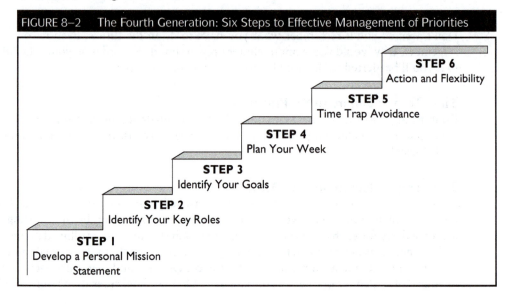

FIGURE 8–2   The Fourth Generation: Six Steps to Effective Management of Priorities

STEP 6
Action and Flexibility

STEP 5
Time Trap Avoidance

STEP 4
Plan Your Week

STEP 3
Identify Your Goals

STEP 2
Identify Your Key Roles

STEP 1
Develop a Personal Mission
Statement

Competency Checkpoints

- Time management is *self-management*.
- Time is an inelastic resource.
- Time-bound and timeless are opposite states of mind.
- Create a time-management program that involves all of you.
- Time and stress are interactive.
- The situation determines whether a decision should be made quickly or slowly.
- There are four generations of time management.
- Typically too much time is spent on category A activities (e.g., perceived or actual crises).
- Underloads can be as frustrating as overloads.
- The first step in building a time-management program is the creation of a personal mission statement. The remaining steps are roles, goals, schedule, time trap avoidance, and action and flexibility.

Flexing the Message

1. In Chapter 7, "Vitality," we examined stress in its various forms (eustress, hyperstress, hypostress, and distress). Use those categories to define how you are currently experiencing your management of time.
2. How much time are you protecting for yourself? Not for family or friends, but just for you? If you have no time for yourself, you're making a big mistake. All of us need time to think, relax, play, and so on. In your next week's worksheet (Structured Exercise 8-4) block out and guard time slots for you—just you.
3. Review the nine time traps. Which one of the nine bothers you the least? Which one is causing you the greatest difficulty in managing your time? What are you planning to do about it?

PROBLEM EMPLOYEES

In reality, problem employees are not a problem. They're actually a situation. And situations won't go away. It is up to the manager to control the situation.

Fact: All organizations have a few problem employees.

Question: What do you do about them? And,

Question: More importantly, are you one of them?

I still think all of the talent in the world doesn't
excuse deliberate rudeness.

—Lee Iacocca

CHAPTER OUTLINE

W̲e all have good and bad days. At times our performance and motivation are not as keen as they should be. This is life—organizational life. This chapter is *not* about occasional mental mistakes or emotional grouchiness. It *is* about those few police employees who choose to harbor and then display chronic dysfunctional behavior. Some actually enjoy being miserable and, if possible, making others the same.

It takes only a few problem employees to wreak havoc in a department. Although few in number, they can develop enough synergy to impede efficiency, lower morale, and ruin the image of the department. It can take the wrongful efforts of only a handful to destroy the hard, honest work of many.

The media and investigatory bodies expose—regretfully too often—embarrassing evidence of problem employees. The answer must not be "It's only a few out of many." The answer must be "We are striving for and will not tolerate bad behavior in our police department." Not only do problem employees attempt to erode morale, but they're costly. Bad behavior must be dealt with *immediately*.

What you allow, you encourage, and what you encourage creates new expectations.

Problem employees are typically thought about from the boss down. Here we'll also examine those few managers and supervisors who cause turmoil and distrust in the department.

WE CHOOSE OUR BEHAVIOR

> *When we deliberately choose not to stay positive*
> *and deny joy a place in our lives, we'll usually*
> *gravitate in one of two directions, sometimes both—the*
> *direction of blame or self-pity.*
> —*Charles Swindall*

Note above the term *behavior*. Basically, our behavior is making choices about our values. From Chapter 2 you learned that a value could be changed by either profound dissatisfaction or a significant emotional event (SEE). At times, a manager can cause one or the other to occur. But this is a rarity. Unfortunately, many managers consider themselves a failure when they cannot adjust an employee's values or attitude.

> **A police manager cannot be held accountable for changing someone's job-related attitudes or values. However, the police manager *is* responsible for controlling an employee's unacceptable choices at work.**

At the root of being a "good" employee is self-control and knowledge that regardless of how tough or confusing the situation, we always retain the power to choose what we think, say, and do. When we send up a smoke screen of helplessness—"You made me do it," "I couldn't help myself," "I had but one choice"—our work ethic runs amok. If we take control, we have control! If we don't, then we're going to be a problem employee. When we accept moral responsibility for our choices (behavior), we take charge of our lives.

Self-Deception

People problems that plague police organizations are really symptoms of the *blame dragon*. The blame dragon is caused by the choices we make about others and ourselves. Unfortunately, some people choose to deceive themselves by deciding that all problems are caused by someone or something else.

> **Self-deception occurs when we betray ourselves by blaming others for our circumstances. Self-deception is the inability to recognize oneself as a part of the problem or a part of the solution.**

Despite its destructiveness, self-deception is very tough for each of us to see in ourselves. Rather than accept responsibility for a problem, employees can first view themselves as a victim, nonetheless very loyal, extremely hardworking, and grossly undervalued. Second, they see co-workers as highly insensitive, totally unfair, always inconsiderate, and basically lazy. All this leads to poor performance that is behaviorally experienced as a lack of motivation, backbiting, lowered trust, and lack of commitment.

The obvious avoidance of or cure for self-deception is kicking aside self-betrayal and stepping forward to accept that you are causing harmful problems, and that you can choose to be a part of the solution.

Consequences

Ignoring or mishandling misconduct is usually time consuming and expensive for these reasons.

Recruitment

Wise potential new hires are likely to know the agency has more than a fair share of malcontents and thus apply to other police agencies. Because they're selective, they are probably the very caliber of person whom you want to employ.

Retention

If you are mismanaging or not managing bad conduct, it sounds an alarm to other police workers that the agency is drifting, in trouble, or lacks leadership. Your exemplary workers are apt to look for an agency with a more professional culture.

Morale

An absence of discipline suggests a lack of integrity within the managerial and supervisory ranks. Poor morale begets lower productivity, which creates performance shortfalls.

Lawsuits

The lawyers love police managers who mismanage personnel issues. Wrong decisions or no decisions by a police manager or supervisor can be disastrous—e.g., costly legal settlements and being forced into retaining the very miscreant who should never have been hired.

Money

All of the above creates a waste of valuable budget dollars and the manager's time. One estimate has police managers spending 20% of their time on combating wrongful behavior. And that's a large chunk of their salary.

HOW?

In looking for people to hire, look for three qualities: integrity, intelligence, and energy. But if they don't have the first, the other two will kill you.
—*Warren Buffett*

No agency (I hope) intentionally hires or nurtures a malcontent, liar, or crook. But it happens. More importantly, *how* does it happen? Roughly, there are three ways an agency can acquire a bad employee. Each category should be objectively probed for structural and contextual deficiencies.

Selection

Here we are looking at recruitment standards, pre-employment testing, background investigations, basic training, field officer training, and probationary periods.

Recruitment

Is the recruitment process proactive and professional rather than a mere newspaper ad, online ad, or wall poster? Is it ho-hum or does it attractively announce the merits and rewards of being a police officer?

Standards

Are the employment standards set for applicants with high intelligence, solid character, good work ethic, physical strength, and empathy, to mention a few?

Pre-Employment Testing

Does the testing include a general intelligence test, an oral board examination, a psychological examination, and a physical agility test?

Background Investigation

Is an investigator assigned to the applicant's personal and work history? Is the inquiry more than a mere letter or telephone inquiry?

Basic Training

Is the basic training program comprehensive and certified by a state certifying body? Is the applicant's competency tested?

Field Training Officer (FTO)

After the academy training, is the probationary officer subject to a formal, certified FTO program?

Probationary Period

Is there a probationary period from which a supervisor and FTO can recommend permanent hire or termination? And is it *used*?

> **Even with the rigorous application of all of the above personnel screening methods, some problem people slip through and become permanent members of a police agency. Nonetheless, the correct management decision must be to take *every* step and make *every* effort to identify them early on and thus preclude them from contaminating the services of a police department. The greater the percentage of problem employees, the less these steps are being diligently accomplished.**

Retention

What are you doing or not doing as a leader to make police work rewarding, exciting, meaningful, and fun? How many of your direct reports have been disappointed by a lack of praise on your part? Does your staff believe that you value their work to the organization? Do you express your appreciation for their work and take it a step further by affirming their personal worth?

Do you know their strengths and weaknesses? Do they really think that you care about their welfare? Are you setting an example that motivates them to try harder, do a better job? Finally, when you screw up and cause a problem for them, do you acknowledge your mistake and apologize to them?

Think about all of the ideas and lessons learned in the previous chapters. Start asking yourself questions about decision making, evidencing values, maintaining integrity, communicating a vision, listening, and so on.

> **Retention depends on job satisfaction and compensation. A leader influences the first, which is the most important of the two. I doubt many police managers would feel it necessary or be comfortable asking the above questions of themselves.**

Rationalization

W. C. Fields commented about handling a nasty, unhappy person with, "At first you do not succeed, try and try again. Then give up. Don't be a damn fool about it." You should use every approach to correct the repetitive workplace monster. One-on-one conversations, psychological counseling, change in assignments, extra smiles . . . whatever. But at a certain point you must recognize you need to redirect your energies, micromanage the individual, and help him or her to find other employment.

STRUCTURED EXERCISE 9-1

The following are some signposts that help in judging whether you played a part in a problem—and also played a part in the solution. Think of a time you were complaining about someone or something else.

- Ask yourself whether in that situation there was anything *at all* that you did to contribute to the problem.

- Ask yourself whether the other person would say there was anything *at all* that you did to contribute to the problem.

- Ask yourself what *they* would say you did to contribute to the problem.

- Ask yourself what effect your contribution would have on the other person and how he or she would respond to it. What might that person do or say in response?

- Did they respond in any of the ways you would predict? If so, then you are most likely acting in a way that invites the behavior you complained about.

- Did you make a change in your behavior? If so, did it improve the situation at all?

- If you did not resolve the situation at the time, what do you think you could have done to resolve it?

Don't keep an employee you wouldn't rehire.

DRAWING THE LINES!

> *The first thing we have to do to get adequate performance*
> *is to get people to come to work.*
> —*Lieutenant Neil Griffin, Watch Commander*

Although the community may disagree with, or be vague about, what constitutes police misconduct, the police cannot.

Granted, without community consensus on the subject, the problem is a highly perplexing one for the police. Nonetheless, wrongdoings must be defined and policies must be set by the agency. *Lines* must be clearly drawn. Essentially, these lines should encompass three forms of misconduct: (1) legalistic, (2) professional, and (3) ethical (moralistic). The first involves criminal considerations; the second may or may not be criminal in nature but does entail professional considerations; and the third may or may not include professional canons but does embody personal ethics. Specific examples of three forms of misconduct are examined later.

Legalistic Misconduct

This type of misconduct can be "corruption" or crimes against people and property. Police corruption is an extremely complex and demoralizing crime problem, and it is not new to our generation of police personnel. Police corruption includes (1) the misuse of police authority for the police employee's personal gain; (2) activity of the police employee that compromises, or can compromise, his or her ability to enforce the law or provide other police services impartially; and (3) the protection of illicit activities from police enforcement, whether or not the police employee receives something of value in return. Crimes against people and property include such behavior as use of excessive force, falsifying criminal reports, and lying under oath.

Professional Misconduct

This form of misconduct can range from insensitive verbal abuse of a citizen to negative body language. On the one hand, a criminal or civil violation may have occurred, while on the other, agency standards of professional conduct may be at issue. The possibilities for wrongdoing in this instance can fall within two rubrics: the law and professional conduct "unbecoming an officer." Again, the distinction between this type of wrongdoing and corruption is that no personal gain for the officer or others is involved. The key question is, What conduct is permissible? Hence there is a need for established policies, procedures, rules, and sanctions that explicitly encompass the conduct of police employees.

Ethical Misconduct

If an officer thinks certain citizens are deserving of aggressive police practices, he or she is likely to behave aggressively, perhaps to the point of overreaction or even physical abuse. Or if the officer thinks certain citizens are deserving of no police attention, he or she is likely to behave passively, perhaps to the extent of refusing to help someone. Ethical misconduct is the very root of other forms of misconduct for which managers must be alert.

WHAT LINES?

> *Negative people are worse than negative occurrences. The argument is over in minutes; the person may hang around for years.*
>
> —*Jeffrey Gitomer*

Police agencies can make three costly mistakes about the legalistic, professional, and ethical lines. First, in not drawing them at all, or clearly. Second, once created, not conveying them to all employees with regular reinforcement. Third, not establishing guardrails that automatically trigger disciplinary responses.

While it doesn't happen often, it does happen that some police employees will employ the "Duh" game when informed about their rule-breaking behavior. Here's one type: "Duh! No one told me that this behavior was bad. So it's not my fault; it's the department's." Another is, "Duh! I don't remember being told about this policy."

I recommend that you and all police managers do at least the following in the way of clearly drawing lines of conduct, thereby attacking the "Duh" tactic.

- Prentice-Hall graciously agreed to allow the preceding section, "Drawing the Lines," to be reproduced. In other words, you are welcome to use or modify as you like the statement about the three types of police misconduct. Put it in manuals, on the walls of your police buildings, *and* have *every* employee read, sign, and date it. The person's manager should do the same. Place the signed form in the employee's personnel folder. *Update* the form annually.

- Figure 9-1 is a government form and is also for your use. Modify it as necessary. Then follow the same exact steps as above.
- Return to Chapter 3 and the Law Enforcement Code of Ethics (Figure 3-1). Again Prentice-Hall has okayed your use of this document. Follow the same steps.

The above recommendations are not guaranteed to stop the "Duh" factor. But I can promise you that it will significantly diminish it. Moreover, it is likely to decrease wrongful conduct in general.

There is one other outcropping behavioralism that merits attention here. It involves *obeying orders*. There is a slogan, "Challenge authority!" A manager who abuses or misuses his authority *must* be challenged and stopped! However, to question a manager's *legitimate* command is a borderline, if not an overt, act of disobedience. You may be recalling the earlier admonition about empowerment. About including people's ideas and hopes in a decision *you're* going to make about their work. Not that *they're* going

---

FIGURE 9-1 California Police Officer Code of Conduct

POLICE OFFICER'S CODE OF CONDUCT

The police department will demonstrate an uncompromising allegiance to the State of California's Police Officer Code of Ethics. Every employee will embrace ideals such as duty, service, respect, liberty, equality, justice, courage, honesty, honor, and integrity. As prescribed by law, each employee will swear to keep this oath:

As a law enforcement officer, my fundamental duty is to serve the community; to safeguard lives and property; to protect the innocent against deception, the weak against oppression or intimidation and the peaceful against violence, or disorder, and to respect the constitutional rights of all to liberty, equality and justice.

I will keep my private life unsullied as an example to all and will behave in a manner that does not bring discredit to me or my agency. I will maintain courageous calm in the face of danger, scorn or ridicule; develop self-restraint; and be constantly mindful of the welfare of others.

Honest in thought and deed in both my personal and official life, I will be exemplary in obeying the law and the regulation of my department. Whatever I see or hear of a confidential nature or that is confided to me in my official capacity will be kept ever secret unless revelation is necessary in the performance of my duty.

I will never act officiously or permit personal feeling, prejudices, political beliefs, aspirations, animosities or friendships to influence my decisions. With no compromise for crime, I will enforce the law courteously and appropriately without fear of favor, malice, or ill will, never employing unnecessary force or violence and never accepting gratuities.

I recognize the badge of my office as a symbol of public faith, and I accept it as a public trust to be held so long as I am true to the ethics of police service. I will never engage in acts of corruption or bribery, nor will I condone such acts by other police officers. I will cooperate with all legally authorized agencies and their representatives in the pursuit of justice.

I know that I alone am responsible for my own standard of professional performance and will take every reasonable opportunity to enhance and improve my level of knowledge and competence. I will constantly strive to achieve these objectives and ideals, dedicating myself before God to my chosen profession—Law Enforcement.

to make but that *you're* going to make! The manager is there to manage; the leader is there to lead; and the staff is obligated to comply.

Some employees pride themselves in asking, "Why are we doing this? Why do you want me to do it this way? You owe it to me to tell me why there is this line!" Successful police departments do not, *cannot* function based on a hierarchy of "whys." They function best on a hierarchy of commands.

You don't owe an explanation for everything you do or ask others to do. Your boss doesn't owe you one either. At times understanding can wait, but *obedience* cannot. In fact, you may never understand some commands until you obey them first. Some of us pick and choose the commands we obey—this is thought of as "partial" obedience. But there is no such thing as partial obedience. You either obey or disobey an order. And when you disobey—even partially—this is *disobedience*.

TYPES OF PROBLEMS

> *Yanking a dog's ears is as foolish as interfering in someone else's argument.*
> —*Proverbs 26:17*

The "three lines" covered earlier are now divided into two categories: unlawful conduct and professional/ethical issues.

Unlawful Conduct
This list is based on federal laws, state penal codes, and local ordinances. The list seems short, but in actuality it is extensive (e.g., burglary, theft, rape, and so on). Here are a few examples.

- Use of excessive force
- Hate crimes
- Part I crimes
- Perjury
- Sex crimes
- Misdemeanor crimes

The first line of investigation is the supervisor. Once she or he has evidence of wrongful conduct, the case is immediately transferred to internal affairs or criminal investigations. This situation is handled like any other criminal case—only with the media banging on your office door.

Professional/Ethical Issues
Here the list of misconduct is very long and not as definitive.

- Low productivity
- Malingerer
- Interpersonal difficulties
- Disloyal
- Insubordination

- Lying
- Cowardice
- Chronic complaining
- Improper dress
- Improper use of e-mail, etc.
- Chronic absenteeism
- Alcohol/drug abuse
- Negative personalities
- Racial/gender discrimination
- Unsafe behavior
- Sexual harassment
- Excessive citizen complaints
- Careless performance
- Reckless driving
- Personal chores at work

Problem police employees are difficult to manage. They tend to upset the morale of the workgroup. Consequently, managers should consider (1) why potential problem employees are being hired in the first place, (2) handling them on the job so that they reach maximum productivity with the least disruption of the team's overall performance, (3) progress documentation and counseling, (4) determining whether problem employees have become so seriously maladjusted that they need professional attention, and (5) release from the service. Progressive documentation will be essential; such documentation includes but is not limited to problems, recommendations, actions taken (results), and Employee Assistance Programs (EAP) offered and utilized (or not).

An agency may be large enough to afford an internal investigations, or professional responsibilities, unit. Nevertheless, having an internal investigations unit does not relieve the manager of the need to maintain discipline. On the contrary, it strengthens it by providing assistance to supervisors in the investigation of alleged misconduct of their team members.

HELPING THE PROBLEM EMPLOYEE

> *When a man points a finger at someone else, four*
> *of his fingers are pointing at himself.*
> —Louis Nizer

What follows does not pertain to the employee who is a law violator or was caught sleeping while on duty—disciplinary remedies are called for and will be covered in the next few pages.

Dysfunctional employees require professional assistance, and some police departments have either full-time or on-call psychiatrists or clinical psychologists. With appropriate approval, you should refer troubled employees to such specialists.

A police leader should attempt to help the problem police employee to improve his behavior only after having reassured the individual that the department wants to help him become a contributing and positive member of the agency. No approach does more harm with a person of this nature than the "better-get-yourself-straightened-out-or-you-will-lose-your-job" threat by the manager. The employee must be convinced that the department's intentions are good and that help is available. Here are some ways to help:

- Listen patiently to what the employee has to say before making any comment of your own. This act on your part may be sufficient to resolve the difficulties.
- Refrain from criticizing or offering hasty advice on the employee's problem.
- Never argue with a police employee while you are in the process of counseling.
- Give your undivided attention to the employee.
- Look beyond the mere words the employee says; listen empathetically to see if the person is trying to convey something deeper than what appears on the surface.
- Recognize why you are counseling an employee. Don't look for immediate results. Never mix the counseling interview with some other action you may want to take, such as discipline.
- Find a reasonably quiet place where you're sure you won't be interrupted or overheard. Try to put the employee at ease. Don't jump into a cross-examination.
- Understand that, depending on the nature of the situation, multiple sessions may be necessary. They should last from 15 to 30 minutes per session. If after two counseling sessions you are not making progress, you should consult with your manager concerning referral to a professional therapist.
- Accept the fact that it is your responsibility as a manger to deal with the situation.
- Look at your task as a fact-finding one, just as in handling grievances.
- Control your own emotions and opinions while dealing with the employee.
- Be absolutely sold on the value of listening rather than preaching.
- Recognize your own limits in handling these situations. You're not a clinical psychologist. You're a person responsible for getting results from your assigned officers.
- Give your people regular, honest feedback. Performance evaluations occur too infrequently these days. Some police managers avoid confronting the issue. They harm their department and also the individuals they are evaluating. Let people know where they stand by candidly discussing their strengths and their development needs. Take ownership in helping them meet those needs as a way to advance their careers.
- Realize that leaders also have to be ready to accept reliable feedback about their own performance.
- Don't make the mistake of thinking you can lead with your feet up on the desk. You lead by your feet being on the ground and constantly visible to your staff— in other words, managing (leading) by wandering around (MBWA).

You can achieve control when the employee responds to one or more of the above approaches. You simply want the person to get back on the right track. A results-oriented attitude should remind us of what we're really trying to achieve here—getting the work done with the people at hand. That is the whole aim of management, and it is precisely the goal that should guide us in dealing with people when they make wrong choices about their behavior.

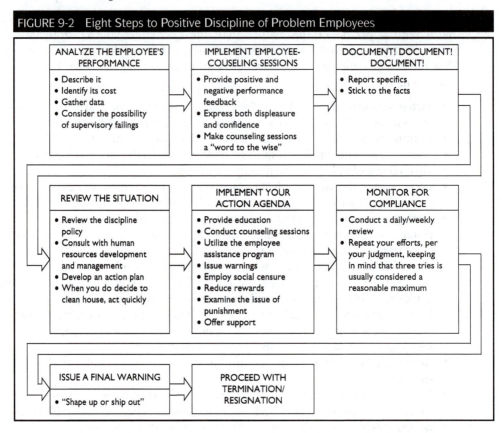

FIGURE 9-2 Eight Steps to Positive Discipline of Problem Employees

If all else fails, you still have your prerogative to use discipline. Figure 9-2 depicts an eight-step process for addressing problem employees. It starts with counseling and proceeds into discipline, which follows.

DISCIPLINE

Don't keep an employee you wouldn't rehire.
—Michael Josephson

Among the complaints heard from both police managers and line officers are that disciplinary guidelines are not clear or that the guidelines don't seem to be the same for everyone. Many disciplinary policies are so voluminous that they are difficult to administer, with a course of action for every possible mischief a police officer might get into. Although some downfalls may be found in the same categorical group, the circumstances and consequences are usually different and deserve additional consideration. Some policies give almost no concrete direction. Perhaps the best (or worst) was "suggested" by one chief who said, "What I'd really like to have is a one-page general order with just three words—and have it work—'Don't screw up!'" I understood what he was getting at when he handed me his department's voluminous general orders.

Internal investigations are impeded at times by how and when officer complaints can be handled. Many states have enacted into law a peace officers' bill of rights. Management is restricted in terms of the kinds of information that can be accumulated (investigation and personnel files) and what information can be made public to inform citizens of corrective action taken by the department.

> **The ultimate responsibility for the promotion of good versus the acceptance of bad behavior on the part of organization members rests with the police chief or sheriff, even though it is delegated via the chain of command and restricted by laws, court, and contracts.**

Types of Disciplinary Actions

- *Verbal Warning.* The purpose of a verbal warning is to allow a police manager to bring to the employee's attention the need to improve his or her performance, work habits, and behavior or attitude and to serve as a warning against further repetition of such unsatisfactory conduct. The commander or supervisor can use the occasion to identify and define the area needing improvement and inform the employee as to how such improvement can be realistically achieved. Supervisors document verbal warnings on an employee incident form or as designated by a division commander (e.g., monthly activity log).
- *Written Warning.* The purpose of a written warning is to assist a police manager to bring to the employee's attention the need to improve his or her performance, work habits, behavior, or attitude after a verbal warning has not resulted in expected improvement, or when an employee commits a more serious offense.
- *Written Reprimand.* The purpose of a written reprimand is to facilitate a police manager in bringing to the employee's attention the need to immediately correct his or her performance, work habits, behavior, or attitude after a written warning has not resulted in expected improvement, or when an employee commits a more serious offense.
- *Suspension.* In the event offenses are continued or repeated and the employee has already received verbal and written warnings, and/or has received a written reprimand from the director of public safety, or if the nature of the offense is sufficiently serious, an employee should be suspended for a specific period of time, not to exceed 30 working days. Such suspensions can be with or without pay and, if for more than one day, are issued on a consecutive working day basis. A suspended employee should not be permitted to work on his or her normal day(s) off, nor take paid leave time, nor make up the time by working overtime in lieu of a payroll deduction for the period of suspension.
- *Demotion.* In instances in which the employee is rated or in a promoted position and the nature of the offense is sufficiently serious, the employee may be reduced in rank.
- *Dismissal.* For a continued series of lesser offenses, or on the first occurrence of a serious offense, an employee may be dismissed from employment. Let's look at this subject more closely.

STRUCTURED EXERCISE 9-2

By the very nature of their task, police officers are sometimes confronted and involved with conflicting and disturbing occurrences. For some this may begin to have an effect on their behavior, whereas others don't appear bothered at all. (Some of these might be personal off-duty occurrences, for example, domestic problems.) Each class participant is to make a list of several situations that he or she believes might fit into that concept. (If nonpolice personnel are in this group, they may list situations from their work or life experiences.) This could even be something such as working with a problem officer.

When this is done, select a group leader to briefly record these situations. Preferably, use a newsprint tablet and fasten the completed sheets on the wall. (The group may wish to store these for later review and comment.) Each participant will read his or her first entry in turn, and so on, until each entry is recorded. Duplicates will be scored with a mark

behind the first listing. When all have responded, discuss the list and its relationship to officers, perhaps officers you have known.

Be sure to leave sufficient time for each participant to prepare a brief scenario (in writing) of how one or more adverse experiences has negatively affected an officer and how that officer has or has not affected others. (Do not use true names.) Submit these to the instructor, who will read and share the results, probably at a later meeting, depending on group size.

The other half of this exercise, at another meeting, is to share your thoughts on how this problem—if it was a problem—might have been or was diminished. Peer counseling is one good idea. Be creative. How would you protect yourself? How would you protect your friend? Discuss positive and negative ways in which some officers deal with this kind of adversity.

The Firing Line

The "firing line" is one test of a department's leadership. Who, why, when, and even how someone is fired goes to the very heart of the character of a police agency, its management, and its leadership. Obviously, it is the responsibility of the leader to cleanse the system of those people who are not contributing or who are impeding the general efforts of all the others. Unfortunately, there are always some people in every agency who simply do not want to work. They may be lazy or disturbed or resentful or otherwise unlawful, but for whatever reason, they don't do their share, nor do they want to.

Easy to See

It is easy enough to recognize bad people in line jobs. In the ranks of management, it is complex. Nevertheless, everyone around such a person recognizes that he or she is a "faker" or whatever word you want to use. Nor will others ordinarily tell the "boss" what is going on. But they will be watching and judging. And it is the duty of the leader to recognize and get rid of that kind of person.

Alert police managers will recognize the clues and will move fast as soon as the facts are discovered. And when they do, they will earn the respect of all the others who are hardworking, imaginative, and productive and who have long resented the freeloaders and violators in their ranks. In that sense, firing people can be a constructive role of a department's management. It clears the air and improves the climate.

Difficult to Do

Firing people is always difficult. First of all, it's the moment of truth for a police leader. You never face the problem of firing somebody without honestly examining the question of how much you yourself have contributed to the situation. Are you firing him or her because the department is under extreme political pressure, because of internal conflicts, or because you dislike the person? If so, then it isn't the officer's fault; it's yours. You are supposed to run the department so that it will be strong enough to weather bad conditions.

Second, there are perplexing and frustrating legal bases to cover. Personnel employment law is complex and often confusing. It seems that everyone wants to be involved—the agency's attorneys, attorneys for the person terminated, civil service boards, other officials who act as arbitrators, and the list goes on. Even with unpleasant repercussions, you must not be intimidated and hesitate to take action. If you do, you'll lose your followership.

> **If the reasons and documentation for firing are valid, then the manager is obligated to move for termination. If others decide to overturn the manager's decision, then they should be held accountable for any possible "wrongful retention."**

Reaction

In physics it is well known that for every action there is a reaction. Every time a police manager takes an action for or against someone in the department, either firing or promoting a person, there is a reaction throughout the agency. The reaction is not simply between the boss and the employee. It reverberates to all the others down the line. They pass judgment on what the boss did and the way he or she did it, and they react accordingly.

Retaliation

All of your decisions, from a verbal warning on through dismissal, must be tied to proven facts and sound logic. Any appearance, factual or not, of you retaliating against an employee can be the basis for rejecting your recommended punishment. It's *not* your job to get even with the malcontent or malefactor. It's your job to *stop* bad behavior.

The Right Thing

Ultimately, a police leader must take action and do the right thing. No one wants his or her leader to be tolerant of incompetence through ignorance, indecisiveness, or weakness. No one will follow a weak manager. That is the worst kind. You cannot rely on the judgment of such people because you don't know what they will do in a difficult situation. Much more respect and loyalty is given to the courageous leader, the one who is not afraid to make difficult and even unpopular decisions, just as long as he or she is perceived to be decent and fair and reliable in his or her dealings with the staff.

Remember—problem employees are few in actual number, but they can, if not controlled, generate enormous adverse consequences for the operations of a police agency and you as a manager. Remember—they range from the gossipy malcontent to the vicious malefactor. Remember—a considerable degree of your success is measured by your ability to identify and discipline those who decide to act criminally, unprofessionally, or unethically.

PROBLEM BOSSES

The most exhausting thing in life is being insincere.
—Anne Morrow Lindbergh

Even with the most careful and sophisticated promotional process, a few employees who should not be managers will percolate upwards. Obviously, every effort (training, coaching, counseling, etc.) should be made to help them develop as managers and leaders. With repeated attempts and no success, they must be reduced in rank or in some other way removed from their position.

Imagine a police agency with one hundred employees, five of whom are serious problems. Now think of this agency with one of those five commanding a division. While problem employees pose a threat to operational effectiveness, they present a horrendous threat when at or near the top of an organization.

Profiles of Problem Bosses

We'll explore several profiles of problem managers. Regrettably, you may be a direct report to one right now. Worse yet, you may fit one of the profiles. As you peruse the profiles, candidly ask yourself, "Is this me?" If "yes," then decide what action you must take to cast aside the negative and put on the positive.

The profiles do not include the really bad bosses—those who lie, cheat, are mean spirited and ill tempered. They should be reprimanded, and if necessary, removed from command. You can read about how much harm they cause in Robert Sutton's provocative and candid book, *The No Asshole Rule* (2007).

Ticket Punchers

A "ticket puncher" or careerist is a boss who daily maneuvers to advance in status, power, and especially rank. You can observe this person jockey for whatever is the best stepping-stone to the next tier above. Promotion is paramount. Accomplishment is incidental. They'll do whatever is necessary to get ahead. Ticket punchers are diplomatic to the point of being devious and insecure. They can be seen thriving on process and giving lip service to progress.

Spotlighters

"Spotlighters" require constant attention and center stage in a police agency. They demand recognition for all of the positive results (from their peers, the media, etc.).

When things go sideways, the spotlighter is quick to disappear and then trains the light of accountability on others. Spotlighters rarely share success with others. They'll go so far as to claim the recognition and praise due others.

Megadelegators

A cousin to the spotlighter is the "megadelegator." Seldom does real work soil the desk or hands of a megadelegator. This manager refers to himself or herself as a "participative manager" and sees to it that everyone shares in doing his or her work. Eventually everyone realizes that the boss is essentially accomplishing nothing while they're working their tails off. (This practice is also referred to as a delegation "dump.")

Micromanagers

The "micromanagers" are either insecure or perfectionistic, or they need to control every aspect of work—theirs and those who work for them. To greater or lesser degrees, they probably possess all three characteristics. The micromanagers will sincerely attempt to delegate work. Regrettably, they find it difficult to share the required authority and power to accomplish it. They fear that the job may not be done on time or precisely the way they want it. They are convinced that only they are capable of getting it right. They do not wait for feedback; they seek it incessantly. (As mentioned earlier, if you have a direct report that is untrustworthy, then *micromanagement is the required style.*)

One Best Style: Mine

"One-best-style" managers are like micromanagers in being well intentioned. They truly want to see you do a good job. This manager believes, however, that there is only one particular style of managing that guarantees success—theirs. All other styles are suspected of gross imperfections and even disloyalty. In other words, if you manage exactly like them, you're a winner. If not, you're incompetent.

Gotcha

The "gotcha" police managers wander around not saying a lot—until they see something wrong. Superficially, this sounds right, doesn't it? The inherent frustration with this manager is that the staff never learns what's right in the first place. These managers expect you to read their mind for what they expect of you, what they prefer, and what the goals of the unit are. There's no clarity—only "gotcha."

Control Taking

The "control-taking" manager craves power. Being in command, being right, and being the authority are the central values you'll perceive in this manager. Force is foremost, control is critical, and being correct is imperative. This person thrives on competition rather than collaboration. When in a conflict, this manager has no concept of a win–win model. Only win–lose makes sense. They will define participative management as "I'll manage and you'll participate!"

Job First

The "job-first" police managers relate well to the ticket punchers. This person is 110% job. Some would label this police manager a "workaholic." Everything else in life is secondary or irrelevant, which includes family, friends, recreation, and fun. They especially question the real value of holidays and vacations. After all, they think, "Your agency comprises your family and friends. Your job is your recreation and fun. Holidays and vacations are unfortunate periods of time that you are separated from it."

Job-first managers are big on family events (e.g., picnics, departmental parties, softball leagues). The spouses and children are expected to participate. In the eyes of this manager, your first allegiance is to the agency. The real heroes are those who leave late or return early from a vacation to further the ends of the department.

These managers are not dictatorial, mean, or manipulative. They simply do not comprehend a greater purpose to life than the job.

The Phantom

The "phantom" manager and the "job-first" manager should not be confused with one another. The phantom is uncomfortable with social interaction. This person attempts to remain invisible—his or her responsibilities are carried out by direct reports and e-mail. They are rarely seen and seldom heard. Another term for this person is "isolationist." This person abhors lively, productive collaboration and interchange.

In some cases, a more socially adept staff person will act as a buffer, a spokesperson, or an alter ego for the phantom. Phantoms exert control in a covert manner. They are uneasy empowering others to do their work. They're probably smart and shy. If you work for a phantom manager, be prepared for (1) infrequent face-to-face conversations, (2) at best, a hurried monthly staff meeting, and (3) a tough time getting policy and operational decisions made.

Coping with Problem Bosses

By this point in your working life, it is likely that you have worked for, or have had working for you, a problem manager. Or you may have experienced being managed by

---

STRUCTURED EXERCISE 9-3

PROBLEM BOSS

In this section, I list several typical problem boss (manager/supervisor) types.

1. After review, the group is requested to add any others that they have observed or are aware of.

2. From the complete list, select the one considered the most difficult type to work with or for.

3. Flesh out the identified problem boss persona with other negative traits—and since no one is all bad, be sure to identify some good ones that one might know or have heard about.

4. Now that the character is properly identified, discuss the immediate and long-range consequences to the organization, those working with or under this boss, and others if this behavior is allowed to continue.

5. Have a discussion to evaluate and to select two options, a primary and a backup, most likely to relieve the problem or bring closure.

6. Develop a strategy for implementation and a schedule.

7. Discuss the probable outcomes both in and beyond the workplace.

one of the problem bosses described above. Regardless of the situation, I'll bet you remember it well.

> Good bosses combat the habits and traits of bad bosses minute by minute. Certain characteristics of a bad boss can be positive, depending on specific circumstances. Over the long term, however, bad bosses lead to bad or inefficient police work.

If you thought carefully about how bad bosses operate as compared to the need for "excellence," "quality," and "speed," you've probably discovered that the good bosses are mainly other or organizationally directed. Conversely, the bad bosses are self- or even inner-directed. Good bosses deal in terms of visions and values. Bad bosses are egocentric and uncaring.

Here is some "trickology" for coping with these stay-away-from folks. At first, the following ten coping tactics may appear only downward oriented. Several of them, however, are actually functional in an upward direction.

1. Doing nothing. Avoid the person, maintain a low profile.
2. Acceptance. Elevate your degree of tolerance, patience, and forgiveness.
3. Managing stress. Develop a stress-reduction regimen that includes everything from jogging to biofeedback.
4. Managing your boss. Figure out what your boss wants and needs. Then give some of it to him or her without compromising your performance or integrity.
5. Talking one-on-one. You already know about setting up a win–win situation. Your boss is not a candidate for a one-on-one relationship if he or she can't take criticism, can't listen, and is vindictive.
6. Talking many-on-one. There is usually strength and safety in numbers. However, it is vital that the group forges a plan and executes it in unison.
7. Indirect feedback. This option ranges from anonymous notes to humorous comments, which must be in good taste and not confrontational or belittling.
8. Transfer. Enough said. But make sure of what/who you're going to get.
9. Laddering around your boss. This is a high-risk, low-chance-of-success solution. It may work, but if your boss's boss supports him or her, you will be in deep trouble.
10. Confrontation. This option is best employed as your last resort. Comment carefully on everything that is wrong. Remain calm. Present your case logically to your boss with his or her understanding that you plan to carry it beyond him or her if necessary.

Competency Checkpoints

- Most organizations have a few malcontents—even rule- and lawbreakers—but while small in number, they can destroy the morale and reputation of a police agency.
- Fortunately, we are able to choose our behavior.
- Self-deception is apt to cause us to blame others for our own misdeeds.
- Sloppy selection, wrongful retention, and rationalization promise a problem worker.

- The three "lines" of misconduct are legalistic, professional, and ethical.
- All employees should read and sign any statement of ethics, policies, and code of conduct.
- A direct and legitimate command requires obedience.
- Having an internal affairs unit does not abrogate a manager's need to exercise discipline.
- There are several corrective steps for keeping a problem employee—the first and most vital is empathetic listening.
- Discipline starts and stops at the top.
- It is not your job to get even; it's your job to stop bad behavior.
- Bad bosses exert pervasive negative influence in the agency because of the sheer authority of their position.
- The last resort for dealing with a bad boss is confrontation.

Flexing the Message

1. Revisit Structured Exercise 9-1. Now, ask the following questions of yourself and then act on your responses.

    a. What is one problem you frequently complain about?
    b. Before today, how did you interpret the cause of the problem? How have you blamed others? How have you acted and felt toward them?
    c. In what ways have you dealt with this problem? Are there things you should have done but didn't? Are there things you shouldn't have done but did? What is the deep truth about your conduct?
    d. List three people you have affected negatively by your behavior regarding this problem.
    e. Can you describe how both you and the other person blame each other for the problem?
    f. Focus on one of the three people you listed above. What could you do to help that person? What kind of help would he or she appreciate?

    Whatever you identified above, go do it. Do it immediately if at all possible. If it can't be done immediately, do it as soon as you are able.

2. Contact two police agencies and inquire about their programs or procedures that they use to either prevent or help problem employees. (For example, some police and sheriff's departments employ or contract for psychological counseling services.)

3. Self-deception and self-denial are twin towers of relational disaster. Return to the section on self-deception. Answer the following questions. First, how do you see yourself in your work relationships (e.g., respected and trusted or overworked and unappreciated)? Second, how do you view your co-workers (trustworthy and genuine or liars and fakers)? Think carefully about these two questions.

4. In the section "Helping the Problem Employee" there are a series of recommendations on how to deal with problem employees. What would you add to the list of recommended tactics? Which tactic is least likely to work?

10 POLITICS

> The question is not "Is this a political police job?" but rather "How political is this police job?"

> A political environment is one in which "who" is more important than "what."

I never give them hell. I just tell them the truth, and they think it's hell.
—*Harry S. Truman*

CHAPTER OUTLINE

1. Governance
   a. Strategic
   b. Ethical
   c. Community-Oriented Policing (COP)
   d. Elected and Appointed Bosses
   e. Public Support
   f. Making Staff Aware
2. The News Media
3. The Dark Side of Political Relations
   a. Political Domination
4. The Bright Side of Politics
5. Police Associations and Unions
6. The Justice System
7. Special Interest Groups
   a. Service Clubs
   b. Informal Leadership
   c. Social Activists
8. Internal Politics
   a. Shared Vision
   b. Openness
9. Survival: "Footsteps"

How would you feel if someone called you a "politician"? Or if they stated that your police agency is highly "political"? These words, along with "politics," typically conjure up negative images such as dishonesty, covertness, or at least questionable practices for the benefit of special interest groups or certain individuals. My definition of politics is "the allocation of power." Just as power can be a force for *wrong* as well as *right,* so can politics!

My approach to the political implications of leadership in a police organization centers on the following overlapping *stakeholders*:

- Governance
- The news media
- The dark side of political relations
- The bright side of politics
- Police associations and unions
- The justice system
- Special interest groups
- Internal politics
- Survival footsteps

Many aspiring police managers, especially those who have risen through a legitimate merit system devoid of political spoils, have thought of police managers as apolitical. This is simply untrue.

Police managers do not operate in a vacuum. They are influenced by, and influence, almost every societal structure around them. They function in an administrative, social, and political environment. Whether they should or not is academic here; the fact remains that they do. It is in failing to sense the political waters that a police manager can be openly "boiled" or subliminally "frozen."

This is not to say that professional, apparently effective, politically astute police managers are invulnerable. There will be times (for some at least) when a manager can no longer function effectively. Whatever police managers are, they are not—and *cannot* be—apolitical!

GOVERNANCE

What does not destroy me, makes me grow stronger.
—*Martin Luther King, Jr.*

For most police leaders, the necessity of participating in the external, political environment is a painful and distasteful part of their job. As they encounter mayors, city council members, civil service commissions, and the media in the course of their regular duties, they feel both vulnerable and corruptible. They feel vulnerable because their jobs, reputations, and careers are to some degree hostage to the views that such people have of their performance, and they feel corruptible not only because they might be asked to do something that goes against their own best professional judgment but also because they might be tempted by the allure of celebrity status to spend more time in the limelight than they (or their organization) think they should. Thus, there are police executives who hope to minimize the political aspects of their jobs.

Strategic

Viewed from a strategic perspective, however, this avoidance reaction is a great mistake. The strategic perspective reminds police managers that they depend on continuing credibility with their boss to ensure a continuing supply of resources to their organizations. Without substantial credibility, their freedom to maneuver—to develop and build their organizations—is quite limited. Even more important, police executives need a great deal of operational assistance from private citizens, community groups, and other agencies of government to perform their tasks well.

Ethical

From an ethical perspective, leaders must be accountable to their political environments for their performance and that of the departments they lead. Thus, for both practical and ethical reasons, police managers must respond to their political environments regularly and often.

Community-Oriented Policing (COP)

There is a third perspective, that community-oriented policing (COP) is forging an external police-citizen partnership. This partnership depends on "customer relations." And customer relations means giving the community the service it expects (more on COP in Chapter 13).

Elected and Appointed Bosses

The police manager's relationship with the elected governing body depends somewhat on the particular form of government. An elected sheriff has a decidedly different relationship with the county board of supervisors than does a police manager appointed by the mayor or city council. In the city manager form of government, the police manager's relationship is substantially different from that in the commission form of government, and so on. There are, however, certain commonalities.

In working through the political relationships with other parts of the justice system, the police manager is for the most part dealing with professionals. The system requires certain minimum educational levels in a rather narrow spectrum of fields. The ultimate goals of the system's parts have at least some intrinsic relationship with each other, and there is some common language.

Conversely, elected officials may spring from a great variety of disciplines and backgrounds. They may be professionally educated or have little formal education. They are not screened in the qualifying sense that civil servants are, nor for the most part have they met specific criteria in terms of their elected office—except for the requirements of age, residence, citizenship, and sufficient votes. Elected officials may serve on either a part-time or a full-time basis; they may depend on their elected position for none, some, or all of their income. Most began their political career at the same level in which they currently serve, whereas most police leaders have worked their way up through the ranks, gaining a variety of experiences and continuing education as they go.

These statements are in no way meant to downgrade elected officials, their backgrounds, credentials, or abilities, or those qualities that tend to assist candidates in popular elections. They are meant, rather, to acknowledge a different set of circumstances that must be taken into consideration.

In cities where the elections of representatives are by district or ward, as opposed to citywide, a great many variables of another kind are likely to be present. Election platforms are, in fact, variables in themselves. Fortunately, most platform commitments involving law enforcement at the local level are publicly announced and open for the manager to consider and deal with. Those concessions that may have been made in *private* are the ones most likely to create difficulty for the police manager.

Public Support

Police agencies that have track records of public support are agencies that are publicly respected. All police managers that know what they're doing seek to gain and hold that respect. Public respect is a positive power, one that is not overlooked by other agencies or by legislative and executive branches of government.

Once again, there has always been and no doubt always will be the temptation for some types of politicians to tamper with the normal course of events over which the police have control—through the budget, for example. But those who are prone to tamper are *less* likely to chance it with an agency that has a supportive public.

Community groups are in some fashion influencing policy either routinely or occasionally, have vested interests or causes, can and do shift their emphasis for a variety of reasons, and change in membership. Community groups can be supportive or can throw up roadblocks.

Making Staff Aware

Police managers, cognizant of citizen groups, should translate that knowledge into a workable form for their staff. In my discussions with managers I found few who were not conscious of the various groups, although there was some disagreement as to the potential power of certain groups and therefore the degree to which they required attention.

At times it is difficult to communicate with political and community groups. The result of this difficulty or lack of sensitivity at the operating level has at times created undesirable problems for most police managers. Where this occurred, almost to a person the managers had been forced to invest many personal hours correcting—or attempting to correct—the resulting problems. Police chiefs have been fired or retired and sheriffs have failed to be reelected because their staff was unaware of political dynamics and constraints.

THE NEWS MEDIA

> *The Project for Excellence in Journalism reports that the struggle to create sustainable media brands is driving "hyperlocal" coverage in newspapers; encouraging citizen journalism on the Internet; and giving rise to opinion-driven television personalities.*
> —*Los Angeles Times, March 12, 2007*

The news media is readily seen as a political force by most police managers. Unfortunately, some managers have not yet developed a clear and concise philosophy and policy statements so that their awareness and support can be transmitted to the operating level. Even if the police manager and the publisher understand and support each other's needs, very little is accomplished if staff on both sides do not.

Clearly, the news media needs news and the police are involved in activities that are often newsworthy. The media must present interesting and factual information to survive economically, and the police need an informed public to cultivate concerned, supportive citizens. If the public believes that there are no community problems when in fact there are, it is not likely to support budgets that call for more police officers and more support services.

Although a policy of openness is essential, police departments are not free to release all information. Laws are clear in most respects as to what information can and cannot be made public. Beyond that, some information released prematurely can prejudice a case in such a manner as to require a change of venue. This typically results in trial delays and other costly roadblocks.

Much of what is newsworthy can and should be released in a timely fashion. While openness with the news media is essential for a good working relationship, there will be times that openness becomes frankness to a fault; the resulting backfire may be less than desirable, especially when that frankness doesn't come across in print with the same flavor it had in conversation. When rebuttal or pressure results from such a faux pas, typical responses are "I was misquoted," "My statements were taken out of context," and "In the future I'll tape my comments for my protection." Such comments are efforts to shift blame to the media, but they do not. Instead, they jeopardize the working relationship that exists between the police agency and the media.

Regardless of the philosophies of the police agency and the media, every police officer will not enjoy a positive relationship with every reporter any more than all police officers enjoy positive relationships with all other police officers. Open conflicts are more likely to arise, however, when the police manager appears to be in conflict with the media or when the publisher/editor appears to be in conflict with the police. The message is, then, that managers should set a high and ongoing priority of working toward that desirable relationship and make certain that their staff and all other department members are conscious of this priority.

The point here is to reinforce the focus on the print media as a powerful *political* unit. The editorial policies of the broadcast media regarding the police are even more dramatic and reach more people. It is no surprise to anyone that the media influence how the public views the police—*everywhere*—or how they influence public opinion in general on issues important to the police. Figures 10-1 through 10-4 provide ideas and guidelines on how police agencies can more effectively relate to the media.

Many police departments do not have formalized media policies, a situation that often leads to confusion and misunderstanding. Even in those that do, policy understanding or discipline can be lax to the extent that releases are made by unqualified people. It is especially confusing when an uninformed officer is attempting to answer

---

FIGURE 10-1   News Media Relations Checklist

ALWAYS:
- Dress properly and check your appearance.
- K.I.S.S.—Keep It Short and Simple.
- Avoid technical jargon or terms.
- Tell the truth—The TV camera is a lie detector.
- Be patient—Equipment problems can occur.
- Relax. Take a few deep breaths. Relax.
- Be on time—It helps you avoid anxiety.
- Know whom you are dealing with.
- Ask what they want to know and why.
- Research—Be as well prepared as possible on the subject of the interview.
- Rehearse—Don't try to wing it. You will crash.
- Exude the positive.
- Prove you and your agency really care about the public.
- Be courteous, friendly, and appreciative.
- Know how to handle "off the record."
- Utilize a public relations professional, if possible.
- Look the reporter in the eye.
- Be a professional.

NEVER:
- Lie—Your reputation and your career are on the line.
- Get hostile—You will always lose.
- Assume anything—Know the facts or say you don't know.
- Criticize others.
- Exaggerate—The facts alone are enough.
- Joke about the interview subject.
- Talk too much or disclose too much information.
- Say, "No comment."

FIGURE 10-2 How to Write a Press Release

A press release is a direct statement to the media about an event, program, or policy. It is a basic tool for communicating information about your institution or parole office to the general public through newspapers, radio, and television.

WHEN DO I ISSUE A PRESS RELEASE?

The media are interested primarily in *news*. From a Corrections standpoint, that includes events such as

- escapes;
- major incidents;
- serious accidents; and
- serious crimes committed by inmates/parolees.

Less obvious but still "newsworthy" are stories with *entertainment/human interest* value. Such stories offer an opportunity to be proactive in obtaining positive media attention for the department. As events unfold in your institution or parole region, look for issues or programs that have a positive news value. Some examples:

- Community service projects (e.g., completion of a park or community building)
- Major events (e.g., anniversaries, dedications)
- Inmate work programs or products (especially if new or unusual)
- Innovative programs (e.g., drug treatment, recycling)

WHAT DO I INCLUDE IN A PRESS RELEASE?

Every press release should include four elements:

1. A *heading* that includes
   - the words "PRESS RELEASE" or "NEWS RELEASE";
   - the name of the organization;
   - the contact person(s);
   - a telephone number;
   - the date of release; and
   - the date/time to be released; most will be "FOR IMMEDIATE RELEASE."

   Use your letterhead if you don't have a specialized press release format.
2. A *title* that *briefly* describes what the release is all about (similar to a headline for a newspaper story).
3. A narrative—the story you wish to tell. In journalistic parlance, the narrative is copy. This, too, should be brief and to the point.

   The first paragraph of the narrative is the *lead*. This is the most important element of the story. In most cases, the lead should answer the 5 Ws:

   - Who
   - What
   - When
   - Where
   - Why

   The balance of the narrative should add relevant information and details *in descending order of importance.*

   If your narrative runs more than one page, you should add the word *more* in the bottom right corner of each page after the first. (Subsequent pages should include the name of the organization and the page number as "page ___ of ___.")
4. A *closure* that symbolizes the end of your material. Generally the closure is the number 30 or the pound symbol "# # #" centered at the end of the text.

> FIGURE 10-3   Why Mistakes Happen in News Stories

WE CAUSE ERRORS BY DOING THE FOLLOWING:
- Giving our own facts incorrectly
- Getting angry at reporters
- Getting too familiar with reporters
- Giving old information
- Giving incomplete information
- Saying too much
- Saying too little
- Using jargon
- Giving vague answers
- Being too complicated for the reporter
- Speaking beyond our knowledge
- Answering a question when the answer should be "I don't know"
- Speculating
- Guessing
- Speaking for others
- Leaking information
- Going off the record
- Not having key messages to relay
- Being unavailable
- Not returning phone calls
- Saying "no comment"
- Making irrelevant comments
- Talking too long

THE MEDIA CAUSE ERRORS BY DOING THE FOLLOWING:
- Getting too close to deadlines
- Misquoting
- Jumping to conclusions
- Not getting both sides
- Not going to the source
- Not attempting to get any response
- Moving too quickly
- Using unauthorized sources
- Using unconfirmed material (rumors)
- Using old (not updated) information
- Using material from other media
- Using inappropriate headlines
- Not giving you a chance to review information (your quotes)
- Employing a multi-layered editing system, which creates errors
- Using human reporters, who are prone to human error
- Using inaccurate notes
- Not being knowledgeable about the product/service

Errors cannot be totally eliminated from stories, but if interviewees work to eliminate their own mistakes, while at the same time being aware of what causes miscues on the media side, it can improve accuracy. It is easier to anticipate reporters' slip-ups and attempt to counteract them.

inquiries relating to policy. Conversely, some police policies regarding the media are overly restrictive. For example, there are police agencies that permit only employees who are assigned to the public information team to give press releases or interviews on any subject.

FIGURE 10-4	Handling Hostile Questions and Situations

1. *Don't repeat hostile questions or words you don't like.* Counter them: "That may be your perception, but it is not accurate. In fact . . ."
2. *Counter the loaded question.* For example, a question that accuses might begin with "Haven't you been . . ." The question can be redirected: "What we have been doing is . . ."
3. *Don't be forced into bad choices.* Try this approach: "Neither is accurate. But I believe . . ."
4. *Beware of "charged" wording.* If a question seems charged or slanted to a particularly negative meaning, reword it before answering: "So it's absolutely clear, what you are asking is . . ."
5. *Don't let machine-gun-style questions throw you.* You needn't stand for rudeness. Answer the most appropriate question in a machine-gun series. Say you'll be glad to answer more questions once you've dealt with the first. If necessary, politely but firmly tell the reporter you'll respond if he or she will not interrupt you.
6. *Defuse hecklers.* Hecklers are not unusual at a press conference. Answer curtly while making it apparent you are seeking the next question from the other side of the room. This body language will usually cut off a heckler.
7. *Get out of the interview at the appropriate time.* When the interview has ceased being productive, or is becoming counterproductive, simply say you've time for just one more question. Reporters often appreciate the help calling a news conference over when it is, and you've politely set your limit. Be prepared to follow through once you've announced your limit.
8. *Don't answer more than you've been asked.* More damage is done by interviewees who digress, or expand beyond the questions asked, than by reporters. Don't give in to the temptation, and don't try to fill in awkward silences. To date, no one has found a way to print, broadcast, or telecast silence.
9. If appropriate, *make a follow-up call to the reporter* so that each of you has the opportunity to correct, clarify, or add to the interview. Use the opportunity to reiterate your key message(s) too!

STRUCTURED EXERCISE 10-1

The following is an example of a police organization with a poor media policy. A laterally recruited police chief of one week's tenure was roused by the watch commander at 4 A.M. A house was on fire in the "projects"; an arson probably caused by an incendiary device thrown into a first-floor bedroom where three small children slept and had died. Arriving at the police station, the chief was briefed by the watch commander. Homicide detectives and other officers were on the scene, as were firefighters.

CHIEF: "Have the news media been advised?" (The department did not have an information officer at that time.)

WATCH COMMANDER: "It's policy not to do that. They can get the story from our report later."

CHIEF: "What about photographs?"

WATCH COMMANDER: "They can get them later, if they want."

CHIEF: "Have the media notified now!"

WATCH COMMANDER: "We don't have nighttime numbers."

CHIEF: "Do you know the photographer's name?"

WATCH COMMANDER: "Oh, sure."

CHIEF: "Look in the phone book."

(Continued)

STRUCTURED EXERCISE 10-1   (*Cont.*)

The police chief and the watch commander were on the scene when the photographer, who expressed his bewilderment at his police notification ("Haven't had one of these in years"), arrived. The resulting photographs were graphic without intruding on the bedroom where the children's bodies lay, although the photographer was shown that room. The resulting story and editorial actually proved helpful. A neighborhood where the police typically received no citizen response came alive with support and information, ultimately leading to arrests and convictions.

The chief and media representatives met to discuss what a cooperative media/police policy should be and how it could be attained without compromising either organization's integrity or responsibility. Shortly thereafter, formal policies were developed and adopted. Of course, there are times when the police cannot release information and times when the media reports police indiscretions, which is as it should be.

While these policies may not please some people on either side, these are the rules and they are understood. According to the chief, there are some slip-ups on both sides from time to time, but they are quickly resolved. As the chief said to me, "It's an old adage that all cops have to learn: It's stupid to get yourself into a contest with people who buy their ink by the barrel."

Discussion

1. What went right? What went wrong?
2. What should have occurred?

THE DARK SIDE OF POLITICAL RELATIONS

> *The louder he talked of his honor, the faster we counted the spoons.*
> —*Ralph Waldo Emerson*

The political relationships discussed thus far have been positive—positive in the sense that they deal with the open, healthy realities of police administration. Competitive political relationships will not be new to the experienced police manager.

A discussion of political relationships would not be complete without some attention to the negative side: corrupt, unhealthy, hidden politics.

Public concern for negative political/police relationships dates back to the very inception of law enforcement. The thought that power corrupts and that absolute power corrupts absolutely—that there will always be those who gain through the misuse of power and influence—is not new. The Great Depression of the 1920s and 1930s continues to be the setting for motion picture stories of police corruption, of payoffs and appointments of entire police departments, and of looking the other way while major crime flourished.

The police are important, influential people. Relationships with them are sought after by all kinds of people. Most may be honorable, but many are not. And corruption seldom occurs in a flash—unless, of course, a police employee has placed himself or herself in a vulnerable position. It could be anything—the need for money, for position, for prestige, for concealment of something in the past. As a police manager, you are valuable not only to your organization and community but also to those people who operate on the "dark side" and would like to have you on their team.

Political Domination

For decades, political domination of certain positions or bodies such as the police has been a fact of life. Admittedly, headway in eroding this has been made by the police themselves in the spirit of professionalism. Chiefs have been recruited from high-profile, high-reputation police agencies to make changes. This can be effective, but there must be a commitment from and complete support by all of the elected officials: no favoritism, no ticket fixing, no *anything* that's not legally and morally correct.

"Well, I'll knuckle under just this once"—but when done, a chief soon learns it isn't once, it's for perpetuity. Even when well-qualified managers with the best of intentions are appointed to top positions in the atmosphere described, knuckling under to some political boss is not uncommon. At some point there is a sense that "My career is at stake; the family, the house—all of the continuing expenses, and the job are at stake." Cooperate or step down. It is at that point that one faces a moral dilemma.

It happens that excellent chiefs with excellent track records suddenly leave—under pressure—for unannounced reasons, medical reasons, or some other vague excuse or are dismissed for "incompetence." However, at some point, men and women of honor must either stand and fight in hopes of winning—or move to another opportunity. Neither choice does a great deal for the organization or the community, but sometimes those are the only choices.

The person who wishes to become a city councilman, mayor, or judge—or even to be elected to a state office—must have some local support. The budding police officer who aspires to managerial responsibilities may at times seek to influence the selection process through public support by this kingmaker. And it may become difficult for all of those seeking support to differentiate between legitimate assistance and that which has a price tag attached to it.

> When tarnished police managers fall—and they often do—the influence peddler is still holding court, still respected, and still plying his or her trade. Corrupt politicians can be a very real part of the police manager's life. It is the morally grounded police leader that not only resists them but also exposes them for what they are.

THE BRIGHT SIDE OF POLITICS

A politician would do well to remember he has to live with his conscience longer than he does his constituents.

—Melvin Laird

When the word *politics* is uttered, people usually envision the dark side. Being told that you are "playing politics" is a criticism. Being told you are a "politician" is even worse—fighting words!

> In reality, all of us are, to some degree or another, political in nature. The root of the word *politics* centers on the structure, affairs, or policy of government. Paradoxically, when you take the *al* off *political*, you produce a word that means "artful" and "having keen sight." Police leaders should have both.

Being political or engaging in politics is, in essence, a behavioral characteristic. Alone, it does not imply a positive or negative value. Once you attach the means and purpose to the concept, you become artful or insightful for either the right or the wrong reasons. Unfortunately, if unlawful methods are used to attain a particular purpose and the means are acceptable but the purpose is unethical, then we label it "political" and those involved "politicians." Conversely, if both the methods and the purposes are legitimate, then being artful and insightful can be referred to as "leadership" and those involved "leaders."

Being political for the *right* reasons and in the *right* way is both a plus and, indeed, necessary. If you opt for being apolitical or nonpolitical, are you not choosing to be clumsy and myopic? Being political can generate acts of leadership and statesmanship.

Usually you hear this advice to a police manager: "Don't become political. Avoid politics." This is virtually impossible. It is foolish to eschew being artful and insightful in your job. Remember that your "politics" must be linked to and guided by your moral character.

POLICE ASSOCIATIONS AND UNIONS

> *A constant battle for dominance threatens a relationship; principled negotiation protects it.*
> —*Roger Fisher and Willian Ury*

In Chapter 11 we examine police associations in depth. However, it is worth mentioning here that a fundamental relationship does exist between the police manager and the police association or union. Police managers must be skillful in forging a mutually supportive relationship. The difficulty is not so much in anticipating the employee organization's strengths and weaknesses and needs but rather in the dealing with shifting relationships and styles as representatives change with annual elections.

Like elected officials, association or union representatives can be expected to represent a wide range of education, backgrounds, personal abilities, personal goals, levels of sophistication, and the like. Some representatives will be easy to work with: keeping confidences, acting professionally, presenting issues in workable fashion. Others may not have such attributes and may feel a need to make outlandish statements. "I had to go in and kick the old man's desk to get this or that concession" is not atypical of what may be said, perhaps out of false bravado or simply because that representative perceives such behavior as a way to impress peers and electors. Or he or she may challenge the manager in front of others, especially large groups. Whatever the basic reason for this type of behavior, an obvious lack of sophistication exists.

Wise police managers recognize the various strengths and weaknesses of the representatives who confront them; wiser still are those who have the insight and patience to invest in training union representatives to accomplish what is possible and proper in a manner acceptable to all concerned. Often, these representatives have great long-range managerial potential, and lessons learned at this stage can benefit the department at a later time.

THE JUSTICE SYSTEM

Plato made the fatal error of equating knowledge with virtue and assuming that if one knows what is right he will do what is right.
—*Thomas Cahill*

Two opposite and distinct descriptions tend to surface in discussions of the justice system. One is that the various components are interdependent and operate with some semblance of a system. The second considers the various components to be independent and autonomous. The courts are, of course, the component most likely to be viewed as free from influence. The truth is that a variety of relationships exist with even the most autonomous court; with those, the political relationship is perhaps the most delicate.

It does little good for a police department to launch a major drive on illegal prostitution if the prosecutor believes that prostitution prosecution should have a low priority. The prosecutor must have priorities, because there are often many more defendants than there are courtrooms and judges. To carry it further, the police and prosecutor may set prostitution as a high priority, but if the court does not, a stalemate continues to exist.

It may not be the court itself but the probation department that takes an opposing view. This can occur if it finds that detention facilities are in short supply and makes recommendations to the court that are likely to result in putting prostitutes right back on the street. The fact is that even though each justice system component makes its decisions properly within its own legal framework, there are no guarantees that all are working toward a common goal, at least in a manner that is likely to relieve the original problem as seen by the citizens and as interpreted by the police.

Some law enforcement agencies, perhaps through frustration, attempt to change the situation through public castigation: "The D.A. only wants to prosecute cases he knows he can win"; "The D.A. doesn't want to try cases—only bargain them away"; "The probation department is filled with sociological do-gooders"; "The judge is on a rehabilitation kick"; and so on.

Politically astute managers will make certain that they are communicating positively with representatives of the criminal justice system's components. Offering an explanation of the problem on a personal basis, without attempting to tell the other party his or her business, is much more likely to produce desirable results than will the confrontational approach.

SPECIAL INTEREST GROUPS

Ultimately the choice we make is between service and self-interest.
—Peter Block

Service Clubs

Groups formed for specific special interests are often overtly political in nature. Perhaps not so obvious, but far from apolitical, are the organizations and groups identified as service clubs, such as church clubs, women's clubs, men's clubs, lodges, chambers of commerce, and the like. These, while basically not politically oriented, have the capability and history of becoming political when confronted with specific or special interest issues.

For example, business-oriented groups are more likely to become interested in or exert pressure on issues that affect business. Parking enforcement is the example most often given. These groups, or at least some members, are likely to become involved in the selection of a new police manager, or at least attempt to. They also tend to involve themselves in issues such as curfews, loitering, "dragging" (slow vehicular parades), high-crime-rate problems, and ethnic gangs.

One of the issues with special interest groups is that they tend to have "experts" in their membership who may enjoy some level of expertise or none at all. In either case, if their area of interest focuses on the police, it is important that the manager meet with these groups personally or be adequately represented. In all likelihood, the groups will be capable of directing some public attention to the topic, attention that can be either positive or negative.

Informal Leadership

Successful groups tend to remain intact, though their original emphasis may shift. Membership will usually be in an evolutionary state, which adds to the flexibility of their interests.

In almost every community there exists somewhere an informal leadership group. Some are informal to such a degree that they sometimes have no chair, no set of rules or dues, or even no regularly constituted place or time to meet. Although informal in terms of not having any official sanctions, they have regular meetings and an elected hierarchy and concern themselves with community issues. "Informal leadership," then, means those people or groups of people whose opinions are respected and sought after by—or fostered on—those who have been elected into formal governing bodies or who are "wannabes" (testing the water).

Social Activists

Groups made up on the basis of social causes have always been present but have never been more vocal than in current times. Groups formed to gain equal employment, to change employment standards, and to fight social injustices are proliferating. While some are more active or more effective than others, none can or should be ignored. Although many lack strong leadership, have never heard of *Robert's Rules of Order*, and have little or no operating capital, all are very real political forces.

In earlier times, a certain minimum level of cohesiveness and sophistication was necessary to consider issues. Such is no longer the case. Although it may be difficult to identify leadership among social activists (at least in some of the newly emerging groups), their need and right to be heard, and to be potentially politically effective, are great.

Whether the group is large, highly sophisticated, well recognized, and respected by the total community at large or is small, newly emerging, and focused on a specific cause, the police manager's need for communication and credibility is the same.

INTERNAL POLITICS

People of integrity are the same in private as they are in public.
—*Joel Osteen*

Internal politics is not a problem; it is a situation. A problem can be solved, while a situation is constantly present and must be dealt with hour by hour, day by day.

A "political environment" is one in which "who" is more important than "what." If the boss proposes an idea, the idea gets taken seriously. If someone else proposes a new idea, it is ignored. There are always "winners" and "losers," employees who are building their power and people who are losing power. Power is concentrated (the opposite of concentrated power is empowerment), and it can be wielded arbitrarily. One person can determine another's fate, and there is no recourse to that determination. The wielding of arbitrary power over others is the essence of authoritarianism—so, in this sense, a highly charged, political environment can be an authoritarian environment even if those possessing the power are not in the official positions of authority.

Very few police employees truly want to work in police agencies corrupted by internal politics and game playing. This is why unethical internal politics is the first of many organizational "givens" challenged by professional police managers.

Challenging the grip of internal politics and hidden agendas starts with building shared *vision*. Without a genuine sense of common vision and values, there is nothing to motivate people beyond self-interest. But the police leader can start building an organizational climate dominated by "merit" rather than power grabs—where doing *what is right* predominates over *who wants what done*.

A nonpolitical climate also demands "openness"—both the norm of speaking openly *and* honestly about important issues and the capacity to continually challenge one's own thinking. The first might be called participative openness; the second, reflective openness. Without openness it is generally impossible to break down the game playing that is deeply embedded in most organizations. Together, *vision* and *openness* are the antidotes to internal politics and deceit.

Shared Vision

If employees are presumed to be motivated only by self-interest, then a police organization automatically develops a highly political style, with the result that people must continually look out for their self-interest in order to survive.

An alternative assumption is that, over and above self-interest, people truly want to be part of something larger than themselves. They want to contribute toward building something important. And they value doing it with others. When police departments foster shared vision, they draw forth this broader commitment and concern. Building shared vision, as discussed in Chapter 4, leads people to acknowledge their own larger dreams and to hear one another's dreams. When managed with sensitivity and persistence, building shared vision begins to establish a sense of trust that comes naturally with self-disclosure and honestly sharing our highest aspirations. Getting started is as simple as convening small groups and asking the participants to talk about *what's really important* to them.

Openness

Many police managers and organizations pride themselves on "being open" when, in fact, they are simply playing a new, more advanced game. This is because there are two different aspects of openness—participative and reflective. Unless the two are integrated, the behavior of "being open" will not produce real openness.

Participative Openness

Participative openness is not only the freedom to speak your mind but also the expectation to do so. Participation is one of two key components of empowerment, and community-oriented policing relies on empowered police employees. In some police organizations, it is almost a rule; they become "participative management" departments. It becomes a norm that everyone gets to state his or her view.

Participative openness may lead to more "buy-in" on certain decisions, but by itself it will rarely lead to better-quality decisions because it does not influence the thinking behind people's positions. In the terms of personal mastery, it focuses purely on the "means" or process of interacting, not on the "results" of that interaction. For example, people might say, "That was a great meeting; everybody got to express their views," instead of judging the quality of decisions and actions taken over time. This is why police managers find participative management lacking something.

Reflective Openness

While participative openness leads to police employees *speaking out*, "reflective openness" leads to people *looking inward*. Reflective openness starts with the willingness to challenge our own thinking—to recognize that any certainty we ever have is, at best, an assumption about the world. No matter how compelling it may be, no matter how fond we are of "our idea," it is always subject to test and improvement. Reflective openness lives in the understanding "I may be wrong, and the other person may be right." It involves not just examining our own ideas but also objectively examining others' thinking.

Reflective openness is based on skills, not just good intentions. These include recognizing "leaps of abstraction," distinguishing espoused theory from practiced theory, and becoming more aware of and responsible for what we are thinking and not saying.

STRUCTURED EXERCISE 10-2

CASE STUDY OF POLITICS

You are a new police chief. Shortly after being appointed, you discover that two of your officers, one a lieutenant and one a former sergeant, had been disciplined a year earlier. Prior to that, these two, aided by the news media, had captured the attention and admiration of the justice system, city government, and citizens alike. They were assigned to the detective bureau and were part of a special drug enforcement team. The two were directly responsible for a substantial number of drug-related arrests and drug seizures. Because of their respective ages and style, the media dubbed them "Batman and Robin." The cases had been developed over a period of time, primarily through the use of warrants. All of those arrested were known drug users and distributors. When arrested, all had substantial drug supplies. And all had previous arrest records—there had been community pressure "to do something about the drug problem."

The popularity of "Batman and Robin" later waned with many when it was discovered that "confidential witnesses" whose names were used to secure the warrants were in fact in prison at the time and had no contact with the officers. Interestingly enough, citizens in the affected areas did not share in this criticism—apparently, an "ends justified the means" attitude prevailed—although the arrestees' charges were later dismissed. Your predecessor recommended discharge

for both officers. The personnel review board agreed. The city council, taking past performance into consideration, reduced the punishment to a division transfer for the lieutenant and demotion to detective for the sergeant, placing his name at the top of the promotion list. Many similar arrests made by these officers were important and untainted.

Shortly after your arrival, you became aware of the situation when you observed that this well-touted detective was always at his desk shuffling papers—reading reports, making assignments, and the like. Further inquiry informed you that the district attorney had wanted to prosecute but settled for keeping the man off the street—no arrests, no reports, and no courtroom testimony. He was persona non grata!

Your dilemma: You cannot discharge the man, you cannot use him in a function that he was actually very good at, and you cannot permit him to testify in any case. He fills a position that could and should be filled by a working detective. You certainly could not promote him if an opening occurred. And you don't wish to destroy any future working relationships that you may be able to develop with the district attorney and courts. But it is your duty to get this man back to meaningful work. Discuss this case as a group but form your solutions independently, keeping in mind the various attitudes, including those of citizens who were supportive. Compare solutions.

SURVIVAL: "FOOTSTEPS"

> *So yes, culture matters, but culture is nested in contexts, not genes, and as those contexts and local leaders change and adapt, so too can culture.*
> —*Thomas L. Friedman*

Regardless of your expertise in managerial roles and your ability to function effectively in the political arena, there are times when it is impossible to continue in a given environment, as many "credentialed" managers can attest. In the last several years I have become increasingly aware of sudden, radical job changes by reputable, successful, seasoned police leaders. The jobs to which they have moved have not always been a step up; some have gone into totally different fields for less pay. What would motivate a successful manager to exchange his or her position for one of equal or even less stature, considering all of the unknowns and financial expenses that career changes bring? After wending my way through a maze of symptoms, I found that a common thread finally began to emerge.

The bottom line, as one police manager put it, was, "I heard the footsteps coming up behind me." Another said simply, "My early warning signals said 'Go.'" A few could point to specific events, but most could not put their finger on any single factor—"It was just a feeling," a feeling of survival, of moving under their own power at their own discretion while still on top. "Better to move to an interim job at the right time than to overstay my welcome."

Career moves of this nature were most always described as difficult; they did not occur without a great deal of thought and sometimes pain—and often relief. Few of those interviewed thought they were compromising; they were simply surviving to fight another day, in another place. There are undoubtedly a multitude of factors that contribute to these unexpected career moves:

1. Police leaders tend to be younger these days and are therefore politically vulnerable for a greater period of time than were their earlier counterparts. Forty-year-old police chiefs are no longer an oddity.
2. Many police managers are employed at the pleasure of the hiring authority and can be discharged without cause (e.g., through political pressure on the hiring authority).
3. Elected governing officials change from time to time. Their replacements may have hidden agendas or may not be in agreement with older members regarding police-related issues.
4. Today's police organizations/unions are politically oriented. Votes of no confidence against the chief are not unusual, and the organizations frequently have a political relationship with hiring authorities and elected governing officials.

There appears to be a process of legitimization of what has in the past been seen as a weakness: making a career move when one hears "the footsteps"; developing an early warning system and reacting to it on our own terms. (It should be noted here that, although the average tenure of a police chief is about five years, many remain with one agency a great deal longer.) Others have a history of periodic moves, particularly when they've done an outstanding job in one department and are specifically recruited to do the same in another location.

Some police manager discharges are certainly warranted. But when a leader is doing the job professionally and well and leaving is a surprise ("he or she was incompetent," retiring for medical reasons, and so on, without further explanation), it is shocking and disturbing to the organization and community and to the manager's family.

Some police managers have been able during the hiring process to negotiate employment contracts. These, of course, are a two-way street—sort of a "prenuptial agreement" between police managers and city/county government bodies—that formalize a number of important issues, such as salaries, adjustments, personal benefits, performance expectations, tenure, and buyout.

Although it may not be pleasant to be employed where working relationships have become unpleasant, it does, except in cases in which one is dismissed for cause, provide the latitude of time or remuneration for orderly transition. Social astuteness can in many cases be as simple as awareness, appreciation, and understanding of responsibilities, priorities, and limitations of others who function in the same arena. That is not to suggest a compromise of your integrity or value system. It is to acknowledge that police managers can make more acceptable and supportable decisions when they are aware of the legitimate functions and goals of others, as well as those who would misuse the police.

The really bright police leaders have intuitive early warning systems that are essential to their sense of survival in the field, if not in a particular organization. They have a sense of when their decisions, for whatever reason, are no longer acceptable, a sense that tells them it is time to move on at their convenience.

Competency Checkpoints

- Politics can be a force for wrong as well as right.
- Many police managers try to (or want to) minimize the political aspects of their jobs.
- There are considerable differences between the nature and background of police managers and those of elected officials.
- Line officers should be made aware of the political issues and stakeholders in their community.
- The news media is an extraordinarily powerful political stakeholder.
- A police association/union can be a strong advocate or an equally powerful detractor. It is critical that open communications be maintained between the union and management.
- All police agencies experience internal politics. It is important that politics be integrated into a shared vision of what the department stands for and where it should be going.
- Participative and reflective openness are necessary to elevate trust in and within a political work environment.

Flexing the Message

1. There is an ongoing debate over which office is the more "political"—sheriff or police chief. The simple answer is, "The sheriff is the more political—it's an elective office!" But, in reality, it all depends on the working environment. In some cases, the office of police chief can be highly political.
2. When the United States gained its independence, it was led by six world-class leaders. Who were they? Were any of them politicians? How many world-class leaders does the United States have right now? Who are they? Why did you select them?
3. What is the difference (if any) between a statesman and a politician? Who are the leading global statesmen in the world today? Why did you select them?
4. Peruse the media for articles/stories about politicians. Within the past seven days, which politicians were discussed and why? How many of the articles were favorable, and how many were negative?
5. What can be done to enhance the speed and accuracy of interactions with the news media? Basically, how can news media–police relations improve?

11 UNIONS

There are always several excuses why police management and union leadership cannot forge a working relationship, but there is never one good reason.

With more than a decade of well-publicized recent history, the existence and at least some functions of police employee organizations (unions) will not be a new subject for even the newest recruit.

There is no right to strike against the public safety by anybody, anywhere, anytime.

—*Calvin Coolidge, telegram to Samuel Gompers regarding the Boston police strike, September 14, 1919*

CHAPTER OUTLINE

1. The Right to Strike
   a. Binding Arbitration
2. The Police Employee Bill of Rights
   b. Employee Organizations
   c. The Impact of Unions on Police Professionalization
   d. Membership and Rank
   e. Collective Bargaining
   f. Restructuring of a Relationship
3. Work Stoppage and Job Actions
   g. No-Confidence Vote
4. Negotiations
   h. Anticipation
   i. Training
5. Quality of Working Life
   j. Top Manager Committed
   k. Top Union Leader Committed
6. Eliminating Surprises and Reducing Conflict
7. A Model Approach

8. Competency Checkpoints

9. Flexing the Message

The police labor movement grew out of the same conditions that triggered the birth and development of industrial unions decades earlier. Low salaries, long hours, no job security, poor benefits, and controls were all perceived to be unreasonable, and there was little, if any, organizational support in job-incurred conflicts. The police labor movement was also propelled by the open circumvention of statutory employment procedures—such as eligibility, assignments, promotion, tenure, and even discipline—by political activists.

The police labor movement, supported at times by sympathetic and supportive governments at the various levels and even by some police managers, has made impressive strides in the improvement of working conditions and benefits.

This is not to say that all police officers everywhere have been positively affected to the same extent. Pay is generally appropriate for the geographical area, overtime work is paid at a higher rate, job security is built in, safety equipment is furnished by law in many states, and uniforms are furnished in most departments; memoranda of understanding (MOUs), a written management–union agreement, are typical. Today, police officers have much better working conditions than they did in the past, yet there is still room for improvement. The associations (unions), of course, did not accomplish all of these changes by themselves.

Some unions have challenged managerial prerogatives in such a way that police managers feel constrained in fulfilling their duties. The days of police management dominance over labor relations are gone forever. So is the era in which the chief or sheriff could simply delegate responsibility for labor–management relations functions to other departmental personnel. Police employees not only want a greater piece of the action in terms of higher salaries and benefits, they also seek more empowerment over their work environment.

THE RIGHT TO STRIKE

In every moment of our existence, we are in that field of all possibilities where we have access to an infinity of choices.
—*Deepak Chopra*

Historically, in many states public employees did not have the right to strike. This was based on widely accepted legal interpretations and various conflicting appellate cases. In general, most state courts hold that strikes by public-sector employees are neither illegal nor tortious. A public employee's right to strike typically is not unlimited. The legislature may prohibit strikes by certain categories of public employees. The legislature may conclude that certain public employees perform such essential services that a strike would invariably result in imminent danger to the public health and safety.

The following standard is used on a case-by-case basis: Public employee strikes are not unlawful unless or until it is clearly demonstrated that such strikes create a substantial and imminent threat to the health and safety of the public. The court stated, "This standard allows exceptions in certain essential areas of public employment" (e.g., the prohibition against firefighters and law enforcement personnel going on strike).

Throughout the United States, legislatures continue to introduce legislation that would provide clear-cut guidelines for the resolution of labor–management conflict. However, little if any of this legislation has found its way into law. Those proposals generally contain items such as *binding arbitration* that, although desired by the unions, are cause for concern to governments.

Binding Arbitration

Binding arbitration for local governments and police managers is a mixed blessing. On one hand, it alleviates the concern that a general strike by police would leave a community defenseless or badly crippled, as well as causing political unrest. On the other, it is viewed as removing the decision-making process from the elected body held fiscally responsible by the taxpayers and placing it in the hands of "outsiders" who have no responsibility to the community.

Binding arbitration is also believed by many to deter or cut short the process of good-faith bargaining; some unions will go to the arbitration process as quickly as possible in the belief that their proposals are more likely to be favored. In some states there is an appeal process if either party contests the decision. Appeals, however, are usually predicated on legal error, collusion, or fraud.

The bottom line is that the concern of elected officials is valid. While it is unlikely that an independent arbiter's decision would bankrupt a local government, it could certainly force officials to reconsider budget priorities that would affect other programs and in turn the community.

THE POLICE EMPLOYEE BILL OF RIGHTS

I found myself highly critical of any leader who failed to lead by example.
—*Major Dick Winters, Easy Company, 101st Airborne, U.S. Army, WWII*

For decades, police officers have repeatedly been reminded of their responsibilities to the community, to the agency, to management, and to their co-workers. The union movement in the police service has focused on another *R*, that of personal rights. In this instance, we find the police employee organization attempting to formalize such rights, as well as others of a protective nature, in management–labor contracts. In fact, many collective bargaining contracts negotiated after 1970 contain a police officers' bill of rights, a document extending broad protection to police officers during disciplinary matters and, more specifically, internal investigations. It was in the 1970s that states began to legislate in this area. Sections 3300 through 3311 of the California Government Code are referred to as the Public Safety Officers' Procedural Bill of Rights Act. The following are titles of sections covered.

Similar provisions are contained in the state of Illinois's Uniform Peace Officers' Disciplinary Act, effective 1983, revised 1991, Sections 725 through 725/7. They appear by title as follows:

Act 725. Uniform Peace Officers' Disciplinary Act

50 ILCS 725/1   Local Government

725/3.1	Place of interrogation
725/3.2	Disclosure of information to subject of interrogation regarding nature of investigation and complainants
725/3.3	Time of interrogation
725/3.4	Disclosure to subject of interrogation of officer in charge, interrogators, and others present
725/3.5	Duration of interrogation sessions
725/3.6	Abusive and offensive language prohibited at interrogation
725/3.7	Record of interrogation—transcript
725/3.8	Advice of rights (before interrogation)
725/3.9	Right to counsel—presence of representative of collective bargaining unit
725/3.10	Admissions or confessions obtained in violation of law
725/3.11	Polygraph or chemical tests
725/4	Constitutional and legal rights

§ 4. The rights of officers in disciplinary procedures set forth under this Act shall not diminish the rights and privileges of officers that are guaranteed to all citizens by the Constitution and laws of the United States and of the State of Illinois.

| 725/5 | Application of Act |

§ 5. This Act does not apply to any officer charged with violating any provisions of the Criminal Code of 1961, or any other federal, State, or local criminal law.

| 725/6 | Supersedure of provisions by collective bargaining agreements |

§ 6. The provisions of this Act apply only to the extent there is no collective bargaining agreement currently in effect dealing with the subject matter of this Act.

| 725/7 | Retaliatory actions prohibited |

§ 7. No officer shall be discharged, disciplined, demoted, denied promotion or seniority, transferred, reassigned or otherwise discriminated against in regard to his or her employment, or be threatened with any such treatment as retaliation for or by reason of his or her exercise of the rights granted by this Act.

Illinois's Section 725/6 is an interesting qualifying provision. As can be seen by the two examples, which are reasonably standard, some states prefer to soften the title (Bill of Rights), while others cut to the heart of the matter (Uniform Disciplinary Act); some contain additional areas, such as political activities provisions. This does not necessarily mean that such additions have been overlooked in those that do not have them; more often than not, they are covered in other state code sections.

Employee Organizations

Police officers' bills of rights are fairly common, as are statutes recognizing public employee organizations and setting forth certain functions, such as meeting and conferring in good faith (collective bargaining) on issues relating to working conditions and compensation. Most states have adopted some form of bargaining for some, and in most cases for all, of their employees. But a few states still do not have formalized statutory bargaining provisions.

Typically, collective bargaining legislation covers the following:

- **The right to join an employee organization or abstain**
- **Conferences for the purposes of meeting and conferring "in good faith" on issues affecting working conditions, wages, and benefits**
- **Memoranda of agreement on mediation when an employee organization and the public agency fail to reach an agreement**

The Impact of Unions on Police Professionalization

A professionally led department is one in which efficiency and managerial rationality are emphasized to the exclusion (or attempted exclusion) of politics, except within the framework of positive political relationships. The struggle for professional status involves the quest for the trappings of professionalism, including autonomy, professional authority, and the power to determine the character and curriculum of the training process—empowerment.

In many instances, police unions have openly challenged management's lead in achieving professional status. Issues develop around advanced education, lateral transfer, development of a master patrolman classification, and changes in recruitment standards.

Police unions appear to push for advanced education and master patrol officer proposals as leverage in their effort to obtain more money for all their members, whereas management sees them as a way of rewarding individual achievement. In my experience, unions have tended to be most supportive in these proposals when tuition and book costs are assumed by the organization and incentives are offered. Lateral transfer, on the other hand, would foster increased professionalization in that increased mobility would help shift the locus of specialization from the organization to the occupation.

More recently, union representatives and chiefs have begun to see and support each other's point of view, with some adjustments. For example, some police departments with union/association backing have acquired often-cited professionalism benchmarks and lateral recruitment and have maintained the following high standards with incentives:

1. Salary above recruit level, but not at top step, depending on previous tenure and experience.
2. Use of aggregate tenure (meeting time-in-rank requirement) to compete for promotions after successful probationary period.

3. Sick leave benefit accumulation transferred, in terms of emergency necessity. For example, if a lateral recruit left behind an accumulation of 30 days sick leave, he or she could draw up to that amount, working off that draw by time on the job.
4. Vacation leave computation formula after one year (not to exceed a certain number of days) aggregated with time on the new job.
5. Time-on-job prerequisite for promotion appointment satisfied by previous tenure aggregated after probationary period.
6. Retirement and medical benefits.

Membership and Rank

The question arises as to whether or not officers rising through the ranks are permitted to retain association/union memberships. The answer is that they may do so unless prohibited by law. However, typically they are restricted, by law, from certain association functions. There are some states that prohibit management personnel from participating in such association activities as voting and negotiations.

Conversely, association member chiefs are not prohibited from appearing in arbitration hearings as witnesses for either side. Such occurrences would probably relate to personnel matters and interpretation of such documents as the police manuals, orders, and MOUs. Preparedness in these areas is always essential.

Collective Bargaining

Like other public employees in most states, police have the legal right to participate in collective bargaining—with some restrictions, since they are a primary source of public safety. Like firefighters, the police are usually restricted from striking.

A very good reason for limiting unions with which police officers can affiliate is the following 1993 Chicago example. City streets and sanitation workers, represented by the local Teamsters union, voted to go on strike. To add to the intimidation, union representatives threatened to picket police and fire stations to prevent the delivery of fuel. The Chicago Fraternal Order of Police (FOP) Lodge leadership took the following stance: "Let them do it; we can get gas at any filling station in town, and we'll continue to do our job."

But what's wrong with the bargaining process? It has always occurred to me that both management and the union begin the bargaining process with a "stork dance." The union—or Police Benefit Association, or whatever—usually begins the process with a list of outlandish demands, and the management negotiators begin with an unreasonable list of salary and benefit cuts. Then both sides go out and violate the bargaining (process) fiat of confidentiality, which upsets everybody else. Elected officials bow their necks, and so does the police membership. Then the veiled threats leak out, and everyone becomes more upset. This can go on for months, even years, sometimes without a contract. The police union concerns become the central focus—not catching crooks.

Restructuring of a Relationship

From the police manager's perspective, the growing prevalence and power of police unions need not be perceived as a threat but rather as a restructuring of a relationship that may, in fact, provide benefits for the proper management of our cities and counties.

For example, unions have been able to remove political influence by insisting on job tenure provisions and, in some cases, merit promotion.

The grievance procedure, which is a standard part of a union contract, forces management and supervisory employees to discuss problems openly as they occur rather than to permit festering sores to develop within the police agency. Union stewards can be trained to assist supervisory personnel in spotting potential employee-related problems, such as sick leave abuse and unsafe working conditions, and practices that can develop and cause long-range harm to the agency.

> **For police chiefs and sheriffs, then, the issue is not to resist or fight employee organizations nor, conversely, to actively promote the unionization of police employees. The issue is to identify and effectively protest their authority in a changing labor–management relationship.**

Whatever else union members are, police managers must never lose sight that they are not contractual employees who come and go. These are career employees, an integral part of their team. Managers must continue to be aware of departmental and employee needs. Too many chiefs with whom I have spoken hold the opinion that "if they think they need it, let them negotiate for it next time around." This may be the posture of some public bargaining negotiators.

It is this kind of thinking, coupled with poor ground rule agreements, that has led union negotiators to enter the bargaining process with traditional management prerogatives on their agenda. Some management negotiators see those issues as "throwaways," in place of money or other benefits; police managers must *not*! Some of the restructuring of the management union connection includes the following.

Management "Unit Determination"
Should the supervisor be identified as a line employee, a manager, or a separate entity? I believe that the supervisor is a separate third party who acts as an intermediary between the police manager and the police line employees. Usually, this is not the case. The majority of police supervisors are union members. Lieutenants and above are counted as management.

Personnel Benefits
Police managers must always analyze their employees' personnel benefits and working conditions in relation to other law enforcement agencies and other public employees. Some issues may be beyond their authority if those issues are controlled by legislation or civil service regulations; they can, however, initiate action to make needed changes. (I do not subscribe to holding legitimate issues, especially safety issues, for the bargaining table.) Chiefs and sheriffs must initiate open communication at all times and be immediately alert to personnel issues. (If they do not assume this responsibility, some other person or group eventually will.)

Grievances
A grievance is an employee's complaint that he or she has been treated unjustly by police management. A system that permits police employees to resolve their grievances fairly and expeditiously can operate within any existing police organizational structure. A grievance system may be viewed as a mechanism for maintaining or increasing

employee morale and as another channel of internal communication. With an effective grievance system, the police manager can receive valuable feedback that is useful in pinpointing organizational problems. Supervisors unfamiliar with or careless about interpretations of the MOU or contractual agreements, especially as related to personnel-oriented problems, are a way of avoiding grievances.

Management Rights

In the past, public employee organizations usually dealt directly with local government in the areas of personnel benefits; police managers were not involved. Collective negotiation has changed that situation. Police managers who do not involve themselves in the negotiation process could find their management capability seriously restricted!

> While the primary concern with the negotiation process by elected officials has been fiscal in nature, the police manager's concerns go far beyond that. The trend has been for unions, in addition to their interest in salary and monetary benefits, to encroach on areas reserved as "management prerogatives." These include such issues as work hours, minimum staffing, disciplinary procedures, assignments, and promotional processes. If not careful, a manager could accidentally surrender the very authority and power he needs to do his job.

Involved but Not at the Table

While I have expressed my opinion that managers (chiefs) must be involved in the negotiations process, it is not my suggestion that they be involved directly in negotiations, even where permitted. This could expectedly place them in an uncomfortable adversarial position with either city (county) management or the POA. While any number of "informed" informal conversations ("feelers") may occur, negotiations in the pure sense are conducted at the bargaining table and are a confidential negotiation process.

Negotiation teams are kept small to avoid confusion and therefore should include people who are versed in the issues, the ground rules, and the constraints of confidentiality. Each team is headed by a spokesperson (negotiator) to whom team members offer advice, usually during caucus sessions. Some groups on one or both sides choose to have professional labor negotiators as their spokespersons. Others choose to use lay negotiators; for example, a ranking administrative aide to the appointed local government administrator, the regular union representative, or even a POA member selected for that function. FOP, for example, trains police officer members as negotiators. Larger cities or counties will often have a labor relations unit that will be involved in some manner.

Whoever else is present, there should always be a very knowledgeable ranking administrative aide who reports directly to the chief. The chief is well advised as negotiations progress and provides input through his or her aide, who is empowered to speak to the team, and especially the negotiator, for the chief. This usually occurs when negotiation sessions break so that teams may caucus.

Although the chief is interested in all parts of the process, her primary responsibility is related to bargaining issues that could impair the way in which she and her management team lead the organization. This, of course, does not preclude chiefs from providing the city or county manager with supportive information relating to salaries and benefits (a form of private lobbying in which chiefs can support an issue that they believe in strongly for officers' needs without creating a conflict in their relationship with management).

WORK STOPPAGE AND JOB ACTIONS

If everything seems to be going well, you have obviously overlooked something.

—*Anonymous*

In 1973 the National (Criminal Justice) Advisory Commission recommended that every state enact prohibitive job action/strike legislation. This has not occurred in every state. However, police strikes are illegal in many jurisdictions, either by statute, ordinance, contract, or charter. For example, FOP's national charter expressly forbids strikes.

STRUCTURED EXERCISE 11-1

The following worst-case scenario actually occurred when some city managers and police officers associations (POAs) were first being introduced to meet and discuss concepts. The scenario is the recollection of a professional labor negotiator's first experience with city government when representing a police officers association.

Board members of the POA had developed some information regarding relative salaries and the like. They had also prepared a substantial "want list" of management prerogatives they believed might "be nice" to have control of. The negotiator expressed some concerns at the number and areas of "wants." "Well, at least try," he was told.

The city's uninitiated negotiator was the city manager, who met with the POA's professional negotiator in private (before "teams") to negotiate. The city manager appeared a little uncomfortable at first but seemed to warm up. Wage negotiations, which the POA negotiator had advised would be aided by conceding "a few" perks the POA wanted, were essentially completed. As he read the "want list," the city manager "just seemed to stare, as if unbelieving." The negotiator expected an explosion, but at last the manager smiled, slapped the table with his hands, and said, "Sounds good to me!" The negotiator "could have cried," but he had done his job! The chief, who was not consulted, was left in a bind. The city manager was happy because he saved some money.

Some of the readers have no doubt observed or heard of similar blunders. Discuss this case, including the elements leading to the faux pas. Discuss any similar blunders reported and ways to avoid them.

I like to believe that most labor problems such as these have all been rectified. They have not. That is why other agencies must intervene from time to time—creating concern and unrest.

Another option, however, identified by union officials as *informational picketing*, was discussed and received union support in most cases. Police managers are usually opposed. Legally done and properly orchestrated, it was believed (by association representatives) to be most effective in terms of getting the issue out to the public and to elected officials who might not have been completely informed.

Off-duty police officers in uniform, supported by family members, carry informational signs and march in front of government buildings. This is scheduled for strategic times in terms of who will be present—for example, significant elected officials. The news media are informed of the date and time, to ensure the broadest coverage. Management had better know the issues, notify proper government officials, and be prepared for media interest in its comments. Cautious and well-planned response is recommended—hopefully, by his or her boss as well.

The desirable result is for supportive political pressure. Typically, where picketing has not been confined to public places, such as at elected officials' homes and businesses, court injunctions have followed.

‖ STRUCTURED EXERCISE 11-2

STRIKE

Police strikes have occurred from time to time. The longest strike in recent history occurred in 1979 in Great Falls, Montana. The uniqueness is not only the strike length (28 days), but also the events prior to and during the event. Great Falls boasts a population of 58,500 served by a police force of 90 sworn and nonsworn personnel.

The Incident

Negotiations had broken down. An impasse had occurred, not so much over financial issues, although they did exist, but related more to communication and philosophical problems regarding individual rights. The new city manager was rumored to disfavor formalized departmental organizations, to have a strike plan ready to go, and to have a history of unilateral actions involving the various city departments. For example, shortly before meet-and-confer time, five police officers were reportedly accused by an anonymous source, through the city manager, of misusing the undercover narcotics fund.

Without permitting the police chief to conduct an investigation, the city manager hired a private attorney/special investigator who was also a polygraph operator. The five officers, without representation, were ordered to be interviewed by the investigator at a local motel, where each, over a several-hour period, was interrogated and polygraphed. No reports were ever forthcoming (to the police department or individual officers) and no formal charges were ever filed. Association representatives wanted some formal closure and a formalized agreement ("police officers' rights"). No one questioned the need for an investigation into the allegations, only into the process. Through his representative, the city manager refused any discussion on the issues; an impasse resulted.

Police association representatives met with the police chief, informing him of the impending strike (which they considered a job action, not a strike) and an agreement setting up a process by which eight patrol officers would report for duty each shift, remain in the police station, and answer only felony calls and significant calls for service from that location.

The police chief advised the assistant city manager (the city manager was not available to the chief), who informed the city manager; the city manager responded by sending city mechanics to confiscate all police vehicles and called in his previously organized "strike-breaking team," which turned out to be comprised of chiefs or assistant chiefs from all Montana class 1 and 2 cities (by population). The "team" patrolled the city and answered calls. This action didn't sit well with Great Falls citizens, its police officers, or—as might be expected—the various police associations, which had never experienced patrol assistance from their participating police chiefs. The chiefs were later recalled, and the Great Falls force went back on the streets. Shortly thereafter, the city manager was relieved.

Wounds healed slowly, and the police chief, who was known by all as a "good guy," retired in 1986. His replacement— ironically, a former (after the strike) association president and negotiator—successfully implemented communication reforms, which will be covered later.

The Irony

Shortly after his appointment, the new chief observed that some "essential" contractual issues that he as an association representative had helped to negotiate were difficult to live with as chief.

The Great Falls, Montana, situation may seem somewhat unusual, to say the least. There were violations of two basic negotiation rules: no open and effective communication, and a general lack of role and negotiation strategy understanding by the city manager and police negotiator. There were several other violations, in both the context of the times and by today's accepted practices.

As a group, identify these issues and how they might have been avoided. Since the irony was not unique, that is also worth comment and discussion.

No-Confidence Vote

Votes of no confidence are typically viewed both as political and as a very disruptive job action. Referred to as an NCV, it is a process whereby an employee group has decided to poll its members as to the level of satisfaction with organization management. The process can be initiated by an individual or by an employee group. In either case it may not be based on fact. NCVs have no legal status but are usually disruptive and can have very negative results for the chief.

It has been said that an NCV is an act of labor terrorism. It is often used when all else has failed to obtain the desired results or as an attempt to capitalize on the community's faith and trust in the rank-and-file officers (who answer their calls and provide for their needs) when attacking the chief.

Here is a list of dos and don'ts for NCV survival.

1. Remember that *you* are the manager (a boss).
2. Do *not* "roll over." Betrayal and discouragement will be felt; do not express these.
3. Do *not* retreat into your office.
4. Do *not* take your case to the news media.

5. Do *not* allow leaving to be an alternative.
6. Work in quiet meetings and get all the issues out in the open.
7. Deal openly and fairly with issues over which you have control.
8. Allow some issues to be resolved by other participants through well-attended discussions. (Everyone is rarely aware of all issues, and all parties are seldom in total agreement.)
9. Open continuing channels and discussion opportunities with which to discuss minor issues before they become big issues.
10. *Never* express negative feelings, and *never, never* take retaliatory actions against NCV participants.

Observers/survivors of NCVs have concluded that NCVs are cyclical and tend to be resorted to most when funding is shrinking.

NEGOTIATIONS

Be careful of your thoughts; they may become words at any moment.
—Ira Gassen

Preparation and interpretation of a negotiated MOU or contract does not end with adoption. New information, new needs, changing laws and ordinances, and a variety of other issues that can influence labor and management are likely to occur at any time. This information must be gathered routinely through different channels and then analyzed and stored for future consideration. Salaries and benefits are always a priority, but other issues may be equally important. Managers must also be up-to-date on financial matters involving not only their own government entity but others as well.

Anticipation

The police manager's task is to know in advance what to expect and what to prepare for. If another jurisdiction/association has made certain gains, it can be anticipated that similar demands will be made locally, and so on. Final preparation for a new bargaining process or negotiation over a disputed issue is much easier and more precise with documented ongoing trends and up-to-date information. Police managers must never assume that other city staff will have gathered all the pertinent information.

Training

With a proper training program geared to police managers (chief and staff) *and* labor association hierarchy, *productive* communication relating to departmental issues can bring viable solutions and trust. The trainer begins with relatively simple problems and gradually increases their complexity as the process becomes more ingrained and trust develops—since some issues *must remain confidential*. These are not to be "gripe sessions," although some gripes do appear, and can be treated as such.

Regardless of how well negotiation teams have come together in terms of understanding and trust in contract development, there is a tendency, when issues arise, to resort to adversarial tactics. When it appears that this will occur, it is time for the trainer to return. It's time for the team to get back to teamwork—to return to win–win solutions.

QUALITY OF WORKING LIFE

None of us, no matter how content we are at work, loves our entire job.
—Marcus Buckingham

Quality of working life (QWL) is a philosophy of management, a process, and a set of outcomes. It is a *philosophy* of management that accepts the legitimacy of existing unions, believes cooperative relationships with unions are worth developing, and believes that every employee has the ability and the right to offer intelligent and useful input into decisions at various levels of the organization. QWL is a *process* to involve employees at every level of the organization in decisions about their work and work-places. QWL also refers to the intended *outcomes* of practicing this philosophy and process, with improvements in working conditions, environment, and practices and in the general climate or culture of the workplace. This same process also brings organizational benefits of cost reduction and quality improvement and personal development benefits that are integral to the QWL concept.

Top Manager Committed

For survival and success of a QWL program, all police managers in the organization must be committed to the program, including its philosophy, its intended multiple outcomes, and its structure and process requirements. Even more, the chief/sheriff must be personally involved in the program and in its steering committee. In my experience, this is the most important factor in determining success. In sites where the top executive has not participated, the program has lagged and eventually folded. In sites where the executive has initially stayed back and then become involved, the program has initially suffered and then picked up.

Personal involvement is not a sufficient condition for program success, but it is a necessary condition to avoid program failure.

Top Union Leader Committed

It is equally important that the top union official(s) be committed and personally involved. The argument is the same as that for the top manager. But in my experience, once the union leadership has committed itself to a QWL program, there has been no problem in having them also personally involved. They don't want to leave this (or anything else of any great importance) to their staff.

Third-party neutral professional consultants will be needed; collective bargaining and QWL are separate but closely interrelated.

ELIMINATING SURPRISES AND REDUCING CONFLICT

The human being is the only animal that thinks about the future.
—Daniel Gilbert

We have been consciously redundant in targeting effective communication and effective listening throughout this book. There seems to be no disagreement among police leaders as to the importance of these functions. But how do busy managers find time? They don't find it; they schedule it formally and search for informal opportunities as they move through their workday.

Some police managers walk with their head down to avoid interruptive small talk. Successful managers are heads-up and searching for it. Scheduling may appear mechanical or contrived, but it need not be. And like police managers, police officers dislike surprises, especially on issues related to grievances or job-related change.

A MODEL APPROACH

From a number of working strategies with which we have become familiar, we selected as a model one that is uncomplicated and working well in a midsize department of fewer than 100 employees. The Communication/Problem Solving Team consists of five members: the association president, three patrol officers, and the chief; members choose the chairman. Meetings are scheduled once each month. Emergency meetings can be called by any team member, but reportedly, this has not occurred for several years. On-duty officers are on "city time." Off-duty officers are on "comp time." At times there is a meeting agenda, but meetings are held with or without one. Occasionally, sensitive issues arise; reportedly, this has not created problems.

The entire team is aware of the need for trust at all times and confidentiality at specific times. However, for the most part, members are expected to take information up and down the organization so that everyone has the same information. The chief has a good feel for department-wide conditions and anticipated problems, and the department has a good feel for administrative posture. Changes are not surprises!

By the time annual negotiations arrive, the issues on both sides—including fiscal parameters and the like—have been "pretty much hashed out." Although he is not a negotiator, the chief makes sure that a contract is usually finalized in about four days.

It is important to note that the team does not put the chief on the spot for instant decisions (giving him time to share information with staff), and the staff does not feel threatened or concerned about being circumvented. The chief is "all over that building" before he gets to his office in the morning, according to one patrol-level officer.

STRUCTURED EXERCISE 11-3

ROLE PLAY

Divide into problem-solving teams consisting of one association president, two patrol-level officers, one sergeant, one lieutenant (so the chief doesn't give away the store), and the chief. The team is to select the chairman. The team's role is to receive and resolve the problem by recommendation and strategy. Team members know that the final decision rests with the chief and city manager, but the chief sincerely wants or needs the team's best efforts.

THE PROBLEM

The city manager has just advised the police chief of an impending revenue shortfall that will substantially affect the coming year's budget. The police department will receive 5% less. Other departments are facing even greater cuts. Eighty-five percent of the police budget is allocated to salaries and benefits. All other operating budget allocations are covered by the remaining 15%, and they were cut to the bone last year. Nonsworn personnel suffered substantial cuts then as well.

A 5% cut would be the equivalent of six sworn positions. The contractual work-length provision will expire at the end of the fiscal year, and there are no employee reduction provisions or other fiscal crisis contingencies.

The chief has called the team together to advise members of the problem. The team is instructed to discuss the issues, which are likely to involve seniority, retirement, minority hiring agreements, rank, employee ratings, and the like, and then to develop potential courses of action. From the list of options, select the most feasible from a collective point of view and develop a strategy for implementation. If more than one option is possible, you may wish to develop a plan to inform all sworn members of the problem and potential options and decide how this information should be presented. Additionally, can an alternative be developed to resolve employee reduction?

Remember, the chief is not abdicating but searching for alternatives, and in conjunction with the city manager will make the final decision. But as a team member, your input will be a valuable resource to the chief and city manager and to the organization as a whole. These are tough decisions and will affect everyone. Teams will select a spokesman to present the process and solutions to the group.

Competency Checkpoints

- The police labor movement was triggered by a history of low salaries, uncompensated overtime, poor benefits, and related issues.
- As employee rights have improved, associations have moved to acquire some management prerogatives and to limit others.
- Employee rights have been codified in many states.
- Police officers' bills of rights have become commonplace. They set forth important guidelines that are generally understood and supported.

- Standards of operation, activity, and mutual respect for managers and unions are important for a successful and positive relationship.
- Managers must understand and participate in the "meet-and-confer" process.
- Once formal organizations have gained recognition, managers must be prepared to devote time to them and to respond to their concerns.
- Managers must schedule time for communicating with employee representatives in order to anticipate and resolve issues of concern.
- Managers must gather and analyze information continuously in preparation for negotiation strategies.
- Managers must work with employee representatives to keep MOUs and contracts alive.
- Management–union training programs will take on great importance through the next decade and beyond.
- During the bargaining process, reasonable requests and rapid agreements are important to morale on both sides.
- Starting a quality of working life program is a long process but is another step toward job satisfaction.

Flexing the Message

1. Interview the president or board member of a police officer association (POA)/union and ask what are its three top priorities or issues. Also ask what the three top priorities are for management. Next, interview a police manager and ask about his or her three main priorities and what he or she believes are the union's top three. How do the answers compare? Any surprises?
2. Obtain and read a copy of a POA's memorandum of understanding (MOU). Does the MOU contain any of the priorities mentioned in question 1? What are or appear to be the leading points (e.g., pay, retirement, health benefits)?
3. Again, interview a police manager and POA board member. Inquire about what they are doing to avoid management–union disputes on a daily basis.

12 | BUDGET

Budget Defined

The budget process consists of activities that encompass the development, implementation, and evaluation of a revenue and expenditure plan for a specific period.

It's all right to chase money. But don't let it catch you.

Those police managers who understand the budget and the budget process can work effectively anywhere in the department.

—Jim Nunn

CHAPTER OUTLINE

1. Revenues
   a. General Fund
   b. Grants
   c. Asset Forfeitures
   d. Service Fees
   e. Foundations

2. Budget Principles
   a. Principle 1: Establish Goals
   b. Principle 2: Develop Approaches to Achieve Goals
   c. Principle 3: Develop a Budget Consistent with Approaches to Achieve Goals
   d. Principle 4: Evaluate Performance and Make Adjustments

3. The Budget As Law

4. Fund Accounting
   a. Funds
   b. Governmental Funds
   c. Proprietary Funds
   d. Fiduciary Funds

5. Budget Designs
   a. Line-Item, or Traditional, Budget

The operative word in the definition for *budget* on the previous page is *plan*. Yes, a budget is basically an action plan. In this instance, the plan conveys the guts of its message in numbers. A successful budget process is much more than the preparation of a legal document that appropriates funds for a series of line items. Good budgeting is an inclusive process that has political, managerial, planning, communication (team building), and financial implications.

With an inclusive budget process, a police agency will produce a budget (plan) that

- Incorporates a *strategic* perspective
- Forges links to the agency's *mission*
- Concentrates budget decisions on *results*
- Ensures effective *communication* with all police employees
- Energizes police *leadership*

Such a plan moves beyond the traditional notion of "line-item expenditure control" to building and maintaining satisfaction via community-oriented policing.

There is an adage: "If you're not planning, then you're planning to fail." With a couple of minor changes, this statement equally applies to budget making.

In short:

The central goal of a budget is to help police managers make informed choices about the provision of services and allocation of available resources.

If, as I believe, the budget is a numerical plan on which police agencies function, how do so many managers rise to such important positions without some preparation in this area? The answer, while perhaps logical, is not rational. Most budgets in large departments are prepared by separate bureaus with whom field and most staff officers have very little contact. Such bureaus are typically headed and staffed by civilian experts trained in the field of finance. Small-department budgets are most likely to be prepared by the department head, while the midsize department typically utilizes one middle-management person on a part-time basis. If fortunate, he or she may be backed up by one or two civilian staff people who have had some outside training.

Most police managers come up through the ranks, but few of them have the opportunity to work directly with the budget process. Therefore, they have little direct interest or concern, except when something needed is unfunded. The lower you are on the hierarchical ladder, the more likely you are to view the budget as "someone else's problem." This is not to say that inputs are not made at the division level, for they are. There is, however, a great deal of difference between divisional inputs and the final document—its presentation, execution, control, and audit. Even in departments with carefully predetermined career ladders that rotate, a manager's budget development experience is a random learning experience.

> A police manager who does not comprehend the budget dance is operating with sunglasses on in a dark room. If you will learn the budget process, you can work anywhere within your agency. (Trust Jim Nunn, above, who, for over 35 years, proved this point.)

REVENUES

> *There are three fruitful friends: an old wife, an old dog, and ready money.*
> —*Benjamin Franklin*

The sources for the police budget are: (1) general fund; (2) grants; (3) asset forfeitures; (4) service fees; and (5) foundations.

General Fund

The vast majority of a department's budget is derived from tax dollars (property and sales taxes). If our economy is upbeat, so is the revenue, and vice versa. Economic forecasting, while an inexact science, should be employed in order to predict reasonable ranges of low-to-high revenue. Traffic and parking fines can be an important part of the general fund income revenue stream.

Grants

Many police budgets rely on successful grant requests to federal, state, and other nonprofit organizations. Today, especially, grant requests for homeland security, traffic enforcement, gang abatement, and narcotics interdiction are popular. Usually the grant requests center on hardware (e.g., information and video technology). But today some grants are including monies for staff and buildings. Some agencies significantly increase their revenues (20% or more) by "working" available grant funds.

Asset Forfeitures

Asset seizure for illegal drug activity is in some geographical areas a highly lucrative revenue source. In many instances, cash, real property, vehicles, and other valuable items are converted into a sizable source of income that equates to budget dollars. The results are twofold: drug-related criminals are deprived of operating funds and profits, and law enforcement gains resources to fight them.

Service Fees

A lot of police managers have created sound reasons for recovering some of the costs associated with providing their resources. Essentially they have found or are exploring avenues for charging a fee on specific services. In a few instances, fee income is 10% or more of the overall budget dollars. There are budget makers who actually calculate the estimated sum into the annual budget with the expectation (based on experience, of course) that the monies will be earned. Here are a few examples of fee-based services.

- Fingerprinting
- Copies of reports
- Repeated false alarms (e.g., burglary alarms)
- Vehicle towing and storage changes (this can be a big number)
- Special events (e.g., parades, sport events, conventions)
- Use of jail facilities (this also can be a big fee generator)
- Service contracts
- Taxi permits
- DUI cost recovery
- Vacation checks
- Repeated nuisance calls (e.g., barking dogs)
- Medical transportation
- Booking fees

Foundations

Relatively new on the revenue horizon is the creation of a nonprofit, which may seem a bit Polyanna. But the track record for those agencies that have established a charitable, tax-deductible foundation has shown promise. Check with other agencies via their Web sites. It is certainly worth exploring.

BUDGET PRINCIPLES

Perhaps the most important value pressing upon the whole budgetary process is accountability.
—*John M. Pfiffner and Robert Presthus*

Four key principles for guiding the budget process are outlined in Table 12-1. These principles are benchmarks advocated by—and clearly meriting the attention of—all public budget makers. The four sections that follow endeavor to comply with their intent.

Principle 1: Establish Goals
Data Gathering
It is advisable to begin gathering needed information months in advance of the budget process, so that it can be evaluated and prioritized and so programs can be developed for consideration. It is also important to have both the officers conducting the survey and those being surveyed understand the time frame necessary to turn identified needs into programs and to provide occasional feedback as plans progress. If not, constituents are likely to suspect a lack of sincerity in the first place. And those surveyed—as well

TABLE 12-1   Four Budget Principles

1. Establish Broad Goals to Guide Government Decision Making
   - Assess community needs, priorities, challenges, and opportunities
   - Identify opportunities and challenges for government services, capital assets, and management
   - Develop and disseminate broad goals
2. Develop Approaches to Achieve Goals
   - Adopt financial policies
   - Develop programmatic, operating, and capital policies and plans
   - Develop programs and services that are consistent with policies and plans
   - Develop management strategies
3. Develop a Budget Consistent with Approaches to Achieve Goals
   - Develop a process for preparing and adopting a budget
   - Develop and evaluate financial options
   - Make choices necessary to adopt a budget
4. Evaluate Performance and Make Adjustments
   - Monitor, measure, and evaluate performance
   - Make adjustments as needed

as the police—must understand that all needs must be considered, along with all other requests, in relation to available funds. Police officers unaccustomed to the budget process are accustomed to action once the plan has been made. A most important part of this process is feedback!

Data Analysis

Financial analysts, who are becoming more visible on the staffs of midsize and large police agencies, are excellent resources. These professionals are very likely to spot trends or unique problems before anyone else does. Since many of them do not have police backgrounds, they tend to view needs solutions nontraditionally rather than the typical police response, which can be stimulating.

Political Considerations

A budget document has political messages. When a sufficient number of citizens pressure their elected representatives in reference to a particular local problem, funds may be allocated; however, it may be that, relative to other responsibilities, this problem has a very low priority. For example, certain youth-oriented programs that attract relatively few young people may have a great deal of surface appeal, but their real value in terms of total community service is questionable. However, at the risk of irrational inputs, a police agency should, within the legal framework, reflect the needs of the community wherever possible.

Clearly, it is not easy to express needs in a rational way. And it is equally difficult to allocate resources to activities and programs in a way that ensures that needs will really be met. Responsibility for the equitable and effective distribution of resources is, in our society, a political ethic.

Although some might not view the budget as a political process, it is. Even though department heads develop the budget request and city managers submit

the finished document, it is the elected officials who make the final decisions: cutting, adding, supporting, blocking, and finally approving. Two kinds of reasoning are at work here: analytical and political.

Principle 2: Develop Approaches to Achieve Goals

Prior to budget preparation, instructions are typically sent to departments by the administrative head (e.g., city managers), setting forth the financial prospects for the coming budget year. Efficiency and economy are usually stressed in requests to hold the line and trim the fat. The administrator may point out specific problems of needed or unwanted services, but it is understood that the police manager—keeping the administrator's personal views in mind—is expected to propose a budget based on that administrator's view of finances as well as the needs of the citizens served. Administrators will review the proposed budget, keeping in mind the views of elected officials; finally, elected officials will review the proposed budget, keeping in mind the values, views, and special interests of their constituents.

In this manner, policies of the administration and elected officials are woven into the budget process. The result is that the finalized budget not only reflects the needs and constraints of the various community and government levels but also has been agreed on as a mandate for departmental activities during the ensuing budget period.

Prior to budget preparation each year, most administrators direct an executive policy message, or budget call, to all department heads. Police managers are expected to work within the guidelines as set forth in the message; any anticipated deviation should be cleared with the administrative head. (For example, the message may state that no new positions will be added.)

In addition to the budget message (most jurisdictions have a budget policy to ensure uniformity in the process), manuals are essential for a variety of reasons, not the least of which is format uniformity. Many different departmental budgets must be pulled together in a single document and therefore must have continuity. Manuals also afford systemization and process clarification.

> While the budget message does trigger certain functions, and the manuals will afford clarification, it is a dynamic process that is ongoing throughout the entire year.

Continual Review

A continual review of programs is necessary to ascertain that they are providing the services for which they were created. Budgets are dynamic, not static, systems; if a program is not performing as expected, its design should be modified or even scrapped in favor of some other important but unfunded project. Some police managers are reluctant to go back through the administrative and legislative process, although they should not be. One mark of a good manager is to be on top of such things and be ready to shift the emphasis if the need is indicated.

Elevated Expectations

There are a number of problem areas connected with year-round preparation, problems such as the allotment of time for planning and for employee and citizen contact and feedback. Although employee and citizen inputs are absolutely essential, they can also be the most difficult to deal with in terms of commitment and implementation. If feedback and ideas are solicited and subsequently not utilized, the feeling of "Why did you ask me in the first place?" is likely to prevail. On the other hand, even if the inputs are utilized but take a year to come to fruition, negative comments are likely to occur. Too many of us equate ideas with actions. Push the button and a reward appears magically. As I said, the tendency among police employees and citizens alike is to expect immediate results.

Input, Reinforcement, and Supportive Data

The vital process of input requires continual reinforcement in the form of an explanation of how the budget system operates. Once the various elements of the department have completed and presented their requests, they are brought together in a formal meeting to fashion the rough budget document.

Police manager heads are expected to review divisional requests in much the same manner that the executive views all departmental budgets. They must separate the wheat from the chaff and consider the supportive data carefully, instilling and developing in division heads the same level of competence expected by top administration. Erroneous or careless data or deliberate padding will lead to exposure and a loss in confidence. Division heads must understand that slanted data of any sort will not be tolerated. Compromised data will surface eventually and can have devastating results.

Principle 3: Develop a Budget Consistent with Approaches to Achieve Goals

After the various department budget proposals have been tentatively accepted by the appointed administrator, they are collated into the final proposed budget document and referred to the elected governing body for study. In this manner, elected officials or their staffs have the opportunity to study the budget in depth before the public hearing. Customarily, the city manager prepares and submits the budget message that accompanies the budget. She may do this in writing or may elect to do so orally at the public hearing. Most administrators prefer an oral presentation because it permits the message to reach not only the legislative body and attendant citizens but also, through the news media, the rest of the community as well.

The message typically summarizes the budget and emphasizes special issues and programs. The budget message is significant for the police department in that it historically sets the tone for the hearing. The hearing in itself in most jurisdictions provides the opportunity for each police manager to present his budget and any supportive data that he may wish to bring to bear.

> The budget summary *must* be clear and concise. It should be distributed to interested citizens and the media.

Preparation

Preparation (with a lot of practice) for the hearing is absolutely essential. Smart police managers often rehearse the budget preparation process, requiring each division head to justify the need for specific requests so that supportive elements can be developed and refined for presentation at the hearing. (Division heads must be required to provide all data—pro and con—for the chief's evaluation.)

Supportive data appear in a variety of forms: oral presentations; handout material (chancy, since it may not be read or understood); charts, slides, or acetate overlays for an overhead projector; films; and, more recently, video, audiovisual, and PowerPoint presentations. Whatever the style, the primary goal is to present the information in its *simplest,* most attractive form. Unfortunately, some elected officials who do not understand will not openly reveal their confusion; instead, they are likely to react negatively. At times, it will be important to provide prebudget on-site demonstrations for the city manager/elected officials. For example, they might benefit from demonstrations of costly complicated proposals such as computer-aided dispatch (CAD) systems.

Timing
Timing of the budget information release is a topic for consideration. There has been a tendency to "leak" budget information, either to certain influential citizens thought to be supportive of particular new programs or to the news media. Obviously, there is a great deal to be gained by properly informing the news media and citizens alike. However, as with every other facet of police management, municipal executives and elected legislative bodies do not wish to be surprised. It is essential that public information about the budget be released *after* it has been received by those in authority.

Study Sessions
Study sessions should do the following:

1. Provide a positive forum for the police manager's programs.
2. Provide elected officials with substantive information beyond the proposed budget document.
3. Provide interested citizens with a broad view of police programs and attendant costs.
4. Provide citizens with an opportunity to comment on priorities.
5. Provide news media with timely information on new special programs and projects.
6. Provide the opportunity for police association representatives to observe the process and report back on the progress of special program funding.

Principle 4: Evaluate Performance and Make Adjustments
Once reviewed, revised, and finally adopted, the budget comes alive, setting in motion the amalgamation of funds to programs and programs to planned results. From the point of adoption to the end of its fiscal life, the budget now becomes a means of control. It is the base from which the police manager determines, through regular audits, that funds are being properly allocated to authorized programs. Additionally, monthly reports should provide a real-time audit. These reports are vital in predicting and controlling the flow of funds so that the last days of the fiscal year are not without funds.

Enough emphasis cannot be placed on the importance of the control-audit function for monitoring not only expenditures and revenues but also program goal achievements.

While the predictors used to anticipate and plan programs for modern police organizations are fairly reliable, they are not infallible. As I mentioned earlier, if an audit reveals that a funded program is not producing the expected results, immediate consideration should be given to modifying it or scrapping it. If the program ceases but the original need still exists, an alternative plan should be developed.

In either case, planned deviation—prior to implementation—from the approved program must be reported to the administrator and the elected legislative body. It is their responsibility to review the proposed changes in much the same manner as the original budget and make recommendations for further revisions or adoption.

STRUCTURED EXERCISE 12-1

DEFENDING THE POLICE DEPARTMENT BUDGET

Your police chief calls you into her office and tells you that she has a family emergency and that you must defend the quarterly budget results at the City Council meeting. What are the six most important questions you should be prepared to answer? Focus on individual line-item questions, such as "Why is the training and travel account overdrawn?" List questions in priority order.

Police First-Quarter Budget Report

Personnel Services	Budget	Expended	Encumbered	% Expended
Full-Time Salaries	$ 1,000,000	$ 260,000	–	26%
Part-Time Salaries	170,000	65,000	–	38%
Overtime	45,000	39,000	–	87%
Fringe Benefits	400,000	85,000	–	21%
Operating Expenses				
Utilities	$ 15,000	$ 8,000	–	53%
Training & Travel	2,000	2,100	–	105%
Office Supplies	75,000	50,000	–	67%
Contracts	100,000	0	$ 110,000	110%
Capital Outlay				
Personal Computers	$ 100,000	$ 6,000	$ 2,000	8%
Office Equipment	45,000	51,000	3,000	120%
Totals	$1,952,000	$ 566,100	$ 115,000	35%

Revenues	Budget	Received	Percentage
Fees & Charges	$ 390,000	$ 55,000	14.1%
Vehicle Code Fines	55,000	45,000	81.9%
Totals	$ 445,000	$ 100,000	22.0%

Modifications

Most budgets need periodic modifications to keep the funding flow in the proper mode. Inflation and other variables make the prediction of certain costs difficult. The bidding process may return surplus dollars to the treasury, while an unexpected rise in the cost of fuel oil, for example, may affect not only the vehicle-per-mile costs but the cost of electricity, heat, and other items as well. Normally, such minor changes are provided for in city charters and state laws and do not necessitate a return to the legislative body. Finance directors usually have flexibility in adjusting funds between the various operating accounts.

Police Manager as Accountant? (No!)

I am not suggesting that police managers become accountants. There should be experienced staff who are expert in this area. (Smaller jurisdictions will be provided such expertise through their finance departments.) Nonetheless, police managers *must* be familiar with monthly accounting reports. They should also have an ongoing internal audit system for regular program review and the ability to superimpose or interrelate the two audits for purposes covered earlier. In larger municipalities with more complex needs, audits will need to be summarized by subordinate experts, but the control and breadth of these summaries should be dictated by police managers themselves so that their financial diligence is sound. Audits are the best indicators for the preparation of the next fiscal budget.

A system of accounting, reporting, auditing, and inspection is essential to a manager's responsibility for due diligence. As a manager, you may or may not be involved in the preparation of a budget, but *your* reputation is on the line when it comes to executing it.

First, the controls must meet the management needs of the expending agency. Next, they must set standards of performance and fiscal integrity that enable elected officials to keep current with public agency productivity and to reassure these officials that no hanky-panky is occurring. Finally, the controls should reassure the public that monies spent are providing the services desired in an efficient and economical fashion.

An Opportunity

To sum up, the budget affords the opportunity to:

1. Understand the needs of citizens.
2. Utilize the knowledge of these needs to develop a budget that will meet the needs.
3. Allocate the agency's resources in harmony with the budget.
4. Ensure that the public's business will be conducted in an efficient and economical manner.
5. Prepare a budget document that also clearly reflects on the policies of elected officials.
6. Help citizens understand the connection between public expenditure and the rendering of public services.
7. Provide controls that ensure that public monies are spent efficiently for the purposes intended.

THE BUDGET AS LAW

*A budget, therefore, may be characterized as a series
of goals with price tags attached.*
—Aaron Wildovsky

All governmental funds (general, special revenue, and others) are established in compliance with *legal mandates*. A governmental unit may raise revenues only from sources allowed by law. Laws commonly set a maximum amount that may be raised from each source or set a maximum rate that may be applied to the base used in computation of revenue from a given source. Revenues to be raised by law during a budget period should be set forth in an *estimated revenues budget*. Revenues are raised to finance governmental activities, but revenues may be expended only for purposes and in amounts approved by the legislative branch in accord with existing laws. This is known as the appropriations process.

An *appropriations budget*, when enacted into law, is the legal authorization for the managers of the governmental unit to incur liabilities during the budget period for purposes specified in the appropriations statute or ordinance and not to exceed the amount specified for each purpose.

When a liability is incurred as authorized by an appropriation, the appropriation is said to be *expended*. At the end of the budget period, managers no longer have the authority to incur liabilities under the lapsed appropriation. However, in most jurisdictions, managers continue to have the authority to disburse cash in payment of liabilities legally incurred in a prior period.

FUND ACCOUNTING

Viewed in another light, a budget may be regarded as a contract.
—Aaron Wildovsky

Funds
Think of a fund as a "drawer" where financial activity is recorded:

- Assets
- Liabilities
- Fund balances
- Reserves
- Expenditures and revenues

Fund Accounting
- An accounting system organized on the basis of "funds"
- Separate "bank accounts"

- Means of controlling government resources
- Cash "pooled" for investment purposes
- Number of funds
- Governed by a standard-setting body—Governmental Accounting Standards Board (GASB), which basically establish the "laws" or rules of accounting in governmental agencies
- Fund accounting is also a means of controlling resources—generally funds are restricted or "earmarked" for specific purposes (e.g., they may not always be available for any type of expenditure)

Government accounting systems should be organized and operated on a fund basis. A *fund* is defined as a *fiscal and accounting entity* with a self-balancing set of accounts recording cash and other financial resources, together with all related liabilities and residual equities or balances and changes therein. The funds are segregated for the purpose of carrying on specific activities or attaining certain objectives in accordance with special regulations, restrictions, or limitations.

Note that the definition given above requires that two conditions must be met for a fund, in a technical sense, to exist: (1) there must be a fiscal entity—assets set aside for specific purposes, and (2) there must be a double-entry accounting entity created to account for the fiscal entity.

States and local governments use seven types of funds to achieve the objectives outlined above. The following seven funds are organized into three categories: (1) governmental, (2) proprietary, and (3) fiduciary.

Governmental Funds

Four fund types are classified as governmental funds. These are:

1. The *general fund,* which accounts for most of the basic services provided by the governmental unit. Technically, this fund accounts for all resources other than those required to be accounted for in another fund.
2. *Special revenue funds,* which account for resources that are legally restricted, other than for debt service, major capital projects, and trust and agency relationships.
3. *Capital projects funds,* which account for major capital projects other than those financed by proprietary or trust funds.
4. *Debt service funds,* which account for the payment of principal and interest on general long-term debt.

Proprietary Funds

Two types of funds are *proprietary funds.* The term indicates that the funds are used to account for a government's ongoing organizations and activities that are similar to those often found in the private sector. The two types of proprietary funds are:

5. *Enterprise funds,* which are used when resources are provided primarily through the use of service charges to those receiving the benefit. They are also used in

situations when it is deemed best to display a matching of revenues and expenses in the manner used by business enterprises. Examples of enterprise funds would be water and other utilities, airports, swimming pools, and transit systems.

6. *Internal service funds*, which account for services provided by one department of government, such as a print shop or motor pool, to another on a cost-reimbursement basis.

   Proprietary funds are considered "nonexpendable," in that the revenues are generated through user charges intended to cover operating costs and expenses.

Fiduciary Funds

The third general category of funds used by state and local governments is called *fiduciary* and includes:

7. *Trust and agency funds,* which account for resources for which the governmental unit is acting as a trustee or as a collecting/disbursing agent. The type of accounting used by trust and agency funds depends on the nature and purpose of the fund. *Agency funds* and *expendable trust funds* are accounted for in a manner similar to governmental funds. *Nonexpendable trust funds* and *pension trust funds* are accounted for in a manner similar to proprietary funds.

BUDGET DESIGNS

*The universe is full of magical things patiently waiting
for our wits to grow sharper.*
—*Eden Phillpotts*

In the latter part of the twentieth century, government agencies were considering one of five budget formats:

- The line-item (or traditional) budget
- The performance budget
- The planning, programming, budgeting system (PPBS)
- The program, or results-oriented, budget system
- Zero-based budgeting

   While exciting and promising at the time, zero-based and PPBS have proved trendy but not helpful. From here on, we'll deal with the line item, performance, and program budgets.

Line-Item, or Traditional, Budget

The line-item budget is so named because its resources are allocated in the budget document line by line. Line-item budgets typically categorize budget items by departments, divisions, or organizational units within the department, listing proposed expenditures under such categories as

1. *Salaries and wages*, which includes the number of positions allocated for each type of classification assigned to the unit, such as police captains, lieutenants, sergeants, police officers, secretaries, and the like
2. *Operating expenses*, which includes fuel costs, repairs and maintenance, service contracts, telephones, utilities, and the like
3. *Equipment*, which includes the purchase of new items, such as automobiles, motorcycles, weapons, and computers
4. *Capital outlay*, which usually covers those items needed beyond the normal operation and utilized over a wide span of years, such as the acquisition of real property, new building construction, or major remodeling

Typically, many line-item budgets also display a series of columns containing recent historical data relating to each of the categories listed above. These columns list the amounts budgeted and actual or adjusted figures for several preceding years, including the current operating budget. Thus, comparisons can be made at a glance by the legislative body and the citizenry, as well as the user department. Some line-item budgets go one step further by displaying separate comparative columns for departmental requests, administrative recommendations, and the legislature-approved figures.

Finalized line-item budgets actually provide several sets of data. The budget summary breaks down expenditures and personnel by department. The second set of data sets forth the workload indicators. The third set of data is much more detailed by item and function. Finally, the fourth concerns capital outlay.

Strengths and Weaknesses

There are both strengths and weaknesses in the line-item budget. On the downside, it is primarily an "inputs" type of budget with no real correlation to the end product. There may be a few broad goals attached to the budget format, but there is no real indication that if *A* is invested, *B* will be the result. (On the other hand, inputs are made from all divisions and units so that each is offered the opportunity to project its needs.) The emphasis is on keeping costs down, with very little indication as to how this allocation of resources relates to the public need. The focus is on requested increases and on new programs. Old or ongoing programs are rarely questioned.

On the plus side the line-item budget is easy to understand for both legislators and citizens. Since citizen understanding is essential, this is an important advantage, for line-item budgets also encompass easy-to-understand accountability.

Performance Budget

A performance budget is a *measure* of the work process of an agency or unit. Expenditures are classified by functions, activities, and projects. The emphasis is on the means and accomplishments to be achieved. The specific activities and work activities are ends in themselves.

Like line-item budgets, performance budgets provide comparative data that is useful for allocating resources. For example, if one police officer on one foot beat can effectively patrol a four-square-block area, theoretically that patrol officer's activities can be projected over similar areas to determine the number of patrol officers needed.

Ideally, the database would furnish other pertinent information that would permit the decision maker to look at alternative methods of delivering services to the same area, such as the patrol car. By utilizing cost accounting and performance data, managers are better positioned to select the most effective patrol method in terms of services delivered per cost dollar.

Unfortunately, police officers' logs continue to be completed in broad generalities rather than in accurately recorded time frames. Unaccounted-for time tends to be lumped under the headings of "other" or "patrol time," because logs are typically filled out at the shift's end and events tend to run together or be forgotten.

Performance budgeting and cost accounting began to fade from the police management scene when the data were found to be unmanageable in terms of available staff person-hours. So while the tenets of the performance budget are excellent, it appears that most experts in the field have found it impractical.

Strengths and Weaknesses

Performance budgeting is more practical for organizations whose production units derive from assembly lines or other work functions that are highly quantifiable, such as paving or sweeping a certain number of street miles. Of course, many police functions are quantifiable. However, quantification often relies on quotas, and "police quotas" are typically resented by citizens and police officers alike. Therefore, in terms of the police budget, the selection of meaningful work units is most difficult and thus an obstacle to accurate, reliable, and usable work measurements.

Program, or Results-Oriented, Budget System

"Program" and "results-oriented" budgets are the same; they both stress *results*.

Many police departments utilize programs to some extent in their budget preparation. An appealing facet of the program budget is that it connects *community needs* and *departmental goals*. Accounts are then related to specific programs rather than simply to line items. The aim of this budget format is to assist legislative bodies in selecting and rejecting programs rather than dwelling on the cost of supplies and equipment. This is relatively simple in certain city functions such as tree trimming or animal control, where the focus is on the program, not equipment and personnel. Police programs that lend themselves to easy application of this system include traffic control, narcotics, youth diversion, school resource officers, crossing guards, and problem-oriented policing.

The program budget process does not include or rely on elaborate cost-benefit analyses. It classifies activities by programs and stated objectives. Choices among programs (or objectives) are made in the political process. In other words, policy analysis and choices among programs are *separated* from the budget process.

While policy analysis and choices (among programs) are decoupled from the budgetary process, the budget does relate proposed expenditures to desired objectives. The program budget is the responsibility of the designated program managers. Typically, the final document is coordinated and presented at the department-head level with the full participation of the program managers.

The typical program budget provides for:

1. A statement of need
2. Legal authority for the program

3. A statement of how it originated
4. Objectives
5. A work plan
6. Multiyear coverage—when it will start and how long it will go, whether closed- or open-ended
7. An explanation of how it will be funded (e.g., grant [asset forfeiture] versus general fund)

Strengths and Weaknesses

The strengths and weaknesses of program budgets can be summarized as follows:

Strengths

- Program budgets allow wide participation in the budget's preparation.
- They constantly probe the environment for emerging needs.
- They provide a vehicle for managing by objectives.
- They focus on social effectiveness rather than simply on cost-effectiveness.
- They reflect administrative and legislative policy.
- They demonstrate high accountability to the legislative body and to the people.
- They are less complicated than PPBS and so are within the reach of more jurisdictions.
- They are likely to produce greater economizing behavior (because they are based on a modified market model).
- They permit analysis of the budget as a line rather than a staff function.
- They equate budget cycles with the specific needs and nature of each program.

Weaknesses

- Legislators have to learn to take the risks associated with the advantages.
- Accounting systems must be revised.
- It is tough to formulate objectives that are sufficiently explicit to manage and budget by.
- Managers may hesitate to take the risk of meeting objectives.
- The different role required of staff may cause dissatisfaction on staff units.
- Data collection can be costly.

RISK MANAGEMENT

[M]ost executives are more receptive when I talk about ethics as a risk management strategy.
—*Michael Josephson*

Why this quote and why this subject sandwiched into a discussion on police budget making? Simply, the budget deals with the allocation of scarce resources. And when officers, dispatchers, and so on, goof up, it can result in an unexpected commitment of budget monies to remedy the mistake. When a felony search knocks the wrong door off its hinges and innocent folks are scared nearly to death, the department is liable for redressing this error. The redress is usually more than a police "oops"; it involves money—sometimes a lot of it. Risk management is making decisions that will minimize an agency's exposure to liability and reduce the loss of personnel and financial resources. This is accomplished through risk identification and assessment, inspections and audits of departmental operations, and maintaining risk information systems and loss prevention programs.

Risk is most effectively managed from the foundation of the organization. In other words, risk management is the responsibility of each and every member of the department. Employees must recognize that police agencies, as a provider of a wide range of services, have a high level of exposure and need to manage public resources prudently. The very nature of police work requires risk assessment and risk avoidance decisions daily. Losses are inevitable, but an agency can protect and conserve its assets by promoting identification and treatment of risk and exposures.

Larger departments will have risk management units or a few employees designated as risk management specialists. Midsize and small police agencies may assign this responsibility to supervisors.

Regardless of where risk management is positioned in the organization, its mission is to quickly and accurately assess and report risk status and present information on corrective opportunities.

Risk management includes:

- Coordinating and tracking the department's response to civil liability claims
- Identifying and evaluating potential risks within the organization
- Providing safe and healthy working conditions
- Reducing liability associated with traffic collisions
- Administering substance abuse programs

THE BEST APPROACH

Since the budget touches everything, changing it will begin to change everything. The budget process has great leverage.
—*Camille Cates Barnett and Darin Atteberry*

I have observed various police agencies attempt to implement innovative budgeting processes, only to have legislative bodies reject them or request adjunct line-item budgets. Legislators without a great deal of expertise in the subject have found the line-item budget easy to understand; it is also an excellent auditing device, but only for expenditures.

Legislative bodies and city managers are often more concerned with how much something is going to cost rather than with how effective it is going to be. They question whether a program is really what their constituents want, will understand, or support.

Frankly, I doubt that there is any rational way to do away with the independent line-item budget because of the accounting responsibilities of finance directors, state legal requirements, and police administrators themselves. And, of course, line-item budgets are the building blocks for all other forms.

The program (results) budget, however, has great potential. It is relatively inexpensive to implement, although some training is necessary for division and unit heads, along with orientation for elected officials. It retains the human element, makes good use of the management theory of empowerment, considers the social element of the community, is easily understood by all, and is an excellent audit instrument for determining whether or not programs are achieving what they are designed to achieve.

The best approach is to combine the traditional line-item budget with the program budget. Many currently have done this and are improving the use of programs. Line-item budgets are most useful for auditing fiscal control; program budgets, for setting goals and working to reach them. Program budgets permit police organizations to break their functions into specific programs, which in turn permit the selection or prioritizing of programs.

See Figure 12-1 for a typical annual city budget program activity description by division. The progression of information can readily be seen and understood. Figure 12-2 shows a typical police department summary.

FIGURE 12-1   Typical Annual City Budget: Program Activity Description by Division

Division		Police Department Program Activity	Staff Years	Bduget ($)
Office of the chief	310	Chief's Office	4.00	378,700
	311	It's-a-Crime Program		20,500
		Subtotal	4.00	399,200
Field Services	314	Field Operations Administration	14.00	2,793,700
	315	Southwest Police Area	50.00	2,668,300
	316	Central Police Area	47.00	2,526,300
	317	Southeast Police Area	50.00	2,632,700
	318	Northeast Police Area	52.00	2,761,000
	319	Patrol Tactical Team	9.00	556,000
	320	Crime Prevention	7.00	194,700
	321	Northwest Police Area	55.00	2,841,200
	322	Traffic	27.50	1,517,100
	337	Juvenile Tactical Team	5.00	318,700
		Subtotal	316.50	18,809,700
Operations Support	330	Investigation Bureau	5.00	548,000
	331	Persons & Miscellaneous Crimes	38.25	2,103,000
	332	Property Crimes/Juvenile	22.75	1,328,100
	333	Identification Section	16.00	528,500
	334	Court/Prosecutor Liaison		2,200
	335	Special Enforcement Section	7.00	456,400
	336	Narcotics Section	14.00	1,140,300
	338	Vice Section	6.00	331,100
		Subtotal	109.00	6,437,600

Division		Police Department Program Activity	Staff Years	Bduget ($)
Administrative	344	Information Services	16.00	389,700
Support	345	Property Evidence	6.00	485,900
	346	Communications	57.50	1,814,900
	347	Records	32.00	873,400
	348	Management Support	13.00	699,700
	349	Career Criminal Apprehension	5.00	123,500
		Subtotal	129.50	4,387,100
		Total Department	559.00	30,033,600

Department: Police	No: 40	Division: Field Services	No: 31	Fund Type: General

Program Activity Descriptions

	FY2003 Actual	FY2004 Estimated	FY2005 Projected

319 Patrol Tactical Team

The Patrol Tac Program is a flexible, uniformed unit responsible for providing police services for unique and specialized situations that cannot be addressed by community-based policing area personnel. They are available to assist with special problems and events. These include parades, gang-related problems, crime scene control, and city parks traffic and crowd control.

	FY2003 Actual	FY2004 Estimated	FY2005 Projected
Budget ($)	513,900	529,800	556,000
Staff years	9.00	9.00	9.00

320 Crime Prevention

This program seeks to increase cooperation between the community and the police department in resisting crime and creating neighborhood cohesiveness through organizational and operational methods that have been demonstrated to be effective.

	FY2003 Actual	FY2004 Estimated	FY2005 Projected
Budget ($)	163,300	180,000	194,700
Staff years	7.00	7.00	7.00

Objective

To conduct 275 neighborhood watch group update meetings

Performance Indicator

	FY2003 Actual	FY2004 Estimated	FY2005 Projected
Number of watch group update meetings	402	250	275

Objective

To perform 1,000 home security inspections

Performance Indicator

	FY2003 Actual	FY2004 Estimated	FY2005 Projected
Number of home security inspections	1,159	1,200	1,000

Objective

To perform 225 business security inspections

Performance Indicator

	FY2003 Actual	FY2004 Estimated	FY2005 Projected
Number of business security inspections	223	200	225

FIGURE 12-2 Typical Police Department Summary

Police Department Summary

The police department provides the professional assistance needed to sustain an effective response to illegal and disorderly conduct in the city. The department strives to enforce the law in a manner that is consistent with the community's interest in ensuring safety, security, and public order.

There are staffing changes proposed in the FY 03 budget in field services and administrative support divisions. Ten grant-funded sworn personnel, one grant-funded community service officer (CSO), and one grant-funded clerical position will be added to the field services division in order to implement a centralized traffic safety program. These proposed additional positions will be funded through a grant from the California state Office of Traffic Safety (OTS). A lieutenant and two clerical positions, as well as motorcycles and other equipment, will be added as an in-kind contribution to implement the OTS grant. The state will pay $425,000 to the city in FY 03 for this program, $311,000 in the second year, and no contribution in FY 05. An account clerk II position will be added to the business office to maintain department accounting services at an acceptable level and perform critical payroll functions. This position will help manage the workload created by an expanded department work force and provide the staff needed to operate computer spreadsheet programs and perform other duties.

Office of the Chief Division

There are no staffing changes proposed in the chief's office. The feasibility study of a colocated/consolidated city/county law enforcement facility will continue in FY 03.

Field Services Division

The grant-funded sworn positions—two sergeants, eight motorcycle officers (police specialists), one community service officer, and a typist-clerk—are being recommended to implement the OTS grant-funded program. An additional lieutenant and two clerical positions will provide in-kind city additions to the traffic grant. The city would also purchase ten motorcycles for the new officers, as well as other minor capital equipment.

Sixteen current motor officers will join the additional officers in this new traffic program. This new unit will approach traffic control as a coordinated, centralized unit, enforcing traffic and traffic-related regulations in all areas of the city. This new unit should also free up field officers for more nontraffic law enforcement.

Operations Support Division

No additional positions are proposed; however, a more concentrated approach will be made against vice and narcotics-related crime.

Administrative Support Division

An account clerk II is proposed to maintain department payroll and accounting. Two communications operator I/II positions are proposed to complete the implementation of 9-1-1 and fire dispatch.

All ballistic vests will be replaced, because they have exceeded the manufacturer's life expectancy. A total of $142,000 has been recommended to purchase vests for all police officers and reserves in the coming fiscal year.

Summary

Eighteen positions are recommended to be added to the department this year, most associated with the state traffic grant. Almost $200,000 in minor capital and special projects is also included. Next year, the city will assume a larger share of the cost of the traffic program, and in the third year, no state funds will be available.

STRUCTURED EXERCISE 12-2

In this exercise, a single copy of a current police budget document will need to be acquired from several small to midsize departments. Six or eight should be sufficient. At this chapter's conclusion, participants will read each of the documents (they won't be very long) and discuss them. Then, as a group, evaluate and rank order the budgets in terms of style, including but not limited to (1) information, (2) clarity of purpose, and (3) thoroughness and succinctness. Next, take the "poorest" and "best" examples. As a group, reconstruct the poorest using clues from the best, even improving on that if you can.

Remember, this is going to be your budget. It represents your department and you personally and is the plan for the next fiscal year. Receiving support from the elected officials has a great deal to do with those issues you used for ratings. Some people in the public eye find it easier to vote "no" on a given item rather than ask questions.

Congratulations, you have had a hands-on real-world budget experience.

Competency Checkpoints

- The main purpose of a budget is to help police managers make more accurate decisions about allocation of resources and provision of services.
- A "service fee" is a means for recovering all or some of your budget dollars for police work.
- The four principles of budgeting are (1) establish broad goals, (2) develop ways to attain them, (3) construct a budget that supports goal achievement, and (4) evaluate performance.
- A budget document is also a political statement.
- The budget function is a dynamic and cyclical process that continues throughout the year.
- A continual review of programs is necessary to confirm that they are providing services as originally intended.
- An effective budget presentation requires (1) preparation, (2) timing, and (3) study sessions.
- The seven types of budget funds are organized into three categories:
  - I. Government funds: (1) general, (2) special revenue, (3) capital projects, and (4) debt service
  - II. Proprietary funds: (5) enterprise and (6) internal service
  - III. Fiduciary funds: (7) trust and agency
- Although there are five types of budgets, the most frequently used are (1) line item, (2) performance, and (3) program (results). (The latter has the highest potential for improving the budgetary process.)

Flexing the Message

1. Reread the opening quote. Jim Nunn is now a retired chief deputy of the San Bernardino Sheriff's Department in California. It is an agency of more than 3,000 employees and 3,000 active volunteers. He served in several administrative positions that he never previously worked as a deputy. Nevertheless, Chief Nunn was adept in comprehending the "money situation." In essence, he could work anywhere because he understood where the monies were coming from and when and where they should be expended. Return to Structured Exercise 12-1, and repeat it using the budgets of other police agencies. With some practice, you'll know where the monies are and how best to allocate them. Your career and your value to your department will be significantly enhanced.

2. Many police agencies ignore or forget the enormous amount of revenue that can be generated through service fees (e.g., charging for fingerprints) or contracting for police services (e.g., providing background investigations for business firms). Think about it—where can police agencies, with their proven expertise, increase their revenues by either charging for provided services or contract for needed investigative services?

3. In respect to risk management, do you know your department's position on coping with operational "errors"? Is it cover-up or pay-up? How much money did your agency pay out last year on liability claims? What action is being taken to reduce costly mistakes?

P A R T

III RESULTS

13 | COMMUNITY- AND PROBLEM-ORIENTED POLICING

Community-Oriented Policing (COP)

Community-oriented policing is an organization-wide philosophy and management approach that promotes community, government, and police partnerships; proactive problem solving; and community engagement to address the causes of crime, fear of crime, and other community issues.

Problem-Oriented Policing (POP)

Problem-oriented policing is a department-wide strategy aimed at solving persistent community problems. Police identify, analyze, and respond to the underlying circumstances that create incidents.

If you want to live in the kind of a town
That's the kind of a town you like,
You needn't slip your clothes in a grip
And start on a long, long hike.
You'll find elsewhere what you left behind
For there's nothing that's really new.
It's a knock at yourself when you knock your town;
It isn't your town—it's you.
Real towns are not made by men afraid
Lest somebody else gets ahead.
When everybody works and nobody shirks
You can raise a town from the dead.
And if while you make your stake
Your neighbor can make one, too.
Your town will be what you want to see,
It isn't your town—it's you.
—R. W. Glover

CHAPTER OUTLINE

1. Service

2. Core Component 1: Community Partnership
   a. Who's Really Responsible?
   b. Parts of the Partnership

3. Core Component 2: Organizational Transformation
   a. Changing Governance Styles
   b. Restructuring
   c. Creating Value

4. Core Component 3: Problem Solving
   a. Underlying Conditions
   b. Community Involvement
   c. Community Priorities
   d. A Two-Way Street
   e. Patrol Officers
   f. All Levels
   g. Interagency Assistance

5. Problem-Oriented Policing
   a. SARA
   b. POP: Basic Tasks

6. Service Plus

7. Competency Checkpoints

8. Flexing the Message

Internal relationships drive external performance. It always has and it always will. There is a reason for this chapter being near the end of this book. It is because everything that we have covered thus far must come first. In other words, for community-oriented policing (COP) and its tactical partner, problem-oriented policing (POP), to happen, a police agency must first concentrate on values, ethics, vision, communication, and all the rest.

The ultimate goal of the police is to provide police services in such a manner as to create a desired change in the customer. What is this change? It's that the customer increasingly places greater value on the service received. It's all about them—the customers.

The entire progression toward COP starts with caring—*really caring*. Police leaders have to really care about their community. The leader must equally *really care* about his staff. In line with Rule 150, the leader must know his staff. This means direct and frequent contacts. Why? To repeat—

Internal relationships drive external performance.

After all, if the boss doesn't care about the staff, why should the staff care about the customer? COP and POP are *not* new policing models. Adventurous police agencies were experimenting with COP nearly 40 years ago. Some followed their path in the 1980s. The deliberate and more skeptical joined up in the 1990s. A few continue to either wait cautiously or outright reject COP. They can be detected by such comments about COP as "Fluff!" "It's just change for the sake of change," "I've been doing this for years," and "I really want a COP program, but it requires more officers."

The rest of the chapter presents a comparison of traditional and COP models, explores the three core components of COP, and finally covers the mechanics of POP.

SERVICE

Service is the lifeblood of any organization.
—*Joe DeLadurantey, Ph.D.*

The central service of the police is to control crime. Crime fighting enjoys wide public support as the basic strategy of policing precisely because it embodies a deep commitment to this objective. The approach to achieving this mission has separated into two distinct paradigms, as shown in Table 13-1.

We are convinced, along with many others, that

Community-oriented policing has a better chance of controlling crime and is more focused on rooting out crime than traditional crime fighting.

TABLE 13-1 Two Policing Paradigms	
Traditional Policing Paradigm	*Community Policing Paradigm*
• Manageable number of problems	• Overwhelming number of problems
• Arrest is a primary tool	• Additional tools to solve problems
• Numbers-oriented	• Results-oriented
• Incident driving	• Proactive problem solving
• "Us vs. them" mentality	• Police–community partnerships
• Citizens call 9-1-1	• Citizens meet and work with police and government
• "We do it FOR the community"	• "We do it WITH the community"
• Reactive policing	• Proactive policing
• We let it happen	• We make it happen
• Police, government, citizens reluctant to share information	• Police, government, citizens recognize value of sharing information
• Citizens do not interact with neighbors and community	• Citizens unite to form active neighborhood and community groups
• Officers focus on call response and criminal arrests	• Officers focus on crime reduction and prevention
• Citizens believe the police should solve their problems	• Citizens are active partners with the police to solve problems
• Government agencies schedule and deliver services	• Government agencies are active partners in solving problems

COP can be categorized into three core components:

- Community partnership
- Organizational transformation
- Problem solving

Yes, "Service is the lifeblood of any organization." Everything flows from it and is nourished by it. COP is not a unit or a position in a department; it is an *attitude*—an attitude of *service*!

CORE COMPONENT 1: COMMUNITY PARTNERSHIP

> *The decision to change or not to change an organization should not be made on one department's experience.*
> —Herman Goldstein

In many ways, the concept of community policing is not new in this country. Before the advent of patrol cars, police officers typically walked neighborhood beats getting to know residents and merchants personally and their problems and concerns intimately.

For a host of reasons—including potential for corruption, perceived lack of efficiency, and the development of sophisticated technology—police departments eventually shifted away from beat walking and began emphasizing motor patrols, which offered broader territorial coverage, quicker response to calls for service, and easier supervision of police officers.

Since the 1970s there has been renewed interest in community policing, with its inherent closer contact between the police and citizenry. Why? People want a sense of police presence. Merely increasing the number of police officers is *not* the answer. A new type of police work is being called for in which the ultimate goal is to increase the *value* of police service to the community. This is being attempted by creating a close working relationship between the police and their customers—especially by making them partners in the control of crime and enhancement of safety.

Who's Really Responsible?

If we believe that the police are the first line of defense against disorder and crime and the source of strength for maintaining the quality of life, what should their strategy be? The traditional view is that they are a community's professional defense against crime and disorder: Citizens should leave control of crime and maintenance of order to police. The COP strategy is that police are to promote and buttress a community's ability to create livable neighborhoods and protect them from criminals.

What about neighborhoods in which criminality prevails, where, for example, drug dealers take over and openly deal drugs and threaten citizens? Clearly, our police must play a leading role defending such communities. Should they do so on their own, however?

Oddly enough, when the police move in to attack dangerous street crime aggressively, the very neighborhoods plagued by disorder often reject their methods. The citizens are not ready to surrender control of their neighborhoods to remote police who show them little respect. Are police the first line of defense in a neighborhood? *No!* Citizens are!

People control crime; the officer is the catalyst. Police departments can no longer take a paternalistic attitude toward protecting the community from crime. Departments need community support coordinated by the police.

Parts of the Partnership
Several vital ingredients in a COP program are

- Emphasis on increasing the quantity and improving the quality of police–citizen interactions
- Some mechanism for consulting with the community on its problems and using community input to develop plans to address them
- Emphasis on the development of the self-defense capabilities of the community
- Increased empowerment of the police officer
- Emphasis on decentralized decision making within the police department
- Enhancing the value of police services

Clearly, successful COP programs require face-to-face interaction between police officers and community residents. Equally important is the assignment of a particular officer to a specific beat over an extended period of time so that familiarity and trust can develop. Some police departments have adopted park-and-walk policies for officers and/or the use of bicycles, horses, motor scooters—even roller skates. Currently, the most common and popular community-policing tactic by far is the foot patrol.

CORE COMPONENT 2: ORGANIZATIONAL TRANSFORMATION

The challenge of inventing a new future is never easy. But against a backdrop of much tougher service needs, it is imperative that we take action on many fronts today. The best defense for any police agency is a potent offense.
—*Norman A. Traub*

Developing a COP program automatically involves

- Changing governance styles
- Restructuring
- Creating value

Changing Governance Styles
COP depends on the abandonment of a management emphasis in favor of a team leadership approach. Table 13-2 compares the two styles of governance. (The team leadership concept supports the "agile organization" presented in Chapter 14.)

TABLE 13-2 Comparison of Traditional Management with Team Leadership	
Traditional Management	*Team Leadership*
• Micro-focus (on policy, practices, and methods)	• Macro-focus (on values, mission, goals, and outcomes)
• Authority is centralized	• Employees are encouraged to identify and solve problems
• Manager is in control	• Leader is the facilitator
• Manager maintains a sense of status quo	• Leader maintains a sense of commitment to the shared vision and to change
• Decisions are based on past practices and rules	• Decisions are based on values, judgment, and consensus
• Management is top-down command	• Leadership functions at all levels of organization

Restructuring

The first step in restructuring for COP is the implementation of programs designed to provide the public with ways to participate in policing efforts. The initial phase does not require a total change in the organization's operating style. Step two, conversely, does require the department to make such a change.

Since step one includes only the implementation of individual programs, the systems that support the organization's policing style, such as recruitment, training, performance evaluation, rewards, and discipline, do not change. Therefore, individual and separate programs do not affect the entire department or the entire community.

Step two encompasses more system-wide changes. The changes are not merely programs that are being implemented; the department's style and configuration also are being modified. Unlike individual programs, style affects the total department and the total community. Reconfiguration involves decentralizing the department into smaller work units so that Rule 150 prevails.

> Implementing a COP program is not a short, quick-fix adventure. It is best seen as a three- to five-year installation endeavor. Long-standing ways of doing police business must be undone and new ones implanted. Expect opposition. Habits are not easily unlearned. COP requires patience, persistence, practice, and a lot of perspiration.

By implementing one program at a time, the department is able to accomplish the following:

- Breaking down barriers to change
- Educating its leaders and line employees on the merits of COP
- Reassuring the line employees that the COP concepts being adopted have not been imported from outside the department but, instead, are an outgrowth of existing programs
- Addressing programs on a small scale before making the full transition to COP
- Providing a training ground for COP concepts and strategies
- Developing a willingness to experiment with new ideas
- Demonstrating to the community and elected officials the values of COP

Creating Value

The values added are twofold: community values and police values.

Creating Community Values

- *A Commitment to Crime Prevention* Unlike traditional policing, which focuses on the efficient means of reacting to incidents, COP strives to confirm that the basic mission of the police is to proactively prevent crime and disorder.
- *Public Scrutiny of Police Operations* Because citizens will be more involved with the police, they will be exposed to the "what," "why," and "how" of police work. This is almost certain to prompt meaningful discussions about the responsiveness of police operations.
- *Accountability to the Public* Until the advent of COP, officers were accountable for their actions only to police management. Now, officers also will be accountable to the community with whom they have formed a partnership.
- *Customized Police Service* Because police services will be decentralized, officers will be able to increase their responsiveness to neighborhood problems. As police–citizen partnerships are forged and nurtured, the two groups will be better equipped to work together to identify and address specific problems that affect the quality of neighborhood life.
- *Community Organization* The degree to which the community is involved in police efforts to evaluate neighborhood problems has a significant bearing on the effectiveness of those efforts. The success of any crime-prevention effort depends on the police and citizens working in concert—not on one or the other carrying the entire load alone.

Creating Police Values

- *Greater Citizen Support* As more people spend more time working with police, they learn more about police operations. Experience has shown that as people's knowledge of the police function increases, their respect for the police increases as well. This increased respect, in turn, leads to greater support for the police.
- *Shared Responsibility* Historically, the police have accepted the responsibility for resolving the problem of crime in the community. Under COP, however, citizens develop a sense of shared responsibility.
- *Greater Job Satisfaction* Because officers are able to more successfully resolve issues and problems, they experience the results of their efforts more quickly.
- *Better Internal Relationships* Communication problems among units and shifts have been a chronic problem in police agencies. Because COP focuses on problem-solving accountability, it also increases cooperation among the various segments of the department.
- *Support for Organizational Changes* COP requires a vast restructuring of the department's organization. Such restructuring promotes the integration of various functions, such as patrol and investigations. The needed changes include new management systems, new training curriculums and delivery mechanisms, a new performance evaluation system, a new disciplinary process, a new reward system, new ways of managing calls for service, and hands-on leadership.

CORE COMPONENT 3: PROBLEM SOLVING

> *An accepted leader has only to be sure of what it is best to do*
> *or at least to have made up his mind about it.*
> —*Winston Churchill*

There is a distinction between "problem solving" as a part of COP and "problem-oriented policing" as a part of COP. Problem solving, or the problem-solving process, depends on community participation in the identification and resolution of a problem. POP likewise is addressing a problem, *but* (and here's the distinction): the police agency (1) is using a specific method such as SARA (discussed later) and (2) typically does not involve community members in the problem identification or response process. The definitions of COP and POP are the basis for separating problem solving from POP.

> *Problem solving* is a broad term that implies more than simply the elimination and prevention of crimes. Problem solving is based on two assumptions. First, crime and disorder can be reduced by carefully studying the characteristics of problems in a geographic area and then applying the appropriate resources and tactics. The second assumption is that individuals make choices based on the opportunities presented by the immediate physical and social factors of an area and that these factors can be affected in a manner such that the right choices will be made.

Underlying Conditions

The theory behind the problem-solving process is simple: Underlying conditions create problems. These conditions might include the characteristics of the people involved (offenders, potential victims, and others), the social setting in which these people interact, the physical environments, and the way the public deals with these conditions.

A problem created by these conditions may generate one or more incidents. These incidents, while stemming from a common source, may appear to be different. For example, social and physical conditions in a deteriorated apartment complex may generate burglaries, acts of vandalism, intimidation of pedestrians by rowdy teenagers, and other incidents. These incidents, some of which come to police attention, are in reality "symptoms" of the problems. The incidents will continue so long as the problem that creates them persists.

Community Involvement

As police recognize the effectiveness of the problem-solving approach, there will be a growing awareness that community involvement is essential for its success. Determining the underlying causes of crime depends, to a great extent, on an in-depth knowledge of community. Therefore, community participation in identifying and setting priorities will contribute to effective problem-solving efforts by the community and the police. Cooperative problem solving also reinforces trust, facilitates the exchange of information, and leads to the identification of other areas that could benefit from the mutual attention of the police and the community.

Community Priorities

For this process to operate effectively, the police need to devote attention to and recognize the validity of community concerns. Neighborhood groups and the police will not always agree on which specific problems deserve attention first. Police may regard robberies as the biggest problem in a particular community, while residents may find derelicts who sleep in doorways, break bottles on sidewalks, and pick through garbage cans to be the number one problem. Under community policing, the problem with derelicts should also receive early attention from the police with the assistance of other government agencies and community members.

Therefore, in addition to the serious crime problems identified by police, community policing must also address the problems of significant concern to the community. Community policing in effect encourages community members to bring problems of great concern to them to the attention of the police. Once informed of community concerns, the police must work with citizens to address those concerns while at the same time showing them how to assist in solving the problems.

A Two-Way Street

In COP, the problem-solving process depends on input from both the police and the community. Problem solving can involve

- *Eliminating the Problem Entirely*   This type of solution is usually limited to disorder problems. Examples include eliminating traffic congestion by erecting traffic control signs and destroying or rehabilitating abandoned buildings that can provide an atmosphere conducive to crime.
- *Reducing the Number of Occurrences of the Problem*   Drug dealing and the accompanying problems of robbery and gang violence will be decreased if the police and community work together to set up drug counseling and rehabilitation centers. Longer-range solutions might include intensifying drug education in schools, churches, and hospitals.
- *Reducing the Degree of Injury per Incident*   For example, police can teach store clerks how to act during a robbery in order to avoid injury or death and can advise women in the community on ways to minimize the chances of being killed or seriously injured if attacked.
- *Improving Problem Handling*   Police should always make an effort to treat people humanely (e.g., show sensitivity in dealing with rape victims and seek ways to ease their trauma; increase effectiveness in handling runaway juveniles, drug addicts, drunk drivers, and the like, by working with other agencies more closely).
- *Manipulating Environmental Factors to Discourage Criminal Behavior*   This can include collaborative efforts to add better lighting, remove overgrown weeds and trim shrubbery, and seal off vacant apartment buildings.

Patrol Officers

Patrol officers are *the* focal point for joint police and community problem-solving endeavors. They are involved with the community on a day-to-day basis, understand its unique physical and social characteristics, are aware of local problems, and when needed, can help community members articulate their needs. Many problems within the community can be successfully handled by patrol officers or their immediate supervisors and members of the community (e.g., determining that better lighting would decrease the incidence of mugging at a local park).

All Levels

All levels of the police organization should contribute to problem solving. For example, crafting a solution to widespread incidents of spousal assault taking place in several communities in an agency's jurisdiction might involve multiple levels of police management. Patrol officers may have noticed a correlation between spousal assaults and excessive drinking by the perpetrators, especially late at night at bars. The officers, their supervisors, and community members might explore ways to close down these clubs with the help of local zoning and city planning boards. Perpetrators with alcohol problems might be required to attend rehabilitation programs run by a city agency. Meanwhile, mid- and senior-level police managers and community leaders might confer with women's groups and other social agencies about providing temporary housing and counseling for victims and their families. In addition, members of the community might be able to repair an abandoned building to house the victims.

Interagency Assistance

The problem-solving process relies on the expertise and assistance of an array of social and government agencies and community resources. Police managers might combine forces with a civil abatement agency to condemn and board up crack houses. One police officer seeking a system-wide approach to the problem of spousal assault formed a team comprised of units from the police department and representatives from women's shelters, the YWCA, nearby military bases, the prosecutor's office, newspapers, hospitals, and social agencies. A tremendous amount of leverage can be attained through the collaboration and partnership of this type of far-ranging alliance.

PROBLEM-ORIENTED POLICING

> *But the "them" we battle isn't the community we serve; it's*
> *the jackals that prey upon it.*
> —*Will Beall, Police Officer*

Problem-oriented policing (POP) emphasizes the value of being able to diagnose the continuing problems underlying repeated incidents reported to police employees and to design and implement solutions to those problems. A police department is practicing POP when it

- Identifies substantive community problems
- Inquires systematically into their nature
- Analyzes community interest and special interest in each problem
- Assesses current responses
- Conducts an uninhibited search for tailor-made solutions
- Takes the initiative in implementing solutions
- Evaluates the effectiveness of solutions

Current police practice is primarily *incident-driven*. That is, most police activities are aimed at resolving individual incidents rather than groups of incidents or problems. The incident-driven police department has four characteristics.

First, it is reactive. Most of the workload of patrol officers and detectives consists of handling crimes that have been committed: disturbances in progress, traffic violations, and the like. The exceptions—crime prevention and narcotics investigations, for example—make up but a small portion of police work.

Second, incident-driven police work relies on limited information, gathered mostly from victims, witnesses, and suspects. Only limited information is needed because the police objectives are limited: Patrol officers and detectives are trying only to resolve the incident at hand.

Third, the primary means of resolving incidents is to invoke the criminal justice process. Even when an officer manages to resolve an incident without arresting or citing anyone, it is often the threat of enforcing the law that is the key to resolution. Alternative means of resolution are seldom invoked.

Finally, incident-driven police departments use aggregate statistics to measure performance. The department is doing a good job when the city-wide crime rate is low or the city-wide arrest rate is high. The best officers are those who make many arrests or service many calls.

A police agency is not constrained to one strategy for accomplishing its mission. It is important, however, that if two or more strategies are adopted, they must be compatible and not confrontational.

See Figures 13-1 and 13-2 for a comparison of incident-driven and problem-oriented policing. These figures were originally published in the article "Personnel Performance Evaluations in the Community Policing Context" by Timothy N. Oettmeir and Mary Ann Wycoff, in *Community Policing: Contemporary Readings,* 2nd ed., Geofrey P. Alpert and Alex R. Piquero, eds. (Prospect Heights, IL: Waveland Press, 2000, pp. 399–400), and are used with the permission of the authors.

The practice of POP seeks to improve on other crime-fighting strategies by adding pro-activeness and thoughtfulness. It differs from COP by its emphasis on an analytic effort. It differs from crime-fighting/incident-driven policing, which focuses on discovering offenders and apprehending them. It assumes that

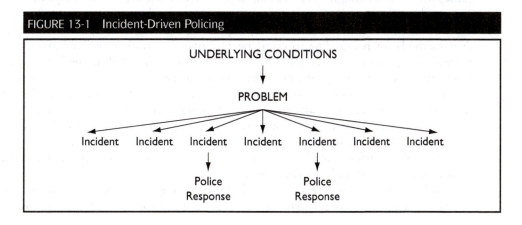

FIGURE 13-1 Incident-Driven Policing

FIGURE 13-2 Problem-Oriented Policing

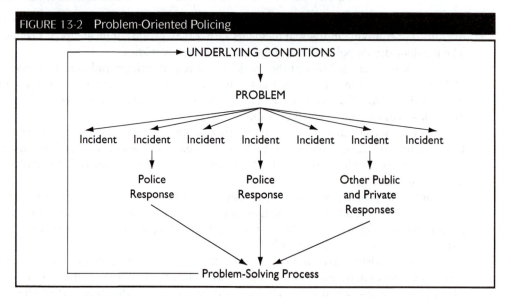

the police can position themselves to detect the underlying causes for offenses and thus respond to them more effectively.

Problem-oriented policing takes a much different view of crime. In POP, it is not automatically accepted that crimes are caused by predatory offenders. (True, in all crimes there will be an offender.) But POP makes the assumption that crimes could be caused by particular continuing problems in a community, such as drug dealing. Hence, crimes might be controlled, or even prevented, by actions other than the arrest of particular individuals. Arrest and prosecution remain crucially important tools of policing. However, creative ideas about the causes of crime and methods to correct it are paramount.

In POP, the applied imagination of police employees, sworn and civilian alike, is forged into a potent crime-fighting tool. Problem identification and problem definition are essential steps in POP. The superficial symptoms of crime are avoided while the root causes are ardently sought. (The common linkage of POP, COP, and the professional crime-fighting/incident-driven strategy, however, remains the same—crime control!)

The subtle but powerful switch in perspective requires police agencies to expand their methods for responding to crime beyond patrol, investigation, and arrests. For example, the police can use negotiating and conflict-resolving skills to mediate disputes before they become crime problems. Why wait for crime to occur? Moreover, the police can take corrective action the second time they are called to the scene rather than the sixth or seventh time, thus making timely savings in the use of police resources.

The police can use civil licensing authority and other municipal ordinances to enhance neighborhood security. Bars can be cautioned on excessive noise, children can be cautioned on curfew violations, and loitering ordinances can be expanded to reduce situations that require police involvement.

Further, other local agencies can help deal with existing or potential criminal offenses. The fire department can be asked to inspect "crack houses" for fire safety regulations. The public works department can be asked to inspect buildings and property for code violations. To the extent that problem solving depends on the initiative and skills of officers and civilians in defining problems and devising solutions, the administrative style of the organization must change. Since POP depends on individual initiative, the agency must decentralize its operations and empower its employees.

Both COP and POP strive for greater crime control. The techniques are sufficiently different, which necessitates separate coverage. COP depends more on community involvement, while POP relies more on police employee problem solving. One strategy obviously contains tactics of the other. The crime-fighting/incident-driven strategy targets crime control. COP and POP also target crime control but add a strong commitment to order, maintenance, and prevention by analysis.

SARA

With time and experimentation, a problem-solving model known as SARA was developed by several agencies. This model also supports a management by objectives (MBO) program and is highly useful in making an agile organization a reality.

SARA means:

Scanning: identifying the problem
Analysis: learning the problem's causes, scope, and effects
Response: acting to alleviate the problem
Assessment: determining whether the response works

A Problem Analysis Guide was also formulated to assist in the application of SARA.

The Problem Analysis Guide (List of Topic Headings)

- Actors
  - Victims
    Lifestyle
    Security measures taken
    Victimization history
  - Offenders
    Identity and physical description
    Lifestyle, education, employment history
    Criminal history
  - Third parties
    Personal data
    Connection to victim
- Incidents
  - Sequence of events
    Events preceding act
    Act itself
    Events following criminal act

- Physical context
  Time
  Location
  Access control and surveillance
- Social context
  Likelihood and probable actions of witnesses
  Apparent attitude of residents toward neighborhood
- Immediate results of incidents
  Harm done to victim
  Gain to offender
  Legal issues
- Responses
  - Community
    Neighborhood affected by problem
    City as a whole
    People outside the city
  - Institutional
    Criminal justice system
    Other public agencies
    Mass media
    Business sector
  - Seriousness
    Public perceptions
    Perception of others

POP: Basic Tasks

This section reinforces the essential components of a POP program.

Task 1: Grouping Incidents as Problems

The first component of POP is to move beyond simple incident handling. It requires that incidents be looked on as symptoms of a problem.

Task 2: Focus on Substantive Problems

Recurring problems are substantive problems, what we think of as police work. Simply, but importantly, substantive problems are those very problems that justify establishing a police agency in the first place.

Task 3: Effectiveness First

Effectiveness is defining for a specific agency, in a particular community, what ought to be tackled and in what order of priority.

Task 4: Setting Up a System

Once the seemingly random incidents have been categorized into groups, a system for the collection of pertinent facts and their analysis must be designed. Systematic analysis includes (1) crime and service statistics, (2) telephone, questionnaire, and individual surveys of those who might have information (e.g., citizens, victims, officers, offenders, other governmental personnel), and (3) literature searches of government and private-sector repositories.

Task 5: Redefining Problems

What at first blush may be a traffic problem may, on further analysis, be categorized as a drug problem. Problem definitions make or break a POP program. There is an enormous difference between thinking tactically about dealing with burglars from a legal standpoint and coping with burglary as it exists in the community. How we perceive and label a problem ultimately determines how we go after it.

Task 6: Who's Interested (or Should Be)?

For example, gangs. Why is the community concerned? What are the social costs? Who is being harmed? There are obviously many other similar questions. To invent a successful action plan to deal with gangs, or any other problems, the police must find out who is interested in it. It is here that POP surfaces—"If it ain't broke, don't fix it." If the agency's approach to spousal abuse is successful, don't fuss with it unless some other tactic can nearly guarantee an improvement.

Task 7: Customized or Canned?

In the 1970s, the criminal justice system was filled with talk of "technology transfer." Many departments borrowed or purchased "turnkey" computers and helicopters, modified workweeks (e.g., 4–10, 3–12, 5–9), and implemented a variety of operational programs (e.g., team policing, neighborhood watch). Most found that canned approaches, when incorporated in any agency, had to be redesigned, or should have been. POP relies on a tailor-made response. Problems are specific to an agency and sometimes a neighborhood; methods of resolving them must be specific. POP is not saying, however, that agencies should shun other innovations.

As Herman Goldstein put it: "The decision to change or not change an organization should not be made on one department's experience." Once again, model POP and COP programs are just that, not road maps to your destination.

Task 8: Take the Offensive

Taking the offensive is accomplished in three ways. First, the initial identification of problems must be constant and systematic. Second, the police must be active in educating the public and placing choices before it. Third, the police should be advocates for their community, reporting, for example, if garbage is uncollected, potholes unfilled, and vehicles abandoned.

Task 9: Decision Visibility

More and more we are seeing officers educating the public on why certain things are or are not done. Decisions are explained. That assists the public in understanding that the police do not have as much authority as they think and that they'll take risks and sometimes fail—they're not infallible.

Task 10: Evaluation and Feedback

Evaluation and feedback are not a concluding POP step. They are designed to support all the other components in making incremental adjustments and improvements. For example, a reliable evaluation should be able to inform the department if its original grouping of problems was valid. Without this task, POP is likely to flop.

Scenario One—Let It Rock   A local restaurant/bar in your area started featuring live amateur rock bands on weekends and the bands draw large crowds of young people. Over the past two months, noise complaints have tripled in the area; citizens have called in and mailed in complaints of excessive trash, drunken bar patrons urinating in their yards, drug use in the area, fights in the street, speeding vehicles, and an increase in property damage. Drunken driving arrests have increased and have been linked to the bar. Also, two of the band's staff members were arrested for possession of firearms. The restaurant owner has ample security/bouncers and has done all he can do to mitigate problems, but he is making a lot of money and is in compliance with all the city's requirements in terms of zoning, permits, business license, and so on. As a *police manager*, what steps would you take using the COP/POP philosophy to ensure this problem was solved?

Scenario Two—Home Sweet Home   Several large shelters for the homeless in neighboring cities have closed down due to funding problems. With the warm summer weather, there has been a sharp increase in the transient population. Your city's abundance of parks with 24-hour bathrooms has become a refuge for a variety of homeless and emotionally disturbed persons. Wide-scale complaints are being made regarding drunks sleeping or passing out throughout the park, human feces in public areas, fights, thefts, and several stabbings, as well as the public restrooms being used for bathing and lewd activity. An article in the local newspaper about the problem and citizen discontent was titled, "Hobo Park Needs Help." As a *police manager,* what steps would you take using the COP/POP philosophy to ensure this problem was solved?

Scenario Three—Fast and Furious   Your beat areas of responsibility consist of primarily industrial areas with wide multi-lane roadways. During nights and weekends, there is virtually no activity other than through traffic and nightshift personnel working inside the buildings. Complaints are starting to become regular regarding high-speed vehicles in the area. Business owners report finding heavy acceleration burnout tire marks, long skid marks, and doughnut-type skid marks in their parking lots and on the streets. They also have been finding numerous beer bottles, trash, and condoms in the area. Graffiti and broken windows are now common calls for service. Gas runs have increased during the weekends and car part thefts as well as window smash thefts of auto part stores are starting to occur. One of your agency's explorers turned in a flyer that advertised a race on Saturday (unknown location) that called for "Street Racers to Take the Challenge." The flyer was one of hundreds circulating through the high school. Last, one of your officers went in pursuit of two custom high-performance vehicles in the industrial area, but quickly lost them after they reached speeds of 120 mph. As a *police manager,* what steps would you take using the COP/POP philosophy to ensure this problem was solved?

Scenario Four—Two-Wheel Terror   In one of your residential areas, there is a disabled veteran who has an assortment of medical problems. He is an alcoholic, becomes angry when he is intoxicated, and often defecates in his own clothing. He is bound to a wheelchair as he only has one leg. He has hepatitis, reoccurring skin diseases and sores, substantial body lice, and a serious asthma condition that requires frequent medications and bronchial sprays. The subject sporadically lives in a house where an elderly caretaker/nurse cares for him and manages his state income checks; however, the caretaker cannot control him. The subject has no family and is in the streets most of the time panhandling in order to purchase alcohol. Several small grocery businesses have restraining orders against the subject and he is the source of continuing complaints. When he drinks, he yells profanity at anyone in the area, disrupts traffic, trespasses onto other people's property, and often falls out of his wheelchair. Most citizens will not press charges against the subject and officers do anything to avoid arresting him, including ignoring minor warrants for his arrest. Twice while in custody, the subject required medical treatment that caused a substantial medical bill to be paid by the city. Last, the fire department is all too familiar with the subject and except for a medical emergency, will have nothing to do with him. As a *police manager,* what steps would you take using the COP/POP philosophy to ensure this problem was solved?

Scenario Five—Build It and They Will Come   A methadone and addiction treatment clinic has opened in your area. This has caused numerous heroin addicts and chemically dependent drug users to frequent the clinic daily. Many of the center's clients are parolees and gang members. The local area businesses have launched continuous complaints, stating that shoplifting is rampant, that drugs are being used in parking lots and alleys, and that their sales are suffering because their customers are intimidated and scared to come to the area. Several fights with injuries have occurred in and around the clinic between opposing gang members. Many of the subjects obtaining treatment or who are on the methadone program tend to hang out in the area after their treatment. One of the nearby business owners is also a member of your City Council and was horrified when his 8-year-old grandson found and picked up an uncapped syringe in the rear parking lot of his business. As a *police manager,* what steps would you take using the COP/POP philosophy to ensure this problem was solved?

STRUCTURED EXERCISE 13-1

This exercise helps you to apply both POP and COP.

1. Participants should be placed in groups of six to eight members.
2. Each group will be given one of the five scenarios on neighborhood issues to use with COP/POP. The instructor should develop scenarios in advance that apply to local issues or, also in advance, have the students identify community problems in their own jurisdictions.
3. The participants will have 40 minutes to discuss among themselves and write their presentations on the easel board.
4. A spokesperson from each group will present their scenario and solution to the group.

SERVICE PLUS

I am convinced that those who are most happy are those who have sought and discovered how to serve.
—Albert Schweitzer

Use of one policing model does not preclude the combined use of compatible elements or models. A confluence of COP, POP, and crime-fighting policing models may well be the ultimate model for the next decade and beyond. Remember, any existing model is just that, a *model*, not a plan to be superimposed on a police organization. Every city, county, and community is unique. Understand that customizing COP/POP through participation by both police employees and community members is the key to developing police services all will accept and support.

COP is not about the police or all about the community. It's all about us—the police and the community they serve. It's about police services that create a customer experience that is valued to the point that the community appreciates and endorses it. This is "service plus." And that is, in summary, COP. Please read again the opening quote and especially the concluding words of hope: "Your town will be what you want to see/ It isn't your town—it's you."

Competency Checkpoints

- The main purpose of the police is to control crime, and community-oriented policing (COP) has the best chance of making it happen.
- The three core components of COP are (1) community partnership, (2) organizational transformation, and (3) problem solving.
- A partnership depends on frequent face-to-face interaction between the police and community residents.
- Organizational transformation includes (1) a new type of leadership, (2) restructuring, and (3) making certain everyone benefits.
- Problem solving must involve (1) line and management staff, (2) residents/victims, and (3) interagency support.
- Problem-oriented policing is a diagnostic tool for uncovering the root causes of an issue.
- The primary problem-solving model is SARA (scanning, analysis, response, and assessment).
- POP is best not approached as a method for improving the police. Rather, it should be used as a way to solve community problems.

Flexing the Message

1. For more updated COP/POP trends and programs, contact the Community Policing Exchange, a free bimonthly publication administered and funded by the U.S. Department of Justice, Bureau of Justice Assistance, and produced by the Community Policing Consortium. For information, telephone (202) 833-3305,

write Community Policing Exchange, 1726 M Street, NW, Suite 801, Washington, DC 20036, or visit www.communitypolicing.org/publications/exchange/.

2. Flex your COP/POP learning experience in this group exercise in which you and other participants role-play assigned characters of various community members, media representatives, politicians, or law enforcement personnel working together to solve a community problem.

   a. Each participant is given a specific role assignment (i.e., a politician, police commander, citizen, business owner, media representative, student body president, religious leader, etc.).

   b. In advance, decide on a crime or community problem. Ideas for some of the community problems could include graffiti, minor thefts, loud parties, robberies, abandoned cars, run-down neighborhoods, and date rape.

   c. The participants are to engage in open conversation with each other (while representing the views and requests of their assigned role).

   d. While still in their assigned roles, the participants should offer proposed solutions to the problem.

   e. After the group has presented some proposed solutions, follow up with a group discussion about how the SARA model could be used to address the issues.

3. Visit a police agency and inquire about their COP/POP programs. Ask if they have any literature on their programs. Also, ask if they have any innovations in meeting community needs.

14 | ORGANIZING

Many of us live two lives. One life is personal, with choices, freedom, interdependency, caring, loyalty, and trust. The other life is organizational, which can consist of directions, control, dependency, indifference, and self-serving. Or if we are fortunate, it may consist of the same qualities we enjoy in our personal life.

The agile organization combined with a management by objectives program presents the best possible structural environment for community-oriented policing.

The best executive is the one who has enough sense to pick good people to do what he wants done, and self-restraint enough to keep from meddling with them while they do it.
—Theodore Roosevelt

CHAPTER OUTLINE

Over the past several pages, you and I explored *the why* of policing. We concentrated on community-driven values of policing and problem solving. We avoided the "hook and book" concept and centered on an overarching value that consists of philosophy, strategy, attitude, and behavior devoted to *service*.

We'll now look at *the way*, or organization, for making *the why* happen. One of the systems thwarts, even destroys any endeavor to deliver COP/POP; the other facilitates it. After reading about the two ways to organize for service delivery, you'll not have to guess which is which. The chapter that follows deals with *the what* we've accomplished—performance measurements.

Since the term *organization* has been used, let's define it.

> *Organizations* are social units (human groupings) that have been deliberately constructed and reconstructed to seek specific goals. Business corporations, military units, schools, churches, and police departments are included; ethnic groups, friendship groups, and family groups are excluded. An organization is characterized by (1) goals; (2) a rationally planned division of labor, authority, power, and communication responsibilities; (3) a set of rules and norms; and (4) the presence of one or more authority centers that control the efforts of the organization and direct them toward its goals.

CONTROL

> *An organization will excel only by amplifying strengths, never by simply fixing weakness.*
> —*Marcus Buckingham*

One, if not *the,* major condition of a police agency that has been most resistant to change is location of control. If control is centralized at the top of an organization, then power is distributed in a top-down, bureaucratic, hierarchical fashion. If control is decentralized, then power is shared in a bottom-up, agile, and open manner.

Control: An Illusion or a Reality?

In moving from the traditional bureaucratic, hierarchical organization to an empowered or agile organization, the greatest issue is control. Beyond money and fame, what drives many managers in bureaucratic organizations is power—the desire to be in control. Most would rather give up anything than control. Yet the perception that someone "up there" is in control is based on an illusion—the illusion that anyone could master the dynamic and detailed complexity of a police organization from the top.

The illusion of being in control can appear quite real. In hierarchical organizations, managers give orders and others follow. But giving orders is not the same as being in control. Power may be concentrated at the top, but having the power of unilateral decision making is not the same as being able to achieve one's objectives. Authority figures may be treated deferentially, lavished with the highest salaries and other privileges of rank, but that does not mean that they actually exercise control commensurate with their apparent importance.

Community-oriented policing depends on distributed control, which means everyone is empowered and thus everyone shares in controlling the organization. Only those organizations practicing empowerment are able to attest that the leader's control is actually increased and not lessened. In reality, true power is not power until it is shared.

Top-Down Control

On paper, the top-down organization looks like a formidable pyramid. It consists of many layers of managers and prestigious job titles; it thrives on written policies and rules; it emphasizes complexity. The manager is the boss, and authority trickles down from there. We refer to this as the *bureaucratic organization*. Here's how six major components of organizations are dealt with in a bureaucratic organization:

- *Service.*   The managers decide on what types and quality of services are best for the community.
- *Community.*   The people served are considered and treated as a faceless, nameless group.
- *Power.*   Power is viewed as having clearly defined boundaries and is centralized at the top of the department.
- *Commitment.*   There is top managerial commitment to their bosses and elite work groups.
- *Purpose.*   The purpose of the department and its divisions is defined by top management.
- *Achievements/advancements.*   Opportunity to achieve and be rewarded (e.g., promotion, a better job) is limited to those that daily demonstrate a commitment to the top managers.

Top-down control relies on a bureaucratic organization to get the mission accomplished. Management is primary and leadership secondary when using this type of governance.

Bottom-Up Empowerment

The bottom-up organization looks, on paper, like a fluid Frisbee. It consists of a few layers of leader-managers with little attention to official emblems of rank; it thrives on flexibility, action, simplicity, and empowerment. The leader is the senior partner, and authority is bottom-up. We refer to this as the *agile organization*. Here's how six major components of organizations are dealt with in an agile organization:

- *Service.*   The leader, in concert with his or her work team, communicates with the community to decide what is best for the customers.
- *Community.*   The people served are viewed and served as individuals, with each being unique.
- *Power.*   Power is understood as being infinite. It is dispersed throughout the agency. Every employee is empowered.
- *Commitment.*   Similar to power, there is an equal commitment by the department to the welfare of all employees.
- *Purpose.*   The purpose of the department and its divisions is determined by people representing all levels and job assignments within the agency.

- *Achievements/advancements.* The changes of career growth and job accomplishments are unlimited and not tied to a particular manager or preferred supervisory style.

   Bottom-up management depends on an agile organization for mission fulfillment. Leadership is primary and management secondary in this type of governance system.

Which One Is Best?

All things considered, and all things being equal, the empowered or agile organization is the more beneficial of the two types for the delivery of high-quality police services. However, in the real world of police work, not all things are considered, and all things are not equal. Thus, before a decision on what form of control system is best for an agency, the following questions or issues must be explored.

- How much tolerance is there for mistakes—taking risks?
- What is the nature of the community, and what do they expect from their police?
- What is the skill level of the personnel?

STRUCTURED EXERCISE 14-1

Visualize an organization—one that you currently work for, or one that you worked for in the past. Next, respond to the following questions about the various dimensions by circling the most appropriate number.

1. Service mix is decided at the top.   Service mix is decided by everyone.

1	2	3	4	5	6	7

2. Community is seen as a whole.   Community is seen as comprised of individuals.

1	2	3	4	5	6	7

3. Power is centralized.   Power is dispersed.

1	2	3	4	5	6	7

4. Commitment is to top management.   Commitment is to all employees.

1	2	3	4	5	6	7

5. Purpose is defined by top management.   Purpose is defined by all levels in the department.

1	2	3	4	5	6	7

6. Achievement is judged by management standards.   Achievement is judged by individual contributions.

1	2	3	4	5	6	7

   Add up the numbers. With a score of 36 or higher, you are more likely working for a governance system that is agile and in need of leader-managers. With a score of 24 or lower, the governance system likely is highly structured and is in need of manager-leaders.

- Do the employees support the mission of the department?
- How motivated is the staff?
- How ethical is the staff?
- How much trust is there among the personnel and among the work units?

Once the above questions have been answered and evaluated, those in power can decide on either a "top-down control" or a "bottom-up empowered" governance system.

The type of control system determines which organizational design should be used. If it's a manager-leader, then the bureaucratic or top-down organization is required. If it's a leader-manager, then the agile or empowered organization is called for. A revolt will occur if the wrong organizational system is applied. Manager-leaders will struggle, if not fail, within an agile organizational setting. And leader-managers will flop in a bureaucratic environment.

Structured Exercise 14-2 is *a keystone for the final part of this section. Review it carefully.*

STRUCTURED EXERCISE 14-2

Several years ago, when I was still a police officer, during roll call a newly appointed sergeant appeared and introduced himself to the 12 of us. He went on to say, "This isn't a democracy. I believe in participative supervision. I'm going to supervise, and you're going to participate. I run a benign dictatorship."

Later that evening, while we were on patrol, my partner remarked, "It appears that this sergeant is the same as the last. Clearly, he is not interested in our ideas or opinions. He's big into control. And if we want to get along with him, then we'd best comply with his orders."

Several years afterward, I recalled this episode. I saw a gross paradox in our daily lives as compared to our organizational lives. First of all, we live with political institutions that celebrate the rights of individuals to express themselves, to assemble, to pursue happiness and individual purposes, and to pick their own political leaders. We pay enormous attention to the rights and procedures of due process. At times, we seem to be on the edge of anarchy and yet we tenaciously cling to our political beliefs. Conversely, when we shift into our occupational life, those beliefs are best ignored. Consistency, control, and compliance become the dominant values.

For many years, I faced the frustrating dilemma of how to most effectively govern an organization. I was convinced that democracy would not work. Can you imagine voting on whether we should wear uniforms, who works what assignments, ethical standards, and whether or not to evaluate employee performance? I was equally convinced that while a top-down autocracy could work, it was filled with such pitfalls as transparent loyalty, weak commitment, low trust, poor communications, and zero risk taking.

If neither one of the above control systems is relevant, then come the questions: What might prove successful? What is the most reliable alternative? Before reading further, think about these questions. What is your answer? Discuss it with your colleagues.

THE BUREAUCRATIC ORGANIZATION

Bureaucracy is here to stay.
—*Anthony Downs*

Most police organizations are bureaucratic in nature and foster top-down, manager-prominent governance systems. Nonetheless, you normally will find a few pockets of agile thinking and leader-managers in charge.

Bureaucracies are organizations that have numerous *formalized rules and regulations*. They are among the most important institutions in the world because they not only provide employment for a very significant portion of the world's population but also make critical decisions that shape the economic, educational, political, social, moral, and even religious lives of nearly everyone on Earth.

The man we know as Ulysses S. Grant was actually named Hiram Ulysses Grant. When Congressman Thomas Hamer appointed Grant to West Point, he mistakenly filled out the application in the name of "Ulysses S. Grant." When Grant discovered in May 1839 that the academy had him registered under the wrong name, he tried to get the error corrected. He was told that it didn't matter what he or his parents thought his name was; the official government application said his name was "Ulysses S." and that application could not be changed. If Hiram U. Grant wanted to attend West Point, he would have to change his name.

Bureaucrats blindly obey whatever set of rules they are given, even if it leads them to make completely illogical decisions. You can keep your people from turning into bureaucrats by regularly reminding them that your organization's rules and regulations are designed to provide guidance to intelligent leaders who use their heads and not ridiculous instructions to robots.

The Four Principles of Bureaucracy

A bureaucratic organization has four givens—division of labor, hierarchy of authority, structure, and span of control. Of the four, division of labor is the most important; in fact, the other three depend on it for their very existence.

The hierarchy of authority is the legitimate vertical network for gaining compliance. Essentially, it includes the chain of command, the sharing of authority and responsibility, the unity of command, and the obligation to report.

Structure is the logical relationship of positions and functions in an organization, arranged to accomplish the objectives of the organization. Classical organization theory usually works with two basic structures, the line and the staff. Both structures can be arranged four ways: purpose, process, people (clientele), and place where services are rendered.

The span of control concept deals with the number of subordinates a superior can effectively supervise. It has significance, in part, for the shape of the organization. Wide span yields a flat structure; narrow span results in a tall structure.

The modern bureaucratic organization evolved from the thinking and practice of

- Max Weber, who emphasized the need for rationality
- Frederick W. Taylor, who concentrated on its scientific aspects
- Luther Gulick and Lyndall Urwick, who formulated principles

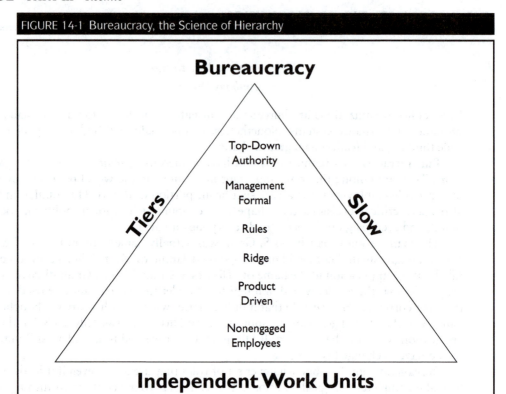

FIGURE 14-1 Bureaucracy, the Science of Hierarchy

Bureaucracy

Top-Down
Authority

Management
Formal

Rules

Ridge

Product
Driven

Nonengaged
Employees

Tiers

Slow

Independent Work Units

Weber: Rationality

Max Weber was a founder of modern sociology, as well as a pioneer in administrative thought. Weber explored bureaucracy (essentially synonymous with "large organization") to uncover the rational relationships of bureaucratic structure to its goals. His analysis led him to conclude that there were three types of organizational power centers: (1) traditional—subjects consider the orders of a supervisor to be justified, because that is the way things have always been done; (2) charismatic—subjects accept a superior's order because of the influence of his or her personality; (3) rational-legal—subjects accept a superior's order because it agrees with more abstract rules that are considered legitimate.

Power and Authority

The type of power employed determines the degree of alienation on the part of the subject. If the subject perceives the power as legitimate, he or she is more willing to comply. And if power is considered legitimate, then, according to Weber, it becomes authority. Hence, Weber's three power centers can be translated into authority centers. Of the three types of authority, Weber recommended that rational structural relationships be obtained through the rational-legal form. He felt that the other two forms lacked systematic division of labor, specialization, and stability and had nonrelevant political and administrative relationships.

Six Safeguards

In each principle of bureaucracy described below, Weber's constant concern about the frailty of a rational-legal bureaucracy is apparent. His primary motive, therefore, was to build into the bureaucratic structure safeguards against external and internal pressures, so that the bureaucracy could at all times sustain its autonomy. According to Weber, a bureaucratic structure, to be rational, must contain these elements:

1. *Rulification and Routinization* A continuous organization of official functions bound by *rules*. Rational organization is the opposite of temporary, unstable relations—thus the stress on continuity. Rules save effort by eliminating the need for deriving a new solution for every situation. They also facilitate standard and equal treatment of similar situations.
2. *Division of Labor* A specific sphere of competence. This involves a sphere of obligation to perform functions that have been designated as part of a systematic division of labor. It clearly defines the necessary means of compulsion and delineates definite conditions concerning their use.
3. *Hierarchy of Authority* The organization of offices follows the principle of hierarchy; that is, each lower office is under the control and supervision of a higher one.
4. *Expertise* The rules that regulate the conduct of an office may be *technical* rules or norms. In both cases, if their application is to be fully rational, special training is necessary. It is thus normally true that only a person who has demonstrated an adequate technical training is qualified to be a member of the administrative staff.
5. *Written Rules* Administrative acts, decisions, and rules are formulated and recorded in writing.
6. *Separation of Ownership* It is a matter of principle that the members of the administrative staff should be completely separated from ownership of the means of production or administration. There exists, furthermore, in principle, complete separation of the property belonging to the organization—which is controlled within the spheres of the office—and the personal property of the official.

Weber did not expect any bureaucracy to have all the safeguards he listed. The greater the number and the intensity of them an organization possessed, however, the more rational and, therefore, the more efficient it would be.

Taylor: Scientific Management

Frederick W. Taylor, production specialist, business executive, and consultant, applied the scientific method to the solution of factory problems. From these analyses, he established principles that could be substituted for the trial-and-error methods then in use. The advent of Taylor's thinking in the early 1900s opened a new era—that of *scientific management*.

Contributions

Taylor's enormous contributions lay, first, in his large-scale application of the analytical, scientific approach to improving production methods. Second, while he did not feel that management could ever become an exact science in the same sense as physics and chemistry, he believed strongly that management could be an organized body of knowledge and that it could be taught and learned. Third, he originated the term and concept of *functional supervision*. Taylor felt that the job of supervision was too complicated to be handled effectively by one supervisor and should therefore be delegated to as many as eight specialized foremen. Finally, Taylor believed that his major contribution lay in a new philosophy of motivating workers and management.

Enforced Cooperation

Taylor consistently maintained—and successfully demonstrated—that through the use of his techniques it would be possible to obtain appreciable increases in a worker's efficiency. Furthermore, he firmly believed that management, and management alone, should be responsible for putting these techniques into effect. Although it is important to obtain the cooperation of the workers, it must be "enforced cooperation."

Five Methods

Taylor prescribed five methods for "scientifically" managing an organization. First, management must carefully study the worker's body movements to discover the one best method for accomplishing work in the shortest possible time. Second, management must standardize its tools based on the requirements of specific jobs. Third, management must select and train each worker for the job for which he or she is best suited. Fourth, management must abandon the traditional unity-of-command principle and substitute functional supervision. As already mentioned, Taylor advocated that a worker receive his or her orders from as many as eight supervisors. Four of these supervisors were to serve on the shop floor (inspector, repair foreman, speed boss, and gang boss) and the other four in the planning room (routing, instruction, time and costs, and discipline). Fifth, management must pay the worker in accordance with his or her individual output.

Impact

Taylor's general approach to management is widely accepted today in production-oriented business organizations. Scientific management became a movement, which still has a tremendous influence on industrial practice. It also had a major effect on the reform and economy movements in public administration and thus also influenced police administration. We see numerous police managers and supervisors (private and public alike) that firmly believe that if material rewards are directly related to work efforts, the worker consistently responds with maximum performance.

Gulick and Urwick: Principles

While the followers of Taylor developed more scientific techniques of management and work, others were conceptualizing broad principles for the most effective design of organizational structure. Luther Gulick and Lyndall Urwick were leaders in formulating principles of formal organization.

The First and Main Principle

Gulick and Urwick proposed eight principles, the first of which (similar to Weber) underlies and influences the seven others—*division of labor*. Their approach rests firmly on the assumption that the more a specific function can be divided into its simplest parts, the more specialized (e.g., homicide investigation) and, therefore, the more skilled a worker can become in carrying out his or her part of the job. They emphasized that any division of labor must be in strict accordance with one of the following four rationales:

- The major *purpose* the worker is serving, such as designing microprocessors, controlling crime, or teaching
- The *process* the worker is using, such as engineering, medicine, carpentry, programming, or accounting
- The *person or things* dealt with or served, such as immigrants, victims, minorities, mines, parks, farmers, automobiles, or the poor
- The *place* where the worker renders his or her service, such as Hawaii, Washington, the Rocky Mountains, beach resorts, college campuses, or sports arenas

No single rationale is better than the others! In practice, the rationales often overlap, are sometimes incompatible with one another, and are quite vague. For example, when looking at a police organization, it would be difficult not to conclude that the four rationales fail to provide a satisfactory guide to division of labor in that organization. Furthermore, it can be seen that the four rationales are prescriptive rather than descriptive, that they state how work should be divided rather than how work is actually divided.

The planning of the division of labor in a given organization is affected by many considerations not covered by the four principles. The division may be determined by the culture in which the organization is situated, by the environment of the organization, by the availability and type of personnel, and by political factors.

Organizations are actually made up of a combination of various layers that differ in their type of division. The lower layers tend to be organized according to area or clientele, the higher ones by purpose or process. Even this statement, however, should be viewed only as a probability. In a police organization, all four rationales operate at the same time.

Seven Additional Principles

Gulick and Urwick went on to underscore seven more principles for organizing.

1. *Unity of Command* A man cannot serve two masters. This principle is offered as a balance to the division of labor and reflects Taylor's "functional supervision."
2. *Fitting People to the Structure* People should be assigned to their organizational positions in an unfeeling, unemotional frame of mind, like the preparation of an engineering design—regardless of the needs of that particular individual or of those individuals who may now be in the organization.
3. *One Top Executive (Manager)* Gulick and Urwick both strongly supported the principle of one-person administrative responsibility in an organization. Hence, they warned against the use of committees and would have choked on the word *teamwork* or *partners*.

4. *Staff: General and Specialized* The classical writers' concern about staff assistance to top management deserves special attention. When management expressed a need for help from larger and larger numbers of experts and specialists, this need immediately raised the question of the relation of these specialists to the regular-line supervisors and employees. In this instance, Gulick recommended that the staff specialist obtain results from the line through influence and persuasion and that the staff not be given authority over the line. The next question to be answered was that of coordination. Top management would have more people to supervise, because they would be responsible for not only the line but also the special staff. The Gulick-Urwick answer to this problem was to provide help through "general staff," as distinguished from "special staff" assistance. Significantly, general staff are not limited to the proffering of advice. They may draw up and transmit orders, check on operations, and iron out difficulties. In doing so, they act not on their own but as representatives of their superior and within the confines of decisions made by him or her. Thus, they allow their superior to exercise a broader span of control.

5. *Delegation* Gulick and Urwick emphasized that the two main reasons organizations fail are the absence of the fortitude to delegate correctly and not knowing how to do it. In larger organizations, we must even delegate the right to delegate.

6. *Matching Authority and Responsibility* It is wrong to hold people accountable for certain activities if the necessary authority to discharge that responsibility is not granted. On the other side, the responsibilities of all persons exercising authority should be absolute within the defined terms of that authority. Managers should be personally accountable for all actions taken by subordinates. Thus, at all levels, authority and responsibility should be continuous and coequal.

7. *Span of Control* Gulick and Urwick asserted that no supervisor can supervise directly the work of more than five or, at the most, six subordinates whose work interlocks. When the number of subordinates increases arithmetically, there is a geometrical increase in all the possible combinations of relationship that may demand the attention of the supervisor.

Bureaucracy Bashing

The words *bureaucracy* and *bureaucrat* have negative connotations. If we do not like an organization, we can label it a "bureaucracy." If we do not like a government worker, we can call him or her a "bureaucrat." This is an injustice to both the organization and the person. To use these terms belies the fact that all organizations of a few or more people—and all workers—are to some degree bureaucracies and bureaucrats, even the agile ones and leader-managers/partnerships. Although they are at times inefficient and frustrating, we need bureaucracies to convert disorder into order.

The four cornerstones of bureaucracy were built on three interlocking theories: rationality of structure, scientific management, and principles of organization. One way of classifying these three concepts is as follows: First, *Weber's writing was primarily descriptive;* however, it did indicate that a particular form of organizational structure was preferable. Second, the theories of both *Taylor and the Gulick-Urwick team were prescriptive;* that is, they expressed the *one right way* to manage and organize a body of people. It is the "one right way" thinking that gets bureaucracies into trouble. The agile organization rejects such thinking with its motto "There are many right ways."

THE AGILE ORGANIZATION AND MANAGEMENT BY OBJECTIVES

Our society is an organizational society.
—*Amitai Etzioni*

Successful community-oriented policing programs require a unique structural-functional valuational chemistry:

- Structural—an agile organizational framework
- Functional—a bottom-up, empowering management by objectives (MBO) system
- Continuity—maintenance of core values
- Change—internal and external cultural and technological values

We will now examine the ten key features of an agile organization. Afterward, we will cover the nine steps for building bottom-up leadership—or management by objectives (MBO).

Key Characteristics of an Agile Organization

See Figure 14-2 for a graphic of the ten characteristics. (Note the juxtaposition of "values" and "vision.")

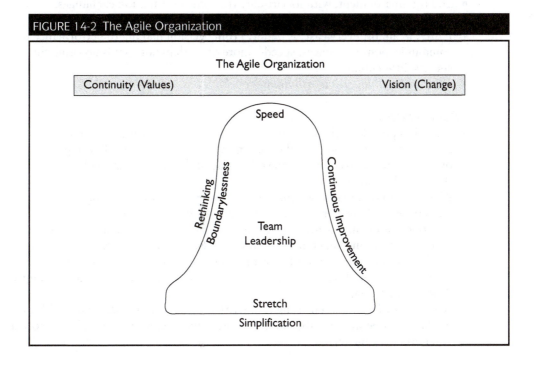

FIGURE 14-2 The Agile Organization

1. Values
- Values are the *enduring* qualities that an organization stands for.
- Values guarantee a *constancy* of purpose.
- Values prevent the department from accidentally sliding away from its founding principles.

2. Vision
- Vision is the *awareness* of incoming demands for policy and operational changes.
- Vision ensures the department *will be prepared* to anticipate and respond to change.
- Vision *helps* the department to be flexible and adaptable.
  (For a refresher on this subject, see Chapter 4.)

3. Size
- Exceeding the line of 150 staff members in a police department is a small change that triggers a big problem.
- Smallness promises "peer pressure," or knowing people well enough that what they think of you matters to you.
- When we get to know one another, peer pressure emerges as more powerful than a boss. Employees want to live up to what is expected of them.
- The Rule of 150 is the crux of "team policing," "neighborhood policing," "area/geographical command," and "community-oriented policing."
- Bigness breeds bureaucracy—smallness ensures agility.

4. Speed
- Today's environment, with its virtually real-time information exchanges, demands that an institution *embrace* speed.
- *Faster*, in almost every case, is better! From decision making to performance to communications to services, speed—more often than not—ends up being the success differentiator.
- *If it's worth doing, it's worth doing poorly.*

5. Boundarylessness
- There is a prevalent obsession for finding a better way or idea, whether it's a source, a colleague, another organizational unit, or a neighboring organization—or even one on the other side of the globe—that will share its ideas and practices.
- Aligned with boundaryless behavior is a rewards system that recognizes the adaptor or implementer of an idea as much as the originator.
- Creating this open, sharing element magnifies the enormous and unique strength of an organization—an endless stream of new ideas and best practices.
- Deploy "seam teams": work teams that link up and integrate two or more operations. Examples are traffic units that work as a common unit to clean up a drug-infested area.
- Bureaucracy bashing is ensuring that written rules, memoranda, and the like, do not hamper operational efficiency. The larger the operations manual, the more it will burden an agency.

- Tier trashing is keeping the number of horizontal levels to a minimum. The more tiers, the greater the inefficiency. Remember: Keep it simple, keep it lean.
- Maintaining a flat organizational structure automatically *pushes* responsibility down to where day-to-day decisions have to be made.

6. Stretch

- In an organization in which *boundarylessness*—openness, informality, and the use of ideas from anywhere—and *speed* are increasingly a way of life, an overarching operating principle—*stretch*—is a natural outgrowth.
- Stretch, in its simplest form, says, "Nothing is impossible," and the setting of stretch targets inspires people and captures their imaginations.
- Stretch *does not* mean "commitments are out." Stretch can occur only in an environment in which everyone is totally committed to a rigid set of core values—integrity, trust, quality, boundaryless behavior—and to outperforming every one of their global competitors in every market environment.
- Stretch *does* mean we are not fixated on a meaningless, internally derived, annual budget number that does nothing but make bureaucrats comfortable.
- A stretch atmosphere replaces a grim, heads-down determination to be as good as you *have* to be and asks, instead, how good *can* you be?

7. Simplification

- Simplify *everything* you do.
- Use straightforward communications to one another and even simpler ones to your customers.
- The efficacy of statistics, budget data, and the like, will be measured by their simplicity; that simplicity will improve their quality, their cost, and their speed in reaching the intended consumer.

8. Rethinking

- On at least an annual basis, compare the performance of an operation or an agency with the performance of all others (benchmarking). Use the best one as the standard to be met by all the following year.
- Conventional policy making ranks programs and activities according to their good intentions; rethinking ranks them according to results.
- Reinventions should be expected and not celebrated as unique.
- Downsizing *per se* is not rethinking—it may cause "amputation before diagnosis." It can cause a casualty rather than be a cure.
- Rethinking is identifying the activities that are productive and those that should be strengthened, promoted, and expanded.
- Rethinking does not give us answers but forces us to ask the *right* questions.
- Focus particularly on:
    —performance objectives
    —quality objectives
    —cost objectives

9. *Continuous Improvement*
- Conduct ongoing evaluations of everything that you do.
- Focus on:
  —performance objectives
  —quality objectives
  —cost objectives
- Link the improvements to some form of an incentive or recognition.
- Show incremental improvements *before* the service reaches a peak or goal.

10. *Team Leadership*
- Team leadership means a swarm of people acting as one—folks that have left behind their self-interest. They manage things and lead people. With people, fast is slow and slow is fast—it takes time to forge a team spirit.
- There is *no* place for halfhearted interest or halfhearted effort.
- Even the most capable managers have trouble in transitioning from an emphasis on command-and-control-type managing (micromanaging) to team leadership. Causes: simple human nature—reclaiming the sandbox for themselves—reverting to old habits.

Transitional tips: (1) Don't be afraid to admit ignorance; (2) think about what you take on, not what you give up; (3) learn when and where to intervene; (4) get used to learning on the job; and (5) learn to really share (let go of) power.

The Nine Basic Steps of Management by Objectives

Management by objectives (MBO) is the curse of top-down control. It is a management system for making an agile organization and empowerment work effectively. It is a system in which overall objectives are clearly stated and agreed on, and it gives people the flexibility to work toward those goals in ways they deem best for their own assigned areas of responsibility. It *decentralizes* decision making. Consequently, MBO is the *essential* delivery system for making community-oriented policing work.

MBO involves development, through a team approach, of mutually agreed on meaningful and measurable objectives. Consistent with employee empowerment, it relies on police managers as well as line officers to construct action plans that are practical, realistic, and achievable. It provides feedback not only to city councils/county boards and command staffs but also to officers in the field in a way that enhances their sense of involvement and professional pride.

The successful practice of MBO is a two-way street. Managers at all levels must be sure that their staff members clearly understand the overall objectives and goals of the department, as well as the specific goals of their particular division or work unit. Thus, managers have a strong obligation to foster good communication and mutual understanding. Conversely, their staff must take sufficient interest in their work to want to plan it, propose new solutions to old police problems, and jump in when they have something to contribute.

The overall success of MBO depends on nine clearly defined steps. The flow as well as the interaction of each of these steps is illustrated in Figure 14-3.

FIGURE 14-3   Steps for Management by Objectives

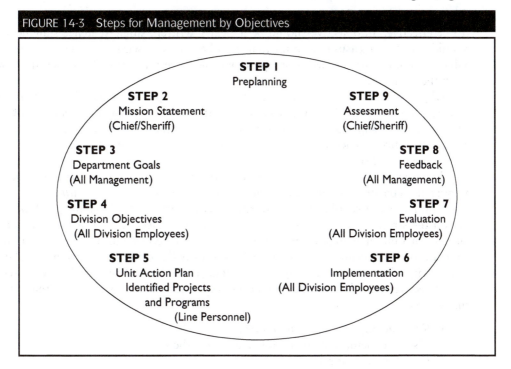

STEP 1
Preplanning

STEP 2
Mission Statement
(Chief/Sheriff)

STEP 9
Assessment
(Chief/Sheriff)

STEP 3
Department Goals
(All Management)

STEP 8
Feedback
(All Management)

STEP 4
Division Objectives
(All Division Employees)

STEP 7
Evaluation
(All Division Employees)

STEP 5
Unit Action Plan
Identified Projects
and Programs
(Line Personnel)

STEP 6
Implementation
(All Division Employees)

Step 1: Preplanning

Proper planning, assessment, and communication are essential to implementing a successful MBO program. The MBO program must have the confidence and philosophical commitment of the chief executive and of the command staff. Ultimately, the success or failure of an MBO program will depend on the support and cooperation of all levels of the department, particularly that of line personnel. Many agencies have found team building to be a successful approach to achieving commitment and understanding.

Step 2: Mission Statement

The mission statement is a mirror of the values and desires of the community. It is a reflection of the ideals and professionalism of law enforcement.

Step 3: Departmental Goals

Ideally, identifying a community's important needs that can be met by effective policing is a task faced by each member of the department and specifically by all management personnel. A meaningful discussion of the needs and concerns of the organization, as well as of the community, must be structured to identify broadly based, yet practical and vital goals that the department wants to accomplish over the next year or more. These goals should reflect the philosophy articulated by the department's mission statement. The management team should concentrate on no more than four—and preferably on only two or three—general goals that are broadly based and encompass practical, department-wide needs and direction.

Step 4: Division Objectives

To be effective, an objective should be a clearly written, single-sentence statement. It should specify a measurable result that is to be achieved within a given time period. Objectives must answer two basic questions: *What* results are to be achieved? *When* must they happen?

Objectives are the ultimate responsibility of both supervisors and managers. To formulate these written objectives successfully, the division commander should obtain input from *both* superiors and subordinates. It is best that an objective be *quantifiable*. Hence the officer is encouraged to tie the objective to the real world and not have it be just a paper exercise.

There are times when attempting to quantify an objective will distort or hamper an important departmental target. In such an instance, the use of a *qualitative* objective is relevant. For example, objectives frequently focus on the professional image of the officer on the street. It is reasonable to restrict such an objective to a qualitative phrase such as "maintaining an appropriate appearance and a courteous manner." To attempt to quantify or delineate this further, such as to provide reference to citizen complaints and specify adherence to a dress/grooming code, could be confusing and complicated.

Objectives must be realistic and motivating. They should comply with the following criteria:

- Keep the objectives few in number.
- Visualize them, write them down, and post them.
- Keep the focus specific.
- Make them neither overly demanding nor ho-hum simple.
- Make sure they are mutually agreed on by managers and line employees.
- Prioritize; determine what actions give the biggest impact.
- Probe for what can be done differently to achieve each of the objectives.

Figure 14-4 shows the linkage of a hypothetical overarching goal (Step 3) to four underpinning objectives. Note that the four objectives are specific and have timelines attached to them.

Step 5: Unit Action Plan

The unit action plan involves spelling out those projects and activities that are necessary to make the departmental objectives a reality. The unit action plan is the ultimate responsibility of the supervisor. It is critical, however, that sergeants, officers, and civilian employees develop projects and programs in a team effort and commit to specific performance measures that support the objectives identified in Step 4.

Officer involvement again is the linchpin to a successful MBO program. Employees tend to be supportive of that which they help create and build. The action plan further provides an opportunity for all employees to have a say in the department's accomplishments. Problem-oriented policing and community-oriented policing underscore that invaluable ideas and information come from the line officers and civilians and supervisory personnel. Even a new employee may have a unique slant on a given problem that would allow the seasoned professional to adapt a fresh perspective to working out an action plan.

It can also be very helpful at this stage to bring in whatever labor or professional organization represents the line officer. This strategy has several advantages. First, the

FIGURE 14-4 Division Objectives

SILVERTHORNE POLICE DEPARTMENT POLICING BY OBJECTIVES

CAPTAIN __NORMAN TRAUB__ DATE FROM __7/04__ TO __6/06__
DIVISION __FIELD OPERATIONS__ SECTION/WATCH __PATROL__

> GOAL: #1
> TO REDUCE MAJOR CRIME THROUGHOUT THE CITY

OBJECTIVE:

1. Introduce and implement the problem-oriented policing model as a mechanism to reduce street crime to all field operations staff by June 30, 2006.
2. Increase number of field arrests by 15% by June 30, 2006.
3. Conduct at least one major target crime suppression project each quarter of the fiscal year.
4. Continue to coordinate with Community Relations to increase participation in the Combat Auto Theft (CAT) Program by 15% by April 2006.

manager will have a solid idea from the beginning of just what opposition there might be to a particular concept. Second, because the police association representatives may have a better pipeline than the administration itself to the street cops, the chief opens still another channel of communication directly to the employees. Third, rumors about "quotas" or other issues are stopped by getting an accurate message to the association or union leaders. Finally, it is a further demonstration that the department recognizes the individual officer's importance to the program.

Each line officer *must* receive detailed information and training clearly explaining the steps of the MBO process. Team-building workshops, division or unit retreats, and other forums that facilitate employee participation and input are extremely useful in developing the action plan. When identifying and selecting projects and programs for the action plan, they must meet two minimum requirements: (1) they must be reasonably likely to produce a tangible result; and (2) the proposing unit must be capable of carrying them out, either with its own resources or with available outside support.

Structured Exercise 14-3 presents an example of an action plan for Objective 1 in Figure 14-4.

STRUCTURED EXERCISE 14-3

ACTION PLAN

In this exercise you are to present an action plan for your agency based on the hypothetical plan shown here. First a blank form is furnished, which is followed by an illustration; also, an action plan statement is underpinned by a project work sheet. The latter is the "real" action in an action plan.

(Continued)

STRUCTURED EXERCISE 14-3 *(Cont.)*

Silverthorne Police Department Policing by Objectives – Action Plan

COMMANDER LT. BILL ROE   DATE: FROM 1/1/2010 TO 7/31/2010

DIVISION FIELD OPERATIONS   SECTION/WATCH DAY

> GOAL: TO REDUCE MAJOR CRIME THROUGHOUT THE CITY

OBJECTIVE

To reduce armed robberies in the downtown business district by 20% during 2005.

ACTIVITY TITLE & DESCRIPTION

To reduce armed robberies in the downtown area by increased activity and programs initiated to target potential victims and identify and/or arrest possible perpetrators.

PROJECT/PROGRAM

1. Increase the number of field interviews by all officers on the watch.

2. Initiate a bicycle patrol of both uniform and plainclothes officers.

3. Monitor crime analysis by reporting district and location.

4. Initiate a business watch and liaison program with local merchants.

5. Maintain periodic hype sweeps and increase narcotics enforcement in the area.

6. Conduct monthly meetings with each officer to evaluate individual performance.

PERSONNEL INVOLVED

Assigned watch personnel—no additional personnel requested other than day watch crime prevention efforts

EQUIPMENT NEEDED

Normal assigned equipment, 50 robbery prevention kits, five bicycles from property locker

OTHER UNITS AFFECTED

Crime Prevention, Investigations, Narcotics

COSTS

Normal budget projection. Request additional 180 hours projected overtime for special/selective enforcement.

RESULTS MANAGEMENT

Monthly appraisal of officer performance and projects/programs. Quarterly evaluation by objective.

NOTES:

Step 6: Implementation

Implementation involves translating the action plan from a planning document to a method of *accomplishing* the department's goals and objectives. The input of line and middle-level staff is reviewed at the division commander level. (Police managers should evaluate pilot programs in one or more selected areas or precincts before committing to department-wide implementation.)

Timing is critical in the implementation stage. If at all possible, implementation at the beginning of a fiscal or calendar year can assist in comparing results and progress to similar time frames and locations in previous years.

Step 7: Project Evaluation

Here police managers and staff assess to what extent the objectives were reached. Have the action plans been successful in accomplishing their targets? Evaluation is the process of determining the amount of success in achieving predetermined objectives. It is, perhaps more importantly, also an exercise in critical thinking and reflection. No set of objectives or means of achieving those objectives is likely to be conceived and executed perfectly. Mistakes will be made. Perspectives will change. Objectives will be reprioritized and/or better formulated. Thus the process of reflection and reformulation begins here with line personnel as well as with their immediate supervisors.

Step 8: Feedback

Feedback is the leading motivator of people. Law enforcement personnel are somewhat unique regarding feedback. By the nature of their jobs, police personnel deal with people and problems continuously and quickly learn to analyze their surroundings and circumstances. MBO can be a powerful motivator if proper feedback is shared at all levels.

Step 9: Final Assessment

As has been touched on in Step 7, evaluation is a process not simply of measuring success or failure. It's one more process of reflection, reassessment, and representation. At the management and command levels, there needs to be at specified points the weighing and assessing of goals, objectives, action plans, and feedback. Analysis at this level may lead the police manager to conclude that certain values, goals, and objectives are firmly in place and integrated into the day-to-day operations of the department, so that lessened focus need be paid to them in the future. Additionally, specific projects or programs that have proved successful might well be shared with other units of the department.

A successful MBO program will be one that asks questions as well as provides answers and one that will enhance a greater sense of pride and professionalism throughout the agency.

CONCLUDING POINTS: AGILITY AND MBO

Police leaders who opt for a community-oriented policing (COP) service model automatically assume a twofold responsibility. First, they must build an organizational structure that counterbalances values (continuity) with vision (change). Leaders must be alert for, and vigorously defend against, "bureaucracy creep." Second, to implement empowerment, leaders must initiate an MBO program.

If COP is to succeed, then departmental rigidity and top-down autocracy must be cast out and supplanted with a constant stream of new ideas, team learning, and individual empowerment. The formula is easy to express (and tough to master): COMMUNITY-ORIENTED POLICING = AN AGILE ORGANIZATIONS + MBO.

Competency Checkpoints

- Giving orders is not the same as being in control.
- Bureaucratic organizations emphasize top-down control.
- Agile organizations promote bottom-up control.
- Organizations are comprised of people who are pursuing a goal.
- Bureaucracies are organizations with a lot of formal rules, rigid structure, division of labor, and many levels of authority, based on the one-best-way set of principles.
- Agile organizations are organizations that thrive on core values, vision, small size, speed, continuous improvement, rethinking, boundarylessness, stretch, and keeping things simple.
- Management by objectives (MBO) is the operating system for making the agile organization function successfully.
- MBO starts with preplanning and concludes with evaluation.

Flexing the Message

1. Revisit Structured Exercise 14-1. Analyze each response to the six questions. What do you conclude from your evaluation of the answers? What should be changed, and what should not? If possible, compare your findings with others in your work unit.
2. Is the police agency that you work for more of a bureaucracy (see "The Four Cornerstones of Bureaucracy" section), or is it more agile in character (see Figure 14-1)? Can you spot any trend toward one organizational form or the other?
3. Read Malcolm Gladwell's *The Tipping Point* (New York: Little, Brown, 2000) about Rule 150.
4. Reread the section on MBO. Pretend you are your boss and that you've decided to create an MBO plan for yourself. What would you include in the plan? Now, write an MBO agreement about your boss. Do you think your manager will sign it?

15 PERFORMANCE

Effective policing hinges on a willingness to take personal responsibility for the level of crime in a community.

What gets measured gets managed.

Not everything that can be counted counts, and not everything that counts can be counted.
—Albert Einstein

CHAPTER OUTLINE

Okay, we've covered leading and managing police personnel. In the last two chapters we first considered an attitude toward policing (*service*) and then a delivery system (*agile organization*) for facilitating it. We'll conclude here by translating the attitude of service into several operable values and then reveal the enormous power of *performance measures* to improve police work.

Premise: The police and their community require high-quality measures of police performance to determine whether or not the organization is achieving intended results.

The technology and techniques for measuring police output are relatively easy when compared to the normative question of "What do we measure?" In other words, what service values merit measurement and why? The "why" is obvious. Three important groups need to know how effective their police are for three different reasons.

- The **community** *wants* and *deserves* to know what they are getting for their dollar *and* other types of support.
- **Police leaders** are *responsible* and therefore *expected* to know the level of deliverable values they are providing to their community.
- **Police personnel** desperately *want* to know *what* is expected of them and precisely what they can do to increase the quality *and* quantity of their work.

Most police agencies are being driven by performance measures that capture only a portion of the value they are contributing to their community.

As you read further keep repeating the opening mantra—*What gets measured gets managed.*

THE MEASURABLES

Be careful to maintain good works.
—Titus 3:8

It seems to me that if I were a police manager, I would want to be judged on *all*, not some of the values that my department is delivering to the community. Yet I find that there are police managers who intentionally beg this question. They either don't care about their accountability or they're fearful of the findings, or both. Those leaders who have established a performance measurement system have been richly rewarded by the feedback (two cases that I'll cover later, the New York and Hermiston, OR, police departments). Here's my point: Performance measurement is a powerful and useful management tool, and either you develop one or someone else is likely to cram one down your administrative throat.

Recognizing Value

Assuming that service is your department's driving value, then we must take the next step and explore what subsidiary values lie within it. This gets a little tricky because decisions about police values and their relative priority are *best* guided by the community in consultation with their police agency. Nonetheless, there are some commonly held ideas about the really important measurables in police work. Those expressed here (plus a couple of my own) are the product of the highly respected Police Executive Research Forum (PERF). The values PERF proposes are *practical* and capable of being measured. (I suspect you are measuring several of them already). Before we discuss them, it's time for a brief review of what we've learned about *principled* values or ethics.

Principled Values

An example of a *practical* and preeminent police service value is—*Reduce criminal victimization.* Two statistical measurements are employed: (1) reported crime rates; and (2) victimization rates. *Principled values,* while related, are different since they imbue such ethics as justice, fairness, integrity, respect, trust, tolerance, and more. They are considered inherently good. We prize them, or we should, above the practical ones. Let me explain.

I know (and you do, too) a way to attain a nearly zero degree of criminal victimization. When you inspect my strategy, you'll be astounded at its potential. In a very practical sense, I'm a genius and a true winner. But in order to maximize this value, I had to violate your guaranteed freedoms. Tactically I used excessive force, fear, and cruelty to wipe out crime. I know you're not in favor of my methods because *your* principles cry out—"No way!" Most societies, nations, and cultures evidence a principled and practical approach to reducing crime. However, there's still a few that do not.

Practical Values

Table 15-1 displays seven performance values, their respective indicators, and *hypothetical markers.* The first six require one type of measurement (internal) and the last another (external) that is examined later on.

"Markers" should be coupled to "measurables." You measure, case in point, criminal homicides per capita, but you *set* (the marker) X number or less per annum. Measurement per se is interesting, but inserting markers is at once challenging and invariably grabs the attention of all police managers. It is here that "What gets measured, gets managed" becomes a wake-up call for all police leaders.

Measurables absent of markers are meaningless.

All performance values, measurables and markers in Table 15-1 are pure illustrations. If you were hoping for a sure-fire, cure-all formula of measuring a department's values, then you're going to be disappointed. I can't and must not do it. *Only* a police leader should decide on a measuring rod for her agency. What I hope to do is help you *imagine* how your agency can better measure the values and outcomes it delivers. And once identified, *act* on them.

The performance dimensions in Table 15-1:

- *Focus on Crime and Not Just Criminals.* Traditional policing targets perpetrators being identified and apprehended. Here the emphasis is on reducing crime and fear while increasing the quality of community life.
- *Champion Community Participation.* The old approach to police work considered the community as a stand-alone nonplayer in crime control. In this instance, the police encourage all community members to fully understand how they can meaningfully impact crime.
- *Assume Accountability.* The police manager and his management team hold themselves totally responsible for leading a caring, honest, and effective department that solves real-time problems.

TABLE 15-1	Performance Table Values, Measurables, and Markers: A Hypothetical Model	
Performance Values	*Measurables*	*Markers (%)*
Reduce Crime	Reported crime rates	−5
	Victimization rates	−5
Apprehend Criminal	Clearance rates	+ 10
	Conviction rates	+ 10
Public Safety	Traffic accidents	−5
	Traffic injuries	−10
	Graffiti/vandalism	−15
	Increased property values	+ 5
	Gang abatement	+ 10
Financial Responsibility	Cost per citizen	−5
	Scheduling efficiency	+ 5
	Budget compliance	100
	Overtime expenditures	−10
	Outsourcing	+ 10
	Service fees	+ 10
Use of Force	Risk management	−10
	Citizen complaints	−15
Professional Integrity	Internal affairs investigations	−10
	Disability claims	−25
	Medical retirements	−10
Community Participation	Satisfaction with services	+ 10
	Response times	−5
	Perception of safety	+ 10
	Volunteerism	+ 10
	Citizen academy	+ 20
	Reserves	+ 5

MEASURING

*You've got to be careful if you don't know where you're going
because you might not get there.*

—*Yogi Berra*

Four types of yardsticks can be used to measure police performance values:

- Statistical: output, rates, ratios
- Oversight: city councils, courts, media
- Community: surveys, neighborhood watch, citizen review
- Pro-steering: collateral assignments, projects that are time-certain, and pinpoint individual responsibility

STRUCTURED EXERCISE 15-1

Examine what your department is currently measuring in the way of performance outputs. Is it only Part One crimes? What else is being collected and documented as a productivity measurement? Who gets the information? How is it used? Now, what can be done to improve your performance measures and in turn your outputs and outcomes?

Statistical

Monthly reporting of crime, apprehension, conviction, and traffic enforcement performance activity is typical of most police agencies. Some agencies are more expansive and track (usually for internal purposes) budget expenditures, use of force, citizen complaints, internal affairs, disability and medical leaves, and response times. This form of measurement is:

• **Logical**	• **Factual**	• **External**
• **Rational**	• **Objective**	

The best illustration of a workable statistical measuring tool is New York City's COMPSTAT. It is setting the standard for other police agencies for these reasons:

1. *Oversight.* It produces hard data that external overseers want.
2. *Accountability.* It makes managers accountable for their performance.
3. *Reliable.* The data is objective, simple, and behaviorally anchored.
4. *Rewards.* Police managers are rewarded based on meeting or exceeding performance markers.
5. *Transparent.* The performance reviews are frequent and open to public scrutiny.
6. *Clarity.* Everyone is clear about measurables and markers. Guesswork is supplanted by hard work.

While primarily designed to hold police managers accountable for crime reduction (an outcome), COMPSTAT has proven equally useful in emphasizing the *process* for achieving the desired results. Here are at least three unintended benefits of COMPSTAT.

1. *Teamwork.* The police managers are required to meet regularly (weekly) and share with one another their successes as well as deficiencies. Enhanced face-to-face communication usually engenders elevated trust and mutual support.
2. *Innovation.* While representing separate unit commands, the managers find they can rely on one another for ideas on how to improve their operations. Such synergy often exposes new avenues of creativity.
3. *Interest.* COMPSTAT removed the boredom out of the traditional "staff meeting" that most found useless and ho-hum. With this process you show up well prepared and ready to concentrate on business or else suffer the consequences.

Before you think COMPSTAT is *the* answer to measuring police values, let me assure you that it isn't. It is excellent for accomplishing its six intended and three unintended consequences. But there are still come measurables left unattended.

Oversight

Those in oversight roles require other values to be measured. City managers and councils want to know about, in addition to crime data, budget changes, citizen complaints, and unusual occurrences. Citizen review boards want facts on internal investigations, use of force, and citizen complaints. Special commissions may demand reports on such issues as affirmative action, correctional facilities, anticorruption activity, and gang enforcement activities. The media will ask for facts on "hot" news to include shootings, demonstrations, and whatever is worthy of a headline. Federal and state reporting requirements are a welcome by-product of COMPSTAT.

Community

Typically the very reason for all of the above data collection is left out of the police performance measurement equation—the *community*. How can a police agency really know if the community and neighborhood residents are feeling secure in their homes and/or their streets? Are they satisfied with the quality and level of police values they are receiving? Many of them have not heard of COMPSTAT, and if they did, they could care less. They'll not see the annual report, and if they did, they probably wouldn't read it. What they do want is to see a police officer on occasion (a smiling one, better yet). When considering citizen input, police managers hesitate because such evaluative findings are:

Psychological	Emotional	Internal
Irrational	Subjective	

If you really want to know what they think about police performance, then you'll have to ask them. In doing so, you will complement COMPSTAT's *facts* with the community's *feelings*. You may have loads of solid data to support your contention that the police are performing well. If the community agrees, great; if they don't, then you're in trouble. For those who allege facts will dislodge, defuse, or compel feelings to change— you're wrong—no matter how hard you "feel" that way.

Every time feelings and facts collide, feelings will bury the facts.

Hermiston, OR, integrates the COMPSTAT methodology with community satisfaction surveys. Hence, it is using a more comprehensive measuring stick for evaluating its work effort. It gets at the *output* while simultaneously addressing the *outcomes*. It tells police managers, officers, and overseers not only, for example, that drug arrests on their part are up and how the community feels about it. Or the number of taggings is down and how they feel about that.

The Hermiston Police Department's Community Questionnaire is distributed twice a year through the city's water billing process. The administration of the questionnaire is cheap and it produces rich results. Along with their version of COMPSTAT, the questionnaire provides a high-quality measure that captures more of the police

---

STRUCTURED EXERCISE 15-2

If your agency has not used a community satisfaction survey instrument in the measurement of its work, why not? Why should it or shouldn't it use such an instrument? Has your department considered a professionalism survey of all employees to include: (1) monthly equipment and uniform inspections; (2) physical fitness and assessment program; (3) ethics training; (4) job satisfaction; (5) worker's compensation; (6) college education and reimbursement; (7) ambience of front desk/lobby; (8) numbers and types of internal affairs and disciplines; and (9) absenteeism and tardiness? There are a lot of important variables to be counted.

---

department's value to the people they police. Ironically, so far, the Hermiston Police Department has been pleasantly surprised to learn that their community felt they were doing a better police job than they did! (See Figure 15-1.)

For more information on citizen surveys, visit the National Research Center Web site at http://n-r-c.com/services/nationalcitizensurvey.html, or the International City Management Association Web site at http://icma.org/ncs.

Pro-Steering

Pro-Steering refers to an accountability system for moving projects to completion. It's analogous to an internal, focused COMPSTAT that clearly affixes responsibility for a particular person to complete a project within a given timeframe. Brief weekly updates of project status are provided at staff meetings. Accomplishments are celebrated and delays explained. So simple, and it works great. An example is seen in Figure 15-2 (space does not permit all of the pages to be shown). A number one priority is within a 30-day timeframe, two is 60, and a three is 90 days.

WHAT REALLY COUNTS?

*The highest reward for a person's toil is not what they get
for it, but what they become by it.*
—*John Ruskin*

I'm sure you've heard the admonition "Work smarter, not harder." Obviously you and I strive to avoid the opposite. Working smarter and not harder is preferable and commendable. But I am finding this slogan is sometimes being overused and abused. In fact, I've witnessed police managers sarcastically slam other managers and supervisors with these words when performance values are below par.

Maybe, just maybe, the answer to poor performance is *not* working smarter or harder. Maybe, just maybe, poor performance (e.g., excessive response time) is caused

FIGURE15-1   Community Questionnaire

Hermiston Police Department Community Questionnaire

PLEASE MARK THE APPROPRIATE RESPONSE	Strongly Disagree 1	2	3	4	Strongly Agree 5	N/A
1. My neighborhood is safe during the day.						
2. My neighborhood is safe at night.						
3. My neighborhood feels safe compared to other neighborhoods in town.						
4. The relationship between police officers and residents is good in my neighborhood.						
5. The Police Department is working to reduce crime in my neighborhood.						
6. My contact with uniformed Hermiston Police Officers has been satisfactory.						
7. Crime in my neighborhood seems to be declining.						
8. The Hermiston Police Department is effective at dealing with:	1	2	3	4	5	N/A
A. Violent crimes (robberies, rapes, assaults, homicide).						
B. Property crimes (burglary, theft, auto theft).						
C. Nuisance problems (noise, graffiti, vandalism, code enforcement issues, etc.).						
D. Traffic enforcement (speeding, DUI, school zone violations, etc.).						
E. Parking and abandoned vehicle problems.						
F. Youth, delinquency, and gang issues.						
G. Drug enforcement (manufacturing and sales of drugs, possession, etc.).						
H. Security at area elementary, middle, high school, and the community college.						
PLEASE MARK THE APPROPRIATE RESPONSE	1	2	3	4	5	N/A
9. If I witnessed a crime in Hermiston, I would not hesitate to notify the police.						
10. If I were the victim of a crime in Hermiston, I am confident that it would be fully investigated.						
11. The Police Department has adequate crime prevention programs.						
12. The Police Department has adequate prevention programs focused on youth issues.						
13. I have confidence in the leadership of the Hermiston Police Department.						

WHERE IN HERMISTON DO YOU LIVE?		YEARS YOU'VE LIVED IN HERMISTON:	
NW	NE	1–5	16–25
SW	SE	6–15	26 or more

AGE		ETHNICITY	
14–17	41–65	Caucasian	African American
18–24	66 & older	Hispanic	Asian American
25–40	Declined	Native American	Other

WHAT ARE THE THREE BIGGEST PROBLEMS IN YOUR NEIGHBORHOOD? (SELECT THREE.)					
	Animal complaints		Juvenile problems		Theft & burglary
	Drug crimes		Noise		Traffic violations
	DUI		Parking complaints		Trash, weeds, junk
	Gangs		School safety		Underage drinking
	Graffiti		Speeding		Violent crime

GENDER				
	Female		Male	

If you could make one recommendation to the Hermiston Police Department about how they could improve, what would it be?

FIGURE 15-2 Pro-Steering: Project Accountability

Escondido Police Department Project List (as of March 7, 2007)

Projects	Assigned	Captain	Priority	Start	Due	Completed	Comments
DIMS	Albergo	Cervenka	1				
Mission Statement	Wrisley	Maher	1				
Patrol Minimum Staffing/ Scheduling	Albergo	Maher	1				
Personnel Records	Houchin	Maher	1				
Pillars—Community Outreach	Loarie	Maher	1				
Pillars—Crime Reduction	Albergo	Maher	1				
Pillars—Professional Conduct	Mankin	Maher	1				
Undocumented Alien Policy		Maher	1				
Criminal Intel Gathering	Carter	Merkel	1				
Checkpoint D.I.	Houchin	Milks	1				
OIS Review and Finalization	Benton	Milks	1				
PERT	Griffin	Milks	1				
Vehicle Release Policy	Griffin	Milks	1				
CompStat Modifications	Loarie	Moles	1				
Drug Court	Loarie	Moles	1				
Massage Ordinance	Carter	Moles	1				
Geographic Policing	Wrisley	Moles	1				
Data Entry Citation Processing	Foster	Cervenka	2				
Front Counter Staffing	Foster	Cervenka	2				
Internal Controls for Cash Handling (Front Counter)	Foster	Cervenka	2				

(*Continued*)

FIGURE 15-2 *(Continued)*

Projects	Assigned	Captain	Priority	Start	Due	Completed	Comments
Public Records Acts Requests	Foster	Cervenka	2				
Q-Tel	Wynn	Cervenka	2				
Records Destruction Policy	Foster	Cervenka	2				
Bilingual Polygraph Operator Policy	Mankin	Merkel	2				
CAFÉ Gang Prevention Recommendations	Mankin	Merkel	2				
Cold Case Team	Provost	Merkel	2				
Geographic Policing	Wrisley	Moles	1				
Diversion Review and Teen Court Recommendation	Mankin	Merkel	2				
Lexis/Nexis Utilization	Mankin	Merkel	2				
Employee Evaluations	Griffin	Milks	2				
Muni Code Review (8 Sections)	Griffin	Milks	2				
Non-POST Training Protocol	Benton	Milks	2				
Spanish for Officers	Benton	Milks	2				
Spike Strips	Benton	Milks	2				
City Tow Yard Recommendation	Loarie	Moles	2				
Crime Analysis Workload Review	Gridiron	Moles	2				
Detail Missions, Responsibilities, and Problem-Solving Protocol (Sector Officers)	Loarie	Moles	2				
Operational Damage	Loarie	Moles	2				
Street Team Mission	Loarie	Moles	2				
DUI Cost Recovery On-Line Form	Loarie	Cervenka	3				
Electronic "Red Book"	Stuard	Cervenka	3				
Field Reporting Software	Lewan-dowski	Cervenka	3				
Office Expansion	Albergo	Cervenka	3				
Uniform Review	Stuard	Cervenka	3				
Website and DI Update	Rodelo	Cervenka	3				
3rd Party Damage	Healey	Maher	3				
Internal Audits	Healey	Maher	3				
Overtime Policy/Tracking	Griffin	Merkel	3				
Code of Conduct Review and Revisions	Houchin	Milks	3				
TRAK	Stuard	Milks	3				
"Did You Know" Formalize	Ramirez	Moles	3				

by insufficient staffing—not enough personnel to properly do the job at hand. In essence, everyone is working as hard as they can. Everyone is applying their hardware, software, and brainware wisely. Nonetheless, the workload is so drastically burdensome that performance values suffer. Two researchers decided to look more closely at the question of police strategy, staffing, and other intervening variables that impact outputs and outcomes. They focused on what really counts in getting the right performance count, and here is what they learned.

Policeonomics

It seems that everyone has an expert opinion on the police and about police work. A few profess to be bona fide experts. It also seems that there is a lot more fiction than fact about policing. The majority of police agencies welcome prudent and helpful thinking. Some agencies proactively seek ideas on how they can be more successful. A host of research disciplines and schools of thought have attempted to assist the police in creating the improvements they desperately seek. Now for some good news—the economists have arrived. Well, one, anyway, in the person of Steven D. Levitt, University of Chicago. (See his celebrated book, coauthored with Stephen J. Dubner, *Freakonomics*.)

> **Dr. Levitt's strength resides in his uncanny, incessant ability to ask questions and to hear the answers without filtering them through his own opinions. For example, why do drug dealers live with their moms? Which is more dangerous, a gun or a swimming pool? What are the factors that really impact violent crime?**

Levitt and Debner show that economics is, at its root, a study of incentives—how we get what we want or need when others want or need it, too. *Freakonomics* talks about how we would like the world to work and then scientifically represents how it actually does work. If you're prone to accept *conventional wisdom* (what best fits your paradigms), then be prepared for some discomforting surprises in their findings. Supreme Court Justice Louis D. Brandeis is quoted in the book as follows: "Sunlight is said to be the best of disinfectants." With this in mind we'll concentrate on Chapter 4 of the book, "Where Have All the Criminals Gone?"

When the crime rate free-fell in the early 1990s, it surprised everyone. So confident were the experts that crime was on an incline that it took a couple of years for them to spot the drop. *What happened?* That's the question Levitt asked and than answered. To do so he studied the crime drop explanations cited in articles published from 1991 to 2001 in the 10 largest circulation papers in the LexisNexis database.

Crime Drop Explanation	Number of Citations
1. Innovative policing strategies	52
2. Increased reliance on prisons	47
3. Changes in crack and other drug markets	33
4. Aging of populations	32
5. Tougher gun control laws	32
6. Strong economy	28
7. Increased number of police	26
8. All other explanations (increased use of capital punishment, concealed weapons laws, gun buybacks, and others)	

Three of the above explanations contributed to the drop in crime. Reread the list, and circle the three you believe helped to reduce crime.

I'll now disclose the top three (for documentation please refer to Levitt and Debner's pages 121–137). Numbers Two, Three, and Seven are accurate. The others are figments of our imagination, conventional wisdom, or wishful thinking.

Let's examine "increased number of police" as a causal factor. From 1960 to 1985 the number of police officers *fell* more than 50% relative to the number of crimes. This 50% reduction in police officers translated into an almost equal *decrease* in the chance that a crook would be caught.

> **The hiring of additional police accounted for approximately 10% of the 1990s crime drop.**

The major contributing factor to a crime decrease is *not* among the eight above factors. Why? *Because it wasn't cited in the media!* It took a young, gutsy economist to disclose and defend it. I'll say no more than that this unreported factor is the result of a highly controversial court decision. Even if you've guessed the answer, read Chapter 4 in *Freakonomics*; it deserves your attention.

Staffing Formulas

For every staffing formula there is an equal and offsetting formula. Stripping away all of the statistical variables, the formulas currently dissolve into two questions with a single answer:

> **How many officers does my agency have per thousand?**
> **How many officers do other agencies have per thousand?**
> **Answer . . . We need more officers!**

Do you know of any agency that thinks it does not need more personnel? I don't. I do believe, however, that there is a better question and a better answer.

> **What does it take for this agency, in this community, to achieve our public safety values?**
> **Answer . . . I personally hold myself accountable for delivering services that make the values a reality.**

So many officers per thousand is a nonsensical staffing formula unless tied to work output and outcome values. Any plea, "We need more officers," should be responded with, "What do we—the community—get for our money?" How much reduction in Parts One and Two crimes, for example, will police management be held accountable for? Reduction in gangs and gang crime? Traffic accidents and injuries? Reduction in response times? Arrests and case clearances? Increased directed patrol crimes? Fewer medical claims?

Police managers tend to request more staff because of a magical thousand-per-officer standard. Police leaders are likely to ask for more staff because it will directly influence accepted police values while holding themselves accountable.

STRUCTURED EXERCISE 15-3

An economist would likely approach police work in terms of the monetary investment or budget dollars allocated for value received. How much are you paying for Part One crimes committed, arrests made, convictions attained? How do these statistics compare with other agencies? What is the dollar cost per called-for service? How many volunteers/reserves does the agency maintain and at what savings? What work can be outsourced (e.g., background investigations, SWAT teams, dispatching) and what savings achieved? Dr. Levitt is uncanny at asking questions of data. Now ask some of your own. Start with the budget and then relate dollars to service and outcomes.

WHAT'S ACCEPTABLE?

Are you aware that every local community and its police agency are unique, just as each one of us is different and special? What's acceptable to me may not be to you. What's acceptable in police work in Seattle may not be in Atlanta. While many police managers are vigilantly searching for common police standards (e.g., response time), they should be creating their own specific set of work values and a system for monitoring them.

Valid performance values and reliable measurables must emanate from a very clear picture of what the community decides is acceptable police work.

STRENGTHS-BASED SUCCESS = OUTSTANDING PERFORMANCE

Success has always demanded character. Those who reach within themselves and draw upon an inner strength fortified by strong values always carry the day against those of lesser character. Moral cowards never win.
—*General Charles C. Krulak, USMC*

The 20th century concluded with most government agencies emphasizing *process outputs* and *correcting weaknesses*. The 21st century has opened with a rebirth of pushing *performance, outcomes,* and *strengths*. We can actually see agencies coupling performance measurements to budget deliberations that ultimately impact community values and service outcomes. This is rewarding. This is encouraging. This is exciting!

The operative word here is *strength*. In 1966 Peter Drucker wrote, "The effective executive builds on strengths—their own strengths, the strengths of superiors, colleagues, subordinates, and on the strengths of the situation." I would then add that the successful leader makes certain that the outputs and outcomes are *counted*. If they're quantifiable, then quantify them. If they're qualitative, then qualify them. When it comes to measuring a police department's success, both hard, real-time data *and* soft, overtime information must be factored into any set of metrics.

Here is my first point: Measuring process and outputs, and shoring up weaknesses guarantees, at best, a mediocre gain in crime fighting and operational improvements. Conventional wisdom tells us that we learn best from correcting our flaws and mistakes. So we start counting our failures! Conversely . . .

Measuring performance, outcomes, and strengths assures us that we're leading police organizations toward what works rather than fixing what doesn't.

This approach assumes that if we want to learn about our successes, we must study and measure our successes. Why? Because you learn little about excellence from studying failure. A leader and an organization will excel *only* by amplifying strengths, never by simply bandaging mistakes.

Now my second point: You can excel by lowering crime, reducing the community's fear of victimization, being trusted by external oversight boards, and so on. But is there documentation to *prove* it? Do you have the facts to show just how really good you are?

I'm convinced that those police agencies who use a performance score card for proving their strengths will discover they're actually *more* proficient, *more* trusted, and *more* successful than they thought or said they were!

In conclusion, with all of their challenges, issues, and occasional mistakes, our police leaders are doing a marvelous job; we can see and experience it by the outcomes of the agencies they lead. All I'm asking is that they more accurately and comprehensively measure their performance and prove me right.

INDEX